Praise for
Dancing in My Mother's Slippers

Fayegail Bisaccia has given us a loving gift in her brave, intimate and transparent journal of her journey into love and learning, grieving and healing, as she reckons and struggles with her parents' mortality. The collective wisdom of this family, their fears, humor, and candor, provides a richness that can inform and inspire anyone who will some day be present for and helping a loved one who is dying . . . that is, all of us.

—Rabbi Marc Sirinsky

Dancing in My Mother's Slippers is a valuable tool for hospice and grief work . . . a great read for book groups . . . a book to bring people together. Reading this book with my ninety-year-old mother made it a lot easier for us to face this passage together. It opened the door to a whole series of rich and intimate talks between us. I'm grateful to have found this book for my own journey and for my work with clients.

—Georgia Moriarty King, mental health therapist

"It is beautiful, profound, honest, well-written and riveting. Grief weaves its way into her daily life in unexpected ways. Resolution, or at least a deeper level of peace for her, comes only after time passes. We see her humanity (she is like us) and then we witness her extraordinarily brave spiritual quest. It gives us courage to look deeper at our own experiences, to hang in there on our own spiritual journey. That is one reason, I think, why she chose to write this book. It succeeds beautifully."

—Anne Batzer

"*Dancing In My Mother's Slippers* is a wonderful day-to-day unfolding of personal grief and family intimacy which leads to a transcendent view. This is where the value lies."

—Olive Streit, counselor

"What made the book worthy is that it is about the living, not the grieving. It isn't regretful. It is about a life that is full of love and honor for parents. It's a model for relationship."
—Judith Visser, Jewish educator

"It talks to the heart, not to the head. It's a word-of-mouth kind of book. I would definitely recommend it to my bereaved clients."
—Sister Dorothy Pulkka, OSB, grief counselor

"I found out I am grieving in a much deeper and more profound way than I had understood or acknowledged before I read *Slippers*. During this year I never thought to seek out other literature on grieving because I thought I had moved on. I went back to everything in my life right away. I thought I didn't need to grieve, at least not much."
—Kait Fairchild

"People who have been through it will find comfort in her honest and compassionate treatment of medical issues."
—Ellen Marks

"*Dancing in My Mother's Slippers* is sensitively and artistically written. Her voice is authentic, self-revealing and forthright. The structure is like a symphony—loving relationships at the crescendo, great beauty, a sense of peace and maturity."
—Ann Macrory

Dancing in My Mother's Slippers

A Journey of Grief and Healing

FAYEGAIL MANDELL BISACCIA

Weaverbird Press

My thanks to Wendell Berry for his poem, "Prayers and Sayings of the Mad Farmer," from *Collected Poems 1957-1982*, published by North Point Press, having first appeared in *Farming: A Handbook*. Part Eight was published here with permission of the author.

—✦—

Inquiries should be addressed to:
Weaverbird Press
PO Box 688
Ashland, OR 97520
info@weaverbirdpress.com
888-804-7787

www.weaverbirdpress.com

Cover and interior design by Christy Collins, Confluence Book Services
Photos by Shianna Walker

♻ Printed in USA on recycled acid-free paper
First edition: 2007
ISBN 978-0-9789122-0-8
10 9 8 7 6 5 4 3 2 1

In loving memory of my parents

Johanna Arbetter Mandell
and
Daniel David Mandell

May they always be remembered for a blessing.

"You turned my mourning into dancing."
— Psalm 30

Contents

A Note to the Reader   xi

Introduction   xiii

Sailing into the Sunset   1

The Final Year   3

    November ~ This, Too, Shall Pass   5

    December ~ A Delicate and Blessed Balance 6

    January ~ Reflected Light   10

    February ~ Beneath the Surface   11

    March ~ Be Willing to Fall   13

    April ~ For Tradition's Sake   13

    May ~ Escape   14

    June ~ Instrument of Your Wisdom   15

    July ~ Snowbells   15

    August ~ Continuum   17

    September ~ Life as the Tide   19

    October ~ Period of Grace   23

Transition   29

    November ~ Life Is Good   31

    December ~ A Silver Pathway   55

    January ~ Devastation   75

    February ~ As Though a Dam Broke   79

    March ~ Better Balance   80

    April ~ Playing Dress-Up   83

    May ~ Where My Comfort Lies   83

June ~ An Occasion for Gratitude   87
July ~ Ready to Move On   89
August ~ I Begin to Realize   92
September ~ Change We Must   95
October ~ Might As Well Get Used to It   96

First Yahrzeit   101
November ~ Free to Emerge   103
December ~ Too Many Feelings   109
January ~ I Have Made It Down This Road   111
February ~ The Love Was There   113
March ~ Background Person   114
April ~ The Challenge of Bringing Order   115
May ~ Emptiness without a Name   118
June ~ Navy Blue Silk   121
July ~ Needing to Go On   122
August ~ Not in Control   124
September ~ Ask Me Any Question   127
October ~ A Thing I Can Do   128

Second Yahrzeit   131
November ~ Seasons of Joy, Seasons of Pain   133
December ~ Down, Deeper   136
January ~ A Fitting Thing   138
February ~ Unhealed Grief   139
March ~ Companion of Forty Years   140
April ~ Five Precious Days   140
May ~ Asking for Her Light   142
June ~ Case of the Blues   144
July ~ Riveted   145
August ~ Kinda Shiny   146
September ~ Fragile Shelter   147
October ~ An Old Friend   150

Third Yahrzeit   153
    November ~ Feel the Loss   155
    December ~ Put the Word Out   158
    January ~ Turning toward Life   161
    February ~ Slug a Pillow   165
    March ~ The Procession   169
    April ~ Inner Promptings   171
    May ~ Feel the Joy   173
    June ~ On Retreat   179
    July ~ Full of Wonder   187
    August ~ She Did Share   189
    September ~ Wise-Old-Woman Time   192
    October ~ It's Not Old That's Hard   198

Fourth Yahrzeit   205
    November ~ A Time of Negotiation   207
    December ~ Remarkable Day   218

Epilogue   225
    I Love You, Sweetheart   227
    Peace   230

Dancing Lesson   231

Hebrew/Yiddish Glossary and Pronunciation Guide   233
Questions to Ponder: A Guide for Readers   239
A Conversation with Fayegail   241
Resources   247
Acknowledgments   251
About the Author   254

A Note to the Reader

Because transliterated Hebrew and Yiddish words are used liberally throughout *Dancing in My Mother's Slippers*, I have paid special attention to making them accessible to the non-Hebrew-or-Yiddish-speaking reader. When new words are introduced, they are set in italics and their meanings, set off by commas, generally follow immediately. These words can also be found in the glossary at the back of the book. The glossary also contains brief descriptions of Jewish holy days and other Jewish practices mentioned in the book that might be unfamiliar to some readers.

Please note that some of the names in this narrative have been changed to protect the privacy of the individuals.

Introduction

Don't you people realize my Mother has died? I wanted to shout. *This is not an ordinary day!*

I drove through downtown Ashland the morning after Mother died. A crowd of people stood waiting to cross the street at the corner of Oak and Main. I saw them in their tourist clothes, office clothes, work-out clothes. Nobody in mourning clothes. They were laughing, talking, living life. It was all wrong.

It wasn't a new kind of day for them. If they'd known of our loss, they would have expressed their condolences, and gone on across the street to the bank.

We buried Mother. Days passed. Friends and family phoned and wrote and sat with us and prayed with us during *shiva*, the first week of the year-long formal Jewish mourning period. People were kind. I thought their presence would be healing. I expected things to be easier by the end of the week. It wasn't so. By the last day of *shiva*, I was moving from numbness into active grief.

I talked with my friend Justin shortly after Mother died. "When my own mother died," he told me, "I felt as if a mighty oak had been wrenched from my heart."

The hole she left was that big. This wrenching feeling . . . I recognized it. I felt it almost from the beginning. There was the gentle passing, and then the ache began, the ache of this gaping wound. Every thought, every sight, every memory brought me back to it.

I returned to my demanding job as the executive director of our local community dispute resolution center, and I functioned. But I crept always along the edge of sadness. A particular comfort in those early times was a letter I received from my dear friend Lu, who had lost her mother the year before. That she understood was a thin, strong ray of light through the pain, and I read her letter again and again.

I yearned for a book that could show me how to do this thing: to live in a world where there was no Mother to laugh with me, talk with me, advise me—hug me. Therese Rando's book, *How to Go on Living When Someone You Love Dies*, was a great help. I appreciated the way she explained things. She wrote about anticipatory grief, the grief I felt even before Mother died. She normalized my experiences after the death, helped me understand my mood swings, helped me know I wasn't crazy. But she didn't show me enough of her own experience. I wanted to know more about what it was like for *her*. I wanted her to show me how I could do it myself.

My relationship with Mother was, is, extraordinary. We were blessed to really know each other as adults, had a chance to grow beyond the mother-daughter complications. We learned to relax our roles, change them for new ones. We became dear friends.

And what do you do, how do you grieve the loss of a mother who is also your best friend, mentor, role model, spiritual sister? How do you grieve your partner in playfulness, supporter of girlish and womanly explorations? Where do you go for solace when your comforter dies? Inside, into the depths of Spirit. Outside, to your family, to your community. Farther out, into the Vastness. Some of this I knew before Mother's death, and some of it I learned in grieving and healing.

At some point I realized that grief could transform me, transform itself, but that it wouldn't really end. There were times when slogging through the mire of confusing thoughts and feelings was all I did. The Dance of Life continued. The balance shifted.

After Mother died, I was absolutely clear about what is important. Then I gradually began to worry about the little things again—the long grocery lines, the apparent slight delivered by a co-worker. Healing went underground, continued on a subliminal level. It was no longer daily in the center of my attention.

Grief had made itself a presence in my life, and I rode it like the bow wave of a speedboat. It drew me along, then I'd move off center and it would toss me into the air, all askew until I'd settle back into the flow.

The journey continues. Occasional dramatic interludes transform the hours, the weeks, of moving through. I look back on the last six years and see the "insurmountable" challenges which my family and I have somehow survived, and I know now that life goes on. We go on. A new kind of wholeness emerges, a whole with a gap in the center, like a bagel, like a doughnut. Life is delectable again. Usually.

I am finding my balance, and I move through my days with a broadening view. I move slowly, reintegrate myself into the world around me. Grief remains. Life will not be held back. Grief and Life entwine like partners dancing—undulating, grounded, steady. Exuberant. Serious. Patient. The dancers move through soft sand, sinking, sinking; glide on glare ice; sail through the air in a joyous leap of faith. There is something to dance about. Yes.

Healing emerges. Grief dashes to the fore—a slip of paper tucked in a drawer, a poem in Mother's hand, a favorite recipe, a special song. Tears flow. The center is missing, but the memories are sweet.

And insights emerge, signs of a deepening awareness, signs of the spiritual journey that began years ago and continues still. My personal spirituality, my life-long practice, has given me the strength to go on. It is the vessel that holds the grief.

⌒⌒

I decided to write the book I'd yearned to read. *Dancing in My Mother's Slippers* is my own story, based on journals I wrote from the time Mother was diagnosed through the four years following her death. This is not a traditional self-help book. It provides no lists or sets of instructions about how to heal yourself.

Perhaps you will resonate with what I have written. Perhaps you will see yourself in these pages. You may realize you're not alone.

In *Dancing in My Mother's Slippers* you will share the joys, the challenges, the healing insights that brought me peace and sustained me along my way. Community offers sustenance. Faith offers solace. Being present offers peace. I pray that as you read this book you will, even in some small way, be comforted.

Sailing into the Sunset

Mother was buried in Jacksonville Cemetery, three feet from a sapling spruce. It was pouring down rain, a suitable day for an Oregon funeral. We huddled together, everyone trying to hunch up under somebody's umbrella to keep the prayer sheets dry. Had to be careful not to slip in the red-orange clay in my high-heeled dress-up shoes. The rabbi said it rained because Mother dearly loved to be near water—at the beach, by a stream, even a creek.

I was dismayed to see water rising in the grave. My brother Gerry had built Mom an aron, a traditional plain pine box. As the men lowered the casket into the grave it tilted, and I realized it was afloat.

I whispered to my brother, "Look, Ger, you made Mama a boat."

He turned to Dad. "Look, Pop. It's a boat."

Mother and Dad had spoken, over all the years, of sailing into the sunset together at their ending time. It was Mama's magic: she brought the rain, and she sailed across, and Dad will, too, when his time comes.

The Final Year

November ~ This, Too, Shall Pass

November 18 – Ashland, Oregon – A Year Earlier

"If we each wrapped our troubles in a bundle," Mother told me, "and we each put our bundles in a pile, when it came time to choose, we'd always choose our own. You never know what someone else's life is like." Grandma used to say that.

Dad started hormone treatments for prostate cancer yesterday. And Mom's going to a gastroenterologist next Monday to see why she has blood in her stool. God willing, it will be something simple.

Mom saw the concerned look on my face as I was leaving last night. She gave me a big hug and said, "This, too, shall pass."

Outside my window, gray clouds roll back, and underneath, an eggshell blue sky. New day coming.

November 23

Thanksgiving morning and we have a lot to be thankful for, in spite of many challenges. Last evening, Uncle Mac passed on. I'm going to Los Angeles with the family to be with Auntie Mim and the cousins.

December ~ A Delicate and Blessed Balance

December 2

Ger and Dad and I went with Mom for her colonoscopy. The doctor talked to us afterwards in the green-tiled treatment room while the odor of disinfectant wafted at the edges of our senses.

"I cauterized two polyps," he said, "but there's a third one, very large, and it's partially obstructing your bowel. The likelihood is that it's malignant. It's got to go, or it will close the bowel up all the way."

"How soon does it have to be done?" Mother asked.

"Sooner the better. I'll have my nurse schedule the surgery today. I'm sorry."

Mom's eyes held his. "Thank you."

Mother wasn't surprised by the diagnosis. She'd suspected polyps. She'd had blood stains in her clothes that wouldn't wash out, and somebody told her that's a sign. But she thought the doctor would take care of them today. I have the impression she's known about this for months and has been putting it off. I can't blame her. It's natural to hope there isn't really a problem.

Mother's calm on the outside, but she's worried about the general anesthetic. She's known people who have developed dementia after major surgery.

Ger thinks we're entering a new phase, the Losing Parents phase. I remember thinking in Los Angeles that we'd all been living in a delicate and blessed balance, and that Uncle Mac's death maybe tipped the scale.

Sunday, December 10

I heard Mom's voice in the night on Wednesday, strong and clear and comforting. Just "Fayegail," like she was waking me up.

I went over to visit her and Dad the next day, and I told her about it. She said she wasn't thinking about me then.

⤙⤚

Lance and I hung out with Mom and Dad yesterday. Talked about the dance we'll have for Dad's hundredth birthday party—seventeen years from now. He says he'll dance with me right after

Mom. There they both sit, with cancer in their bodies, calm, lively, joking, full of life. It's hard to think of them as ill, even with Mom running to the toilet every twenty minutes. Maybe that's the whole point: *They* are incredibly healthy and whole, in spite of what's going on in their bodies.

December 13

We took Mom to the hospital this afternoon. Her surgery is tomorrow. She seems calm, accepting of whatever outcome. She and I had some quiet time while the others were in the cafeteria.

"I know the cancer may have spread," she told me, "but I'm expecting a complete recovery."

"God willing, *Imahleh*."

"If Dr. Hudson doesn't get it all, I don't want chemo, or radiation either. I don't want to live that way."

"I hope we'll never have to make that decision," I said, my eyes misting over.

"Fagel, if I had it to do over again, I'd have paid more attention to those early symptoms. I was so intent upon recovering from my second hip replacement, I didn't want to think about cancer."

We were quiet for a while.

"I've had too many surgeries," she told me. "This will be my seventh."

Mom's afraid, and feeling concern for Dad. He's pretty worried about her. I asked Mom how we could help him, and she said, "Just keep emphasizing the positive."

Ger and I signed the folks' advance directives this week—no life-support or tube feeding. They both want to die at home with palliative care and family around. I'm glad they specified that.

December 14 – Lance's Birthday

Mom's having a procedure this morning. I can't remember the name of it. The big surgery is at twelve-thirty.

I'm shivering with anxiety, and the pressure in my chest is intense. I'm trying to drop into Silence to hold it off, into that place deep inside where there are no words, no thoughts, no emotions—only Silence.

Friday, December 15

Mom has ovarian cancer. Dr. Hudson didn't suspect. Nobody did. When he went in, he found a tumor twice the size of my fist in her ovary. The cancers are scattered throughout her belly, and most of them are inoperable. He took out what he could. No symptoms until the cancer hit the bowel. What an insidious disease this is.

We're all in shock. I've been telling relatives and close friends what's happened, but I know reality eludes me. It's hard to switch my thoughts from *I know they'll get the tumor out, and Mother will be fine* to *They got most of the tumors out, and Mother isn't fine.*

Not sure what's next. We talk with the oncologist on Monday. Tears keep welling up. Whatever will change in our lives is unimaginable right now. I'm afraid.

Thoughts go to my job as director of the mediation center. This is such a big transition time for us. I'm worried that the whole organization will fall apart, and I won't be there to save it. I guess I need to trust the Universe to keep things running smoothly. It's beyond me.

I hurt. The pain in my chest was really strong when I awoke, but dropping into Silence has helped it dissipate. I went to Elias for acupuncture last week, and he said I have a "heart block." Apt name for the sensations I'm having. My heart feels like someone is squeezing it so hard the blood is stuck.

Poor Poppy. He went outside the waiting room to cry after we talked with Dr. Hudson. He'll need an immense amount of support now. We all will. Thank God we're a close family and have lots of friends. Risa, my friend from work, sent us presents yesterday—a whoopie cushion and a jar of bubbles and two narcissus bulbs in full bloom.

This whole thing is so unfair. Mom's been working hard to be able to walk again after her joint replacements, and now this.

December 16

Hope is returning. Who can know whether Mom's healing will involve a physical remission or the growth of our spirits, or both? But we do know this: we'll all make the journey together.

I sat quietly with Mom last night, in meditation. Maybe we dozed. The room was filled with power, and with love.

December 24

Panic attack in the night. Awoke overwhelmed, knowing I'd never be able to do all my work and care for Mom, too. *Who can I talk to? Somebody who's lost a mother. Lu offered. She'd be good, but it's Christmas Eve.*

I remembered to ask inside for help, and felt a flood of loving energy. I started to relax. So much pain and fear. How will I manage?

Come back to Deep Self, I hear. If only I can remember.

I am so grateful to have spiritual practices that can anchor me as I bob around in all this fear and pain.

Went to the pond with Lance this morning. Sat awhile with the big maple that leans over the creek, and I realized I've been grieving Mom's passing while she's still with us. Best to celebrate her life now, and grieve later. I don't mean to ignore the pain, but I need to be present with it, and not hurry into a future of what-ifs.

December 25

Ghastly conversation with a friend two weeks ago, and it's still with me. I told him we'd just found out that Mom has ovarian cancer, and he said, "You mean she's dying." Flat, cold, totally insensitive to my state of shock. I wasn't ready to articulate that, hadn't even taken it in. I was furious with him for the brutality of it.

"*My* mother died from ovarian cancer," he said, and I saw he was speaking from his own pain. I couldn't get my breath. I'm barely able now to acknowledge that Mother might be dying.

Maybe now that I've written this in my journal, I can move on.

December 27

Lance went on the Internet to see if he could find alternative therapies for Mom. He learned about an Ojibwa herbal formula for pain control which is said to strengthen the immune system.

We bought some at the food co-op under the name of "Essiac." That's the name backwards of a Canadian nurse, Rene Caisse, who used it successfully with many patients.

Mother's using it. She makes the tea in the soup kettle and bottles it for the family. We can all use an immune system booster, considering the stress we're under. It's our solidarity practice. We take it morning and evening, and say a personal prayer. Mother told me she's created her own ritual: She lovingly prepares the tea for herself and her family. Then she drinks it, envisioning a waterfall that enters her body and flushes out the cancer cells and leaves her comfortable and refreshed.

December 28

Had an acupuncture treatment with Elias this week, and he says I have deep insecurities. No surprise. I'm afraid I won't know how to live once my mother is dead. How will I find my new place in the world?

I made a list of things I can do to help Mother:

1. Laugh when the opportunity presents itself.
2. Field phone calls whenever possible.
3. Take Essiac and pray.
4. Take care of myself.
5. Help with chores.
6. Spend time, just the two of us.
7. Spend time alone with Pop.

January ~ Reflected Light

January 1

New year beginning. God willing, it will be filled with light—and with healing!

Dad asked me, "Why do doctors recommend chemotherapy if it's so toxic?" Good question.

January 9

Ben* and his sweetheart, Julia, are in town, and they're staying at our house. Julia and I went to take a contact improv class, but it was canceled. Exciting to think about it, though. It's the first time I've known I could find energy to dance after work. Maybe it's the Essiac.

January 10

Elias worked with me an hour and a half this week with needles and plant spirit medicine. I had a huge release. He said it had to do with adjusting to Mom's illness—and with letting her go.

He put an acupuncture needle into my solar plexus, and I felt an immense rush of panic. I saw that it's the future I fear.

With the panic came a vision: I looked out onto a dark pavement, a city street at night. It was wet, and the whole way was illuminated with silvery light. It was a narrow street, but it got wider farther out, like an inversion of the perspective drawings we used to make with rulers in elementary school.

This vision is a gift, a reminder that though the path seems dark, it is illuminated, and I will be able to make my way along it. It's a hopeful vision. The street is illuminated with reflected light. I must watch for light reflected to me from my surroundings, from people who love me.

How self-centered I am through all of this. I focus more on my own loss than on Mother's, I fear.

February ~ Beneath the Surface

February 6

Dream

I come across snow and discover a huge ice floe—like a slide—blue-white, and a sort of bowl with a pool at the bottom. The only way to get home is to slide down the ice. I watch other people before me, and they slide into the water and spring straight out, stiff-bodied, as though they've been ejected, as though they've hit a trampoline beneath the surface of the pool.

* Lance's son

A kind man, an older gentleman, approaches. He encourages me. He slides down, pops out of the pool like a piece of toast from a cartoon toaster, and lands on the opposite shore. I stand at the top of the floe looking down, and I wonder whether I myself will ever have the courage to slide down.

February 7

I've been pondering yesterday's dream. I saw that the ice floe was an immense fear, maybe of change. The people who did slide down the ice weren't concerned or fearful. The way they popped out of the pool was comical. They knew just how to do it.

Watching them, I felt as fearful of landing in the icy water as of rushing down the ice. I didn't believe I'd survive. Here is my precipice, perhaps—my opportunity to enter the Void, not with a leap, but with a slide, a hair-raising slide.

Maybe the pool is death. The most obvious thing is that it's Mom's death, but when I consider it, I think it's the death of my old self, and the emergence of someone new. It's about dying to an old way of being. My job is to let it go. I ask myself if I could find the courage to do that.

I like what Wendell Berry says about living:

> When I rise up
> Let me rise up joyful
> Like a bird.

> When I fall
> Let me fall without regret
> Like a leaf.

February 11

Went to a Greek dance class last evening. Dancing helps.

March ~ Be Willing to Fall

March 3

My dear friend Ginger took me cross-country skiing yesterday. It was my first time. Glorious day, and we hardly needed our sweaters. We skied out behind Mount Ashland. Had a picnic at the ski hut, warmed ourselves at the fire pit and fed snacks to the birds who hang out there. Altogether lovely.

I noticed I did pretty well as long as I stayed focused, but when I got distracted, I often fell. I also noticed I was uncomfortable when I felt out of control (as usual). As I learned little tricks, like grabbing with the side of my feet, or using my knees or my poles more effectively, I felt more secure. One lady we met on the trail showed me how to cross my poles and lean on the cross while getting up. Life was easier after that. We also met a friend of Ginger's who taught me a way to turn around on a slope in deep snow. That helped, too.

All in all it was a delicious experience, and I improved as the day progressed—more ease, less fear, maybe even a little grace. Ginger says I'm a natural. I must admit that skiing four and a half miles and falling ten or fifteen times has left me feeling every muscle in my body, but I don't think I've damaged anything.

The whole adventure felt like a metaphor for how to live a good life: relax, enjoy nature, stay focused, don't worry about being in control, accept help from friends, and be willing to fall.

April ~ For Tradition's Sake

April 3 – Passover Eve

I walked through the folks' front door at eight this morning and the kitchen timer was buzzing. Nobody in sight. I turned it off as Mother came hurrying up the hall.

"Morning, Mom. Smells good in here. What are you cooking so early?"

"Chicken soup. I haven't put in all the vegetables yet, just the onion."

"Well, I can do that. Why don't you sit down for a few minutes and drink something hot?"

I put water on to boil, then found carrots, a parsnip, dill in the fridge and took them to the sink. After they were in the soup kettle, I took out some milk and poured it into Mom's hand-painted porcelain bird mug, the one that was Grandma's.

"*Imah*, where's Grandma's chopping bowl? I might as well start chopping the pecans and apples for the *charoses* so it'll have time to mellow before the *seder*."

"It's on the shelf by the back door."

I got out Grandma's double-bladed chopping knife and the big wooden bowl and went to work. One thing I always make by hand is the *charoses*—for tradition's sake.

"Ma, remember that time in high school Carole Berman and I tried to make *matzoh* balls? They turned out so hard we went out in the street and bounced them back and forth like tennis balls."

Mom laughed and sipped her milk and water. "Your dad likes them that way," she said.

May ~ Escape

May 9

I noticed a pattern today. I no longer know what to do with free time. A few years ago I would have reveled in the luxury of an evening on my own. Last Tuesday night Lance had plans without me, and I worked at the office 'til twenty after ten.

What am I avoiding? Odd that I, who have loved solitude so much, no longer permit it in my life. Even as I write, I see I do so to escape the quiet of my heart. I've thought of a dozen people I could visit.

May 10

I looked back through my journal this morning. I've hardly written anything about Mother in the last few months. Maybe I immerse myself in work to escape thinking about her.

June ~ Instrument of Your Wisdom

June 17

Sometimes it's hard to hold faith that my daily practices are enough, that Life will support me if I don't try to make things happen. God, let me be an instrument of your wisdom. I feel so much fear sometimes—and so much peace in other moments.

—✦—

I've had a pain in my breast lately, and I see it's about nurturing. I need to nurture myself. I need to be careful not to make nurturing me the last priority.

Maya-cat just asked me to let her into the closet, and she found herself a nice kitty-sized basket on the shelf. Now she's curled up inside, no parts showing, and purring like a hive of bees.

July ~ Snowbells

July 15

Lance and I spent the weekend at the coast with Mom and Dad at Bandon. Mother walked on the beach for the first time since the auto accident nine years ago that caused her rheumatoid arthritis to flare. She and Dad used to walk on the beach in Ventura every day before that.

I wanted more than anything to be with her when she did it, and it's finally happened. I wept for joy to see her and Dad strolling along the shore, chatting, shoulders nearly touching. Was a foggy day, and the fresh salt wind blew their hair about their heads like halos. Dad wrapped himself in that old red and white Peruvian blanket I keep in the trunk of the car. He carried a golf club, and Mother, a borrowed ski pole. I feel happy and misty every time I think of the incredulous expression on Mom's face as she stepped out onto the sand.

July 24

Lance and I went to some friends' for dinner last night with Mom and Dad. The men left the table, and Mother told this story about renewal:

"We were hiking with friends at Lake Moraine, and we came across the scar of a devastating avalanche. Everything in its path had been swept away. There were no trees, no bushes, nothing to indicate the lush forest that had been there before. But we could see what it must have been like, because the surrounding areas were still heavily wooded. And there on the earth beside the trail, snowbells were blooming. There they were: delicate white flowers raising their heads in the midst of all the devastation, and they assured me life does go on."

July 25 – Letter from Me to Mom

Dear *Imah*,

Last evening I heard your snowbell story for the first time. It is beautiful and moving. If you've told it to me before, I mustn't have understood. Our walk on the beach in Bandon is *my* snowbell story.

Probably, I won't send you this letter. What happened to you at Lake Moraine all those years ago is so sacred that I'm afraid if I talk with you about it or write to you about it, I might desecrate it. I'm grateful you shared it with me, because it's something I can always carry with me.

I wish we'd talk more about our inner lives, although I know you and I are much alike. Maybe talking about it isn't as important as what we sense in each other. We are blessed to be good friends.

Oh, *Imah*. I just realized the summer of our trip to Alberta must have been the year that Grandma died. I've yearned so much to know how you dealt with your own mother's death. Now I see that's why you told the story.

Last night you spoke candidly about the havoc inside you. You seemed at once defiant and accepting, and I felt the tears in my eyes and knew we were each afraid we'd upset the other. But I don't think I felt so upset as moved by the beauty of who you are, and by your courage. You truly are teaching me to live every day in a beautiful way, just being yourself, living life each moment. From the outside you seem at peace with yourself. I wonder if you have any regrets.

August ~ Continuum

August 3 – Mother's 81st Birthday

I'm grateful Mom's still with us. What a challenging year it has been, full of love and laughter and tears and yearning and praying and rejoicing and counting blessings.

We all went to a *bat mitzvah* celebration today. Lance and I were both moved by the warmth of the family and the feeling of community.

I felt happy and at home in the *shul*, in the synagogue. It was hard to reach out to people I don't know, and I regret that, but it was nice to greet the many people I do know.

It means a lot to me that Lance went and that he enjoyed it, even though he's not Jewish. Maybe it's time for me to go to services more often, and to be more involved with the Jewish community. I'd like to find a way to be involved that's comfortable for both of us.

August 14

I need to let go my urgency to learn everything I can about Mom, all she knows, all her wisdom. I'm sure I've absorbed a lot without realizing it. Mother and Dad have both taught me a lot, not by talking, but by being who they are.

And Mother and Dad say their own parents are still nearby and helping them. They've all been gone for years. I guess there's no rush. I put too much emphasis on words. So much comes in silence.

August 15, 3 a.m.

Mom had a CT scan. She has cancer in her groin and extensive liver involvement. It's in her aorta, too. Still no pain, thank God. She says except for the groin, it may all have been there since the surgery. I don't think Mom ever thought the cancer was in remission. I let myself hope so. I don't know, maybe she did, too.

This news wasn't as shocking as the results of the surgery. We're already used to the idea that she is on this continuum from healthy, vital life to stillness. We *all* are, of course, and the cancer makes a poignant reminder.

I've been thinking about this as a transition time, but now I see that this is simply what Life is doing right now. I'm not waiting for something to happen. It *is* happening. I'm not waiting for something to happen to *me*. Life is happening to all of us. We're not a single drop of water holding shape. As soon as we hit the river, we're absorbed. We're not a single drop of water moving from one place to another, but all of it, a big vital flow, rushing along full of life and boisterousness and change. Seeing it that way, I feel less need to prepare for *something*. What is left to do is to engage in the flow, immerse myself in it, let it carry me. Safety comes in no-resistance.

August 16

I'm afraid. How will I manage at work? If Mom becomes more ill, I know my job will cease to be so engrossing. I've been increasingly concerned that I'm not seriously preparing someone to step into my shoes when I'm not there. How do you be an attentive daughter and a responsible director all at once?

August 21 – Mother and Dad's 58th Anniversary

I wrote a meditation this morning:

A Daily Meditation

Source of Life, grant me grace and dignity to live this day.
Give me patience to notice a fleeting smile,
    a moment of tenderness.

Help me face today's challenges
with wisdom and with courage,
    courage to take a stand when I must,
        and to surrender when I have done all I can.

Forgive me the mistakes I make today,
    and help me to forgive myself.

Remind me to cherish a sunlit patch of grass,
 birdsong, a blossom in the yard.

Help me recognize the changes in my body,
 and the changes in those I love,
  as a part of life.

And with all of that, Eternal One,
 help me to rest quietly in Your love
 and to find peace in every breath.

September ~ Life as the Tide

September 4, 3 a.m.

Maya woke us up with a mouse. She let it loose in the bedroom, and when I tried to catch it under the bed, I found two corpses—a bird and some other unidentifiable being—and a flower. It looked like an offering to some kitty god, or maybe it's her critter cemetery.

September 12

I noticed yesterday that when I get into work mode, I do everything too quickly: walk, talk, move, eat. My heart races. I still carry an image of myself as a calm, centered person moving easily through her days, and I am not that person anymore.

September 14 – Rosh Hashanah

Last night was our Traditional Holiday Dinner. A few weeks ago, Ger told Mom that this time, for the first time in years, he would eat chicken and brisket instead of his usual vegetarian fare. He didn't say, "because this will be your last *yontif*," but it hung heavy in the air.

Mom and Carolyn and I cooked all day, even though Mom has been chipping away at preparations for nearly a month. We were all exhausted. There was a last-chance feeling—*we'd better get this, we'd better learn how to do this*—and we weren't as chatty as usual. Still, it was a precious time cooking together, just the three of us. The men cleaned up.

We were all pretty steady, except Mama teared up during the *Shehekianu*. "You abound in blessings, Eternal One our God, Sovereign of all time and space, who has kept us in life, sustained us and allowed us to reach this moment." It's her favorite prayer.

It's a sad time for our family, yet what Lance said is true, too: Mother and Dad have lived full, meaningful lives. How fortunate we are to be here together to celebrate that, and to continue to learn from them, from their warmth and dignity and love.

I have a sense of connectedness with Mom. Last night, when Mom was in the bathroom, she was thinking we should check the brisket, and at the same moment I said to Carolyn, "We should check the brisket." When Mom came back and mentioned it, I was swept over with the knowledge, no, the relief, that she will always be there helping and teaching me, and that I will know her thoughts whenever I need to. I didn't *think* all those things. It was a simple knowing, and a reassurance, and Mom knew it too.

I sit here stroking Maya, and she's silky to my touch.

September 18

Had a vivid image yesterday, of surfing. Sometimes I ride the waves, sometimes I get tumbled and tossed and nearly suffocate, then I'm up out of the surf, and riding again. I am resilient.

I saw Life as the tide, sometimes at ebb, peaceful, empty, soothing, vast. Then high tide, with its tumultuous rollers and crashing waves and fullness and excitement and danger. And always the tide goes out and comes in again, like breath. This is the rhythm of our lives, and somehow that knowledge, that image, is tremendously soothing to me. That is the duality. We are the sea ebbing and flowing, Life itself. This vision gives me courage and peace. It helps me to know I can continue.

September 20

Today, for the first time, I am sensing an ending time for my involvement with the mediation center. It's not that I'm burned out. Rather, I realize that my work will soon be finished. I look forward to a quieter mode of life.

September 24 – *Yom Kippur*

Our whole family went to break our fast with friends tonight. Dad and I were chatting in the living room and suddenly, he turned gray. I ran to the dining room.

"Mom! Ger! Something's wrong with Dad. Call 911." Gerry made the call, then hurried to Dad's side. We settled him into an easy chair and Mom hovered nearby.

"We were sitting there chatting, and suddenly Dad got icy cold, then soaking wet. You can see his hands are shaking, and he wasn't talking right. Look how his eyes have gone vague."

Ger loosened Dad's clothes, and I went to get a damp cloth for Dad's forehead.

The EMTs arrived quickly and moved Dad to the floor with his legs up. They gave him oxygen and took off his shoes.

"Has he had anything to drink?" the burly one asked in a relaxed voice.

"Just one glass of wine," I said.

"Has he eaten anything?"

"No, he's been fasting all day. *Yom Kippur* is just ending, and we're about to start dinner."

The slender one nodded. "That'll do it—drinking alcohol on an empty stomach."

Dad's face was starting to get its color back. "Just let him rest for a few minutes and he'll be fine." The medics left and Dad rested a while. Mother was remarkably calm.

When we returned to the dining room and Dad saw all the concerned faces, he grinned. "You should know by now that I'll go to any length for a little attention," he said, and the party resumed.

September 25

Ger and I went up to the woods on *Yom Kippur.* Talked about Mom and Dad and what next. We both realize this is one situation where you can't plan ahead or prepare much. Things are simply unpredictable. The challenge is to be in the moment.

September 30

Mother and Dad are with Ger and Carolyn at McKenzie Bridge. I'm glad they're having some time away together.

Mother's disease is progressing, and she doesn't want to go to the doctor. I don't blame her. I probably wouldn't go either. She always waits until the last minute, but I can't help thinking she'd be more comfortable if she sought to relieve her symptoms *before* they became intolerable.

———

Lance and I have both been irritable lately, and we went to see Rabbi Marc. We had a good talk. As we described our challenges he said he thinks it's a timing issue. He suggested two things to us: First, come fresh to each other every day. That includes dropping old baggage. Second, make a special time at the end of each day to check in, and to clear the air if necessary. Notice whatever hard stuff comes up during the day, save it, and talk about it then. Mother and Dad have done that for as long as I can remember.

Yesterday I saw exactly what Rabbi Marc meant. Lance and I were impatient with one another while we were trying to decide how to redo one of the beds in the garden. If we'd acknowledged the tension then and left it until later to discuss, I know the day would have gone more smoothly.

———

Lance and I had a great weekend off. Delectable loving on Saturday morning, and a movie, shopping, and dinner on Sunday. After we saw *Spitfire Grill*, which I thought was a powerful lesson about love and judgment, he said, "Let's go buy you something special to wear."

We went to a new shop called Iris Blossom that sells elegant handmade clothing and chose a luxurious brushed rayon blouse that's a color of the sea, a blue teal that is perfect with my coloring. It's a casual thing—or dressy. Slips off the shoulder, just a touch. I've rarely spent as much on any garment, but Lance enjoyed gifting me. I felt so sensuous in it, I wore it right out of the shop.

Then we ate Caesar salad and minestrone and warm sourdough at Macaroni's, and took a walk in Lithia Park. Last thing was a nap on the couch before bed. Deliciously renewing day.

———

It's sad. People are coming to see Mom, maybe for the last time. We've been setting markers as I used to do running: just make it to the white car, just to that second red one. Just until Cousin Beth comes. Auntie Mim will come soon. Maybe that's what keeps us going. Otherwise, we're all doing pretty well staying in the moment. Better not to jump into the future. Lots of fear there.

Mama gets terribly bloated some days, and she gets dull backaches that make her uncomfortable. But she has better days, too, thank God.

October ~ Period of Grace

October 1

Had a special lunch with my friend Lu today, and we talked about mothers dying. She asked me if I have a wish or a vision. I have two: that we'll all be present when Mother dies, and when Dad dies, too, and that I'll have that conversation with Mother about what it was like for her at Grandma's ending time. I have to know how one survives without a mother.

October 2

Mom and I are reading *Final Gifts*, by Callanan and Kelly, but not together. Even though we're not discussing it, there's a kind of sharing as we both read about the poignant end-of-life experiences of the patients and their families. It's an excellent book. Comforting.

I feel numb, or peaceful, I'm not even sure which. I've come upon a time of quietness, of less talking. I hope I can quiet my mind as well. I need to pay special attention to staying level within, and to focus on breath, slow the chatter, quiet myself, quiet myself.

Sunday, October 6

Dream

I am walking by a river near my house. The water is high, and I'm afraid it will flow over the banks. I see a mossy pallet that has become lodged like a gate, and it occurs to me that the water might go down if I remove the blockage. I do. It comes out easily, and the water level does go down. I am pleased.

Then I glance downstream and see that a man and a young girl are together in a little boat. Suddenly there is a huge head of water, presumably built up from the water I released when I removed the pallet. It rushes along and catches the boat. The boat shoots up into the air. The man slips over the stern into the water. The girl remains in the boat alone, and it carries her quickly downstream.

As soon as I see the man go overboard, I rush home to call 911 and report the accident. The man and the girl are both too far away for me to help them. It's the only thing I can think of to do. It's out of my hands. I feel I have abandoned them, but I don't know another way to help.

I recognize this as a teaching dream. It woke me up and the images remain clear. The river is my life right now, full almost to overflowing. It's not really scary until the last stop is removed, then it crashes willy-nilly out of control. Is Mom the pallet—soft on the outside, strong within, and holding things in place? When she's gone, will it set off a terrible chain reaction? I would never, God forbid, want Mom to feel I am hurrying her on her way.

I am the little girl being carried out of control downstream—all alone, at the mercy of the river—out of control and not having any idea about what will happen to me, or what will happen to my father.

And the man—also me?—thrown into churning water. What about him? Will he survive? Will he be safe? This feels like Dad, but also like me as the director of the mediation center. I can't see where I'm going. The bow is straight up in the air blocking my view. How can I see to steer or right the vessel?

When the terror passes, I rely on my faith, but I fear it isn't strong enough. Faith washes over me in waves, and in between I am devastated, terrified, doubtful. Then it surges again, and I am reassured. I try to be present. It's the worrying in the middle of the night that's the hardest, and I'm so exhausted.

October 9

It's been great to have Auntie Mim and the cousins here from Los Angeles. Mom's energetic a lot of the time with relatives visiting.

Cousin Bob called from Sacramento and asked what he should tell Auntie Es and Uncle Joe about Mom. Mom said, "Don't tell them anything. I expect to get stronger. I don't feel like I'm on my way out yet."

Bob's wife, Kate, said she figures Auntie Es knows inside how ill Mom is, but she doesn't *want* to know. She's pretty much stopped asking how Mom is doing. I sure hope our generation can manage to be more open with each other.

October 16

We're starting hospice. Mother is seeing the social worker today. Seems like a turning, but toward what, I don't know. Relief from some of the symptoms, I hope. And maybe we'll have a better sense of where we are along this path we're on. Who can know how long we'll have Mom with us? Only God, I guess.

I'm glad we'll have the support we need, especially Dad. We've all drawn closer lately, closer than ever, but Dad's not asking us kids for any comfort on a verbal level. Maybe he'll be able to talk with the hospice people.

I feel detached from work, yet it's terribly demanding right now. I'm trying sincerely to stay in the moment and out of my racing mind. Just breathe!

Friday, October 18

Some interesting insights today. I realize I no longer need Mom to talk to me. I get a lot of joy helping around the house and making things easier for her and Dad, and I know I'm expressing my love and devotion. At least for now I've gone beyond the need for guidance from her about how she coped while Grandma was dying and how I shall cope without her. Now I trust that I shall know when the time comes.

The fear seems to have subsided, too, but I'm not cocky about it. These things have come in waves before. Anyway, I'm grateful for this period of grace, however long it lasts.

October 20

I'm aware, from being with Mom these weeks, that I indulge in much unnecessary and distracting mental chatter, and I see that quiet is satisfying. I see Mom resting. She draws back inside throughout the day, just resting in some place that leaves her face peaceful. I want to share that quiet peace.

October 29

Life seems to be tugging at us to reexamine our roles. Ger is asserting his position in the family as firstborn. He's the one who knows how to manage things, invest, take care of the rest of us. I have other realms of expertise. Fortunately, we complement each other and appreciate each other's contributions, so I'm fine with him in the role of Elder Brother.

Pop needs our support, but he's still The Father, and I don't want to take away from him what he needs, that is, to be Mom's primary caregiver. That's been his job for many years, and he cares lovingly, eloquently.

I'm torn. I'm constantly being drawn away to the office. My heart is divided between wanting to be with Mom and feeling the responsibility to keep things going at work. I wish I could be with Mother all the time. Of course the others are able to care for her, but I want to do it myself. We all want to feel needed by Mom. That is, we all want to feel that we can help her passing be as easy, as comfortable, as possible.

October 30

Relatives are pouring in—floods of people, waves of emotion. It's hard. Every time someone leaves, Mother has a low day, nausea and weakness, depression, even. It's hard for her to say goodbye. She puts on the green velvet dressing gown we bought for special occasions, and she looks regal. When people come, she's cheery and loving and supportive, counsels them, talks with them. She musters all her energy for this last time they'll be together. It takes a tremendous toll, but she does it over and over again.

Mother has always been the comforter and the advisor. She shares her wisdom with everyone who needs it, any time, and sometimes at a cost to herself.

Cheryl, the hospice social worker, brought up funeral arrangements. She says death's not imminent, but making it until Thanksgiving is iffy. I think Mom will wait until Auntie Mim comes again next week, but of course I don't know that.

Mom's very much alive. At times her voice is strong and clear, but sometimes she's so tired she only rests or sleeps, eyes closed, face peaceful. Thank God for the peace. She seems to have accepted her situation with grace, but she's not talking to me about anything but her physical symptoms. Maybe she never will. Ger wonders what she thinks about these long days. I wonder if she thinks at all. One might get tired of thinking by the end of a long life. I must remember to mention that to him.

October 31

I've noticed that correct posture helps me breathe better. Last night I told Mom I'd been conscious of my carriage since she mentioned it the other day. I'd always thought of myself as a person with good posture. Mother says I've developed a stoop that comes from hurrying; I'm always leaning into my day. I see it's true, for when I straighten my shoulders, my center of gravity drops, my head is higher, and I must walk more slowly, and with grace. I told Mom I carry her like a little bird on my shoulder to remind me.

Transition

November ~ Life Is Good

November 1

November already. Is this the month I shall lose my mother?

The other evening I came late to dinner. The only place left at the table was Mother's place. I sat there and instantly regretted it. I could hardly bear to sit there opposite Pop, in a place where I did not belong. It's Mother's place and probably always will be. I could barely look at him, felt shame for having done it, needed to force myself to stay, rather than make a big fuss during dinner and get everyone to move over and make space for me. Last night for *Shabbos* dinner we were an odd number again. Someone had placed the *challah* and wine and candles in Mother's place, and I was relieved to see it.

We meant to carry all the ritual things into the bedroom on a glass platter so we could share the *brachot*, the blessings, with Mother. She hasn't left the bedroom since last *Shabbat*. That was the first night of the morphine. Last night, when we were ready to say the *brachot*, Mother told us to do them in the dining room. She didn't want anything in the bedroom, not even another set of candlesticks for herself.

It's the first time I can remember her not lighting *Shabbos* candles. Even in the hospital, where real candles aren't allowed, she used the electric *Shabbos menorah* Rabbi Marc brought.

I felt wrenched apart by her decision, as though my heart had been torn out. It is her commentary: I am no longer divided equally between the two worlds. I have made my choice, to move now toward the world beyond. Or maybe she was saying another thing. Maybe, because we believe that *Shabbat* is our gateway to *haolam haba*, the world to come, Mother chose not to say the blessings, chose not to enter *Shabbat*. Maybe she's not ready yet to walk through that gate, was afraid she couldn't come back. Who can know?

Here I am in my mind, trying to make sense of something that is purely a matter of the heart. Whatever it was that prompted Mother to decline the *brachot*, it meant for me, I realized later, another little death in a whole series of little deaths.

Perhaps that is the way we can prepare ourselves. Each change, each step we take toward the final transition is a little death which carries us closer to acceptance, to letting go of her. The swelling, the morphine, the decision not to dress, hospice, staying in the bedroom, now the *brachot*. Each choice is like a sign for us: Death is nearer. We'll go slowly. We'll get used to this. Then the next shift comes, and the prior one doesn't seem so bad. Another step, another step, and soon we find ourselves living in equanimity with the last one.

Hospice becomes a friend, a lifeline in a sense. Our nurse, Eileen, is a source of love and of reassurance that we won't be left alone not knowing what to do. Each little death is a step towards acceptance, but also a weaning away from life as we once knew it. We have been so safe, altogether safe, in our love for each other, and now it is clear that nothing will ever be the same again. We are all, even now, in new territory.

In the past, our crises were temporary. We always knew we'd come out on the other side, somehow or another. Now we aren't so certain at times—or rather, only some of us will come out, and only God knows in what condition.

Dad is treating this, in some ways, like all the other crises. He has faith that Mother will find a way to do her magic once again and pull herself back to us. So maybe these little deaths are especially for him, to wean him from her, who is his lifeline. It seems to me that each one brings a subtle change in him.

Everyone's worried about him. He seems so fragile, so lost. Rabbi Marc talked to Carolyn about it. Eileen said she and Cheryl are also concerned. I see it two ways: Either he'll follow Mother quickly because he can't bear to be here without her, or something else will shift in him, and he'll heal and resume an active life. I feel in him a powerful inner strength, but whether he'll use that life force to stay or to go is yet to be seen.

My work at the mediation center is being left to its own dance. I'm doing what I can, but much of my time is spent asking other people to take on my usual responsibilities or thinking, *What can we let go until later?*

What a time this is. Half of me is in this busy work-and-ending-time world, while the other half rests in a vaster awareness, where I trust that all is well and that everything moves according to some divine plan. I feel like a yo-yo some days. I can hardly bear to think of myself adrift in this world with my parents gone. On the other hand, I have faith that we shall not be separated, that love is everlasting. I sit, pen in hand, thinking, thinking, trying to make sense of all this. But when I look into my heart, I see that my heart trusts the One, no separation.

It comforts me to think of the psychic bond Mother and I share. I told her last night I'd been thinking about *Rosh Hashanah*, and how we both thought of checking the brisket at the same moment. I said I like that wherever we are, when we're not together, we can think messages to each other. Mother squeezed her eyes shut two or three times and changed the subject.

I can talk to Mom in signs and images and metaphors because she sees the world, in many ways, as I do. Rather, I see as she does. She's taught me about signs, and about trusting them. About guardian angels. About snowbells.

Back to this thing about standing tall. The other day, I was telling Mother that good posture helps me breathe better and feel better. Now I see another thing: Walking consciously puts me in touch with my own power, wisdom, the vaster self within me, the part that keeps me going. When I stand tall, and breathe tall, self-doubt goes away. I have a feeling of confidence and well-being that's hard to notice under other circumstances.

I love noticing this now, in conjunction with Mother's suggestion. I'll forever associate her with this way of moving. It's so like her. When I hurry, I am stooped, hobbled. When I stand tall and take my time, I feel centered and grounded and appropriate. I slow down, and I breathe, and I remember Source, and I feel safe. What gifts these are, and what a simple practice. I have a sense of mastery when I stand tall. I feel solid.

November 4

I'm feeling stressed and panicky, and I'm only part way through my day. God knows if I'll make it. Oh, of course I will. I need to beat the furniture or kick it, scream, cry, *express*.

Tried crying. Sounded too fake. Didn't want to hit or kick anything. Afraid I'd hurt myself. Settled on toning. Loud, bellowing sounds came out. Made me feel a little better. Don't know who to call. Don't know what to do. I am terrified, and here's this other part of me saying, *This is the human, little, scared part. Don't forget the cosmic part.*

Then here's Maya, perfectly calm, climbing up onto my lap, smelling of fresh air like a kitty just come in, and reminding me there *is* somebody here for me. That's what Lance said this morning before he left for work.

I said, "I don't want to be alone today."

"Maya's here," he reminded me.

⤙⤚

Finally went to work around three-thirty. On the way from the parking lot, I walked along the alleyway. All along the building, fallen leaves were scattered. I was walking directly into the sun, my vision impaired by its brilliance. Though I could barely see to walk, I could see each leaf reflecting the sun's golden light. A thought came into my mind: *The way is illuminated, but I can only see to take one step at a time.*

It was such a gift, a comfort, to have that reassurance. Surely I shall find my way if only I can take one step, and then another, and then another. Some days I am challenged to trust that one step at a time is sufficient. I don't know who to ask for help right now. I suppose I need to trust that the right people will come.

November 5

Mother got a wheelchair yesterday and joined us at the table for dinner. She seems revitalized, shiny, and regal. It was heart-melting to have her out with us, to see her enjoying her family and her home.

———

I realized this morning I'd be better off to think of Mother as chronically ill, with occasional acute episodes. It helps me get out of that horrible space of waiting for her to die. I don't mean I'm *waiting*, in the sense of wanting, but it sometimes seems that we are poised, waiting to see what our next response needs to be. It's confusing. Most of the time Mother doesn't *appear* to be precariously on the edge of death.

Some days I feel like we're teetering between two worlds, one of celebration, one of mourning. The more fully we can celebrate Mother's good days and appreciate them, the healthier this process can be for all of us. The wheelchair helped me see that we'd given up too soon. Thank God for hospice!

November 6

Had a powerful massage last evening. I realized I need to dance. It's a good way for me to get my feelings out where I can look at them.

I connect with Mom when I'm dancing. I have memories of her dancing at home with Dad. I wonder whether, if she had danced more, had expressed more, she might not have had such debilitating arthritis. She held her feelings close.

When I told Mom I connect her with grace and dancing in my mind, she said, "But I feel so clumsy."

"I remember you and Daddy, the way you'd glide around the family room on Virginia Drive," I told her. "Waltzing." She liked that.

Dancing will be another way of staying close with Mom, *another* bridge. I'm always searching for them.

November 7

Had a really good family talk, and I'm sorry Lance wasn't there. Ger and Carolyn and I were talking in the den about how often we should stay at the house with Mom and Dad.

Dad came in from the bedroom. "I like having you kids in the house. It's good backup."

"Let me go check on Mom," I said.

When I got into the bedroom, Mother looked hurt. "I don't like it when you're all talking about me in the other room. I can't hear what you're saying, and I have a right to know."

So everybody came back into the bedroom, and I told her about our conversation. "So, I was worried that you folks felt a little crowded with people always in the house," I concluded.

"No," she said. "I agree with Dad. It's comforting to have you here." I'm glad they feel that way. It's comforting to me, too.

After everyone else left, I curled up on the bed with Mom and we had another cozy talk. I love the private time I have with her. I told her about my new way of seeing her illness: chronic, but sometimes acute. "That's the way I see it, too," she said.

We talked about how everybody always feels better hanging out with her—she's like a magnet. "I don't know whether that's good or bad—it's just the way it is," she said. "Cheryl came on her way home from her last client yesterday," Mother continued. "She told me we're a great family. I have the feeling a lot of the families Cheryl works with are troubled. I hope I'm not taking her time from people who really need it."

"Coming to you is probably a respite for her, Mom. A good thing after a hard day." She seemed pleased at that. Lance and I haven't met Cheryl yet.

"I think I've reached a plateau with the swelling," Mom said after a while. "For the last two days I've taken only ginger tea, no Compazine or morphine, and I haven't had any nausea or pain. I think the Compazine was making me queasy."

It's not the first time a natural remedy has helped Mom. She's never had much tolerance for pharmaceuticals. She's even started to eat again—bland things like toast and a touch of cottage cheese. "I'm not really hungry," she told me, "but I want to eat to keep my strength up."

Mom spoke of "this stage" of her illness, and how for now she and Dad can manage things like getting her up and into bed and walking to the loo, and getting into the wheelchair. She's rallied, and I guess she's decided to stick around awhile. "With this disease," she said, "one can never know what the liver will decide to do. One never knows whether it will be a day or a week, and the important thing is to take it a day at a time." What an amazing woman is my mother.

November 8

Mom likes having us there. I'd be there constantly, as Ger is, if things weren't so demanding at work right now. Ger thinks I feel guilty for not being there more. Maybe, but I think it's more that I envy him the flexibility his work as a property manager affords him. Still, I see I'm not willing to abandon my work to be there all day—and I think Mother would be appalled if I did. I am trying to find a balance, and I think I'm okay with the way things are right now.

I'm grateful that we're all together supporting each other. I'm grateful that, in the midst of this, we all feel blessed.

Mom seems weak again. She had a spurt of energy, no pain, no nausea for two days, but night before last she had another episode, and yesterday she was still pretty tired. Her legs have begun to swell and feel tight in their skins.

The nurse has been coming more often, and Mom hasn't moved her bowels in three days. The good news is that it isn't causing her any discomfort. She's been eating again, but apparently the food collects rather than processes, and then she vomits it up.

November 9 – *Shabbat*

Last night Marc came to dinner. His family has gone to New York. He brought a delicious lasagna that Catherine made before she left. Mother joined us at the table for *Shabbat* dinner. It looked to

be a supreme effort for her to sit so long in the wheelchair, and
when I said goodnight, her voice was terribly weak.

———

I was puttering around in the kitchen after everyone went to bed.
I noticed the drawers were less tidy than usual, the food was all in
different places in the fridge, and I realized the last jar of Mom's
homemade red pepper jelly is almost empty. Mother's influence
is withdrawing, more every day, from the daily round. I felt a
sadness, not intense, but sweet, almost—gratitude for all Mother
has been to us. At the same time, a knowing swept over me that
things will never be the same again. I wonder where we are going,
what will become of us, in this time approaching.

Part of me wants to straighten things out, put things back where
they belong. Yet I need to find peace with the passing of this or-
derly predictability. The pickled herring goes on the rotating tray
at the bottom of the fridge, and the root beer goes in the rack on
the top shelf, left. Forks are separated into little stacks by size in
the drawer. What details have I missed? What will I never be able
to put back the way it was?

———

We're all raw and hurting and tired and sad. I've noticed before,
though, that it's in times like this that people sometimes make the
biggest personal breakthroughs—when we're exhausted and our
resistance is down.

November 10

Relatives are here from Los Angeles again. It gives Mom a big lift
to spend time with them.

November 14

Yesterday Mother had a terrible episode of retching and vomiting—hours long. Ger called hospice, and Eileen came and gave
her a Compazine suppository and switched her nausea medicine
and upped her morphine dosage.

The vomiting started right after the L.A. relatives left. I've been
thinking for days that Mom was operating on sheer willpower,

sitting up for long hours and chatting, laughing. It's almost as though now she can let go.

Plans are on for relatives from the east to be here for Thanksgiving. I don't imagine Mom will make it 'til then. She's exhausted. Her breaths were odd last night—long in between and then a little jerky shallow inhalation and a puffy exhalation, and sometimes rattly or moany.

Dad and I cried together and then sat silent, holding hands. He is almost totally sad now, and lost to his grief. He has a bad cold—his whole body is crying.

Don't know how long Mom can hold out. Not sure what's keeping her here. She's not able to lie down because of the pressure from the fluid in her belly. It stifles her lungs and makes her retch. Last night she slept in Daddy's easy chair—maybe she will from now on. She has a partial bowel blockage, too.

I can't even imagine how it will be not to share my days with her. She is my solace, even now, when she's so ill. She's still putting other people's needs first. I wish she could go on now instead of suffering so much.

November 15

I'm at home and blasting our wood stove to get rid of the creosote. Doing it always makes me uneasy. It's the intensity of the flames, the concentrated power, like the sea in a storm. It's nurturing, life giving, then suddenly unrecognizably violent and threatening, then calm and nurturing again. Perhaps that is the way of all things in nature and in human behavior, too—the vacillation between might and tranquility. I see there is power in the calm, too, gone deeper, quiet, waiting.

I'm pouring sweat waiting for the creosote to burn off. Lot of waiting these days, and waiting isn't okay with me. I keep wanting to be present, only in the moment, and I keep being dragged away by my fear. Back to center, thrown off again, a raft out of control in white water, bouncing from rock to rock.

I shut down the stove and the roar subsided, but it's still a raging box of flame. No terrible roar, just the crackling and snapping of iron, and rain in the background. Fire and water, breath of life, in the midst of dying. Sadness is always just over the edge, never far away. Comes in a flash, recedes as fast.

———

Maya's coat is luxuriant. What a comfort she is—glue cat. She stays by me much of the time I'm at home these days. She knows I need her.

Saturday, November 16, 11:45 p.m.

Mother died at 8:20 this evening. Carolyn and I are at the funeral home keeping Mama company tonight. We'll be here until 8 a.m. Then the *shomrim* will come, the people from the *chevra kadisha* who will sit with Mother and help her transition from this world to the world to come. Strange to be in this foreign place. I'm glad Mother died at home.

The funeral director hugged me when I went to shake his hand. What is it that makes strangers want to hug me? It's a thing I dread about the next week—that all the people who come will want to hug me, and I'll wind up needing to comfort *them*, instead of vice versa.

———

What a nightmare the last twenty-four hours have been. No, that's not true. It didn't last that long. I woke up at two o'clock and heard Mother and Dad talking. Mom needed to get up. She hadn't slept yet and was already exhausted. She was awake the whole night, and I sat up with her. She finally dozed at a quarter to eight this morning.

Mom had a good day yesterday. She had energy, and she and Ger even played cards. Ger told me it was the best day he's ever had with her. He talked about how close they felt. I'm happy they could share that. I was in a mediation training all day, and I missed it.

I don't know how Pop is managing to walk about. He hardly slept last night either, has been primary care giver all the weeks— months. Guess you do what you must. None of us can say we should have done things differently. We've been a loving team and plenty there for each other, as we'll continue to be.

This morning I tried to help Mom with a suppository in the

bathroom. No success. She was totally exhausted, needed oxygen on the toilet. No way to help her by myself, and I needed to call Dad and Ger. Thank God it didn't happen in the night. There's no way Dad and I could have lifted her off the toilet by ourselves.

That was at eleven, and Mom never got better after that. We got her back into Dad's big chair—coached by a hospice nurse over the phone. Eileen was out of town, and the weekend nurse promised to send someone over around two this afternoon.

Mom needed to go to the bathroom again and collapsed, dead weight, on the floor as Dad and Ger were trying to get her there. The nurse, Trudy, arrived just as it happened. She hadn't realized it was so bad, and it took her a couple of minutes to get her bearings. By that time, we were all pretty scared.

Used lots of oxygen—a full tank. Then hospice brought an oxygen machine that worked pretty well. It was a noisy thing. Took oxygen right out of the air and ran it into Mom through a tube that hooked around her ears and passed under her nose, same as with the tank. It was unsettling to have it there, but at least we didn't have to worry about running out.

God, we are so lucky that Mother didn't live like this for weeks or months. I don't think she ever had intense pain though she had mighty discomfort toward the end with the backaches, the shortness of breath, the nausea.

We loaded Mom up on morphine at the end, in the last several hours, but we couldn't get her breath rate back to normal. At one point, Mother called me from the other room. She was gasping.

"It's okay to go, *Imah*." I told her. "We'll help Poppy. We'll take care of each other." After a while her breath slowed, and she seemed to be asleep.

As Trudy was leaving the house, Mother suddenly looked pleased and said, "Susie!" and got a tender, peaceful expression on her face. Then she threw back her head and gazed, eyes wide open. I thought she was having a seizure, but then she relaxed, and a while later the peaceful look came back.

I followed Trudy out and told her what I'd seen, and I told her I thought Sue Libit, Mom's dear childhood friend who had also died of ovarian cancer, had come to help Mother across. Trudy agreed this might be the day, and I shared that with the family.

Mom's breath was slower, more peaceful, came less and less often. I joined Dad and Lance and Carolyn in the kitchen for some supper while Ger sat with Mom. Then I went back in and sat beside her, and Mom's breathing gradually slowed until it stopped.

I'm grateful I was with Mom at the moment of her transition. I wanted to be. I thought I was alone with her, but Lance remembers he was there, too. And Dad remembers holding her in his arms as she breathed her last breath. I don't know whether Ger and Carolyn were there, or not. I wonder what else we all remember differently.

———

Carolyn shared a perfect image with us that she'd heard in a lecture given by Rabbi Larry Kushner: that creation is like the ocean, and each life rises up like a wave, crests and returns to its source.

Now Mother's body has been cast off, and she has become, once again, indistinguishable from the vast sea of life. No matter where I am, I have the chance of encountering her essence, in the sparks she sends out, in the light she has shared, in the creek, in the stars. She is everywhere, in every flicker of flame.

We could see she wasn't in there anymore. Her empty body sat in Daddy's big chair, jaw slack, mouth agape, as though she'd had a shock at death. That isn't so. Her passing was gentle. Then why did her face change afterwards? Maybe to remind us that she truly has withdrawn. The body is no longer appealing, must be guarded and honored, yes, but it's no longer my Mother. That body, full of life, bore me, and now it's been cast aside like the husk of a seed.

———

I just realized why we say *Kaddish* so long, why we mourn publicly for a year. That way we make it over the whole cycle of hurdles with the community supporting us, and we know we can live through another year on our own.

———

It's three-thirty, and I am fading. I'm *so* grateful Mama died peacefully. What a hellish day.

Tuesday, November 19

Had an important talk with Lance Sunday evening. I realized that my work now is to grieve with clarity, and to let feelings flow through without stopping them—sadness, laughter, whatever is there.

Sometime in the night I came to understand that all that I need is within me, accessible to me. I didn't want to let go needing Mother. The very needing held her here in some magical way. Now I see her wisdom, compassion, knowledge, even, are inside me. I feel her inside me, feel her guiding me. With her passing I find I am willing to accept my own womanliness—without requiring Mother to be my intermediary.

When I phoned Mary Margaret to let her know that Mother had passed, she spoke of woman-time as circular. That is, all of the Grandmothers and Mothers are not only behind us, but also ahead of us, drawing us toward knowing, prompting us toward wisdom, toward fulfillment, toward the Woman Way.

I can't remember just how she described it, but I can feel this drawing out of my woman power, promptings to be my fullest, wisest self, to be a channel for the eternal feminine.

Papa gave me Mama's cozy slippers. He said, "You are walking in your Mother's footsteps now."

"Thank you, Daddy," I told him. "I am honored." He also gave me Mama's gold necklace—the bird in the teardrop. I've always loved it best of all the things he made for her.

I phoned our long-time family friend Ilse to tell her of Mother's passing. "You're so much like your Mother," she said. "That will be a great comfort to your father right now. He'll see her in you and be comforted."

"I hope so," I told her. "I hope seeing her in me doesn't make him hurt even more."

Another friend told me that in the time since his father's passing, his relationship with his father has deepened beyond anything he could have imagined. That surprised and comforted me.

I haven't written anything yet about the funeral. Gerry built the *aron*, the casket, with a woodworker friend of his, a simple pine box with rope handles. It suited Mother's elegant simplicity. I am moved that he made it for her.

We all spent a lot of time planning a memorial booklet to share with people who attended the funeral. Lance did the layout and had it printed on pale blue paper.

We put in this poem by Annie Johnson Flint that Mama has carried in her wallet since Grandpa died:

> God hath not promised
>> Skies always blue,
> Flower-strewn pathways
>> All our lives through;
> God hath not promised
>> Sun without rain,
> Joy without sorrow,
>> Peace without pain.
>
> But God hath promised
>> Strength for the day,
> Rest for the labor,
>> Light for the way.
> Grace for the trials,
>> Help from above,
> Unfailing sympathy
>> Undying love.

We also used the Emerson quote that hangs in the bathroom and the Desiderata and the Serenity Prayer Mom kept under the glass on her dresser, Debbie Friedman's *Misheberach*, the *Kaddish*, of course, and the Twenty-third Psalm—a contemporary translation Rabbi Marc shared with us.

The cover of the booklet said, "Johanna Arbetter Mandell, a woman of valor" and gave the Hebrew and civil dates of her birth and death. The graphics Lance chose were a flying crane and a crane at rest in a marsh—Mama in flight, Pop waiting at home for now. There was another poem Rabbi Marc gave us called, "We Remember Her." It was perfectly Mom.

———

Mother was buried beside a young spruce in Jacksonville Cemetery. It was pouring rain, and I was concerned to see that water was accumulating in the grave. Rabbi Marc said the rain came because Mother loved water so. But then, as they lowered the *aron* into the grave it tilted, and I realized it was floating. I touched Gerry's arm and whispered, "Look, Ger, you made Mama a ship."

He turned to Dad. "Look, Pop! It's a boat!" Mother and Daddy had spoken, over all the years, of sailing into the sunset together at their ending time.

I'm sure the rain and the floating casket were a special gift from Mom to show us she's okay, still doing magic, still *being* magic. It was comforting to all of us that she did that.

———

Today Dad asked me to clear out all Mother's personal stuff from the bathroom. Aunt Mick offered to help. It was a comfort to do it together. I thought it would be hard, but it wasn't so bad. I didn't even cry.

The really hard thing was saying goodbye to Auntie Mim when she left for L.A.

———

Rabbi Marc's wife, Catherine, was in Los Angeles visiting her mother, and she came home especially to be with us, and of course, to honor Mom. I felt so happy to see her at the funeral, holding the umbrella over Rabbi Marc as he read the service. She flew up, and now she has to fly back down to get her car.

Catherine and I had a good talk yesterday after the service, and she helped me a lot. She warned me that sometimes people turn to those in deep mourning to be comforted, rather than to comfort. One of the relatives did turn to Ger, feeling bitterly disappointed with himself, angry and ashamed, because he'd never come up to see the folks while Mom was alive. Maybe he needed our forgiveness in order to forgive himself.

November 21

Every day gets harder, not easier. I thought it would be the other way around. I asked Rabbi Marc about it, and he said, "You're beginning to learn the depth of your loss."

Best to stay in the moment, and be with it. It hurts. I hurt. But I *am* willing. "I dread going back to work next week," I told him.

"This isn't next week yet. Stay here." I know what he says is true.

⤚✦⤙

Yesterday Pop and I took a walk at Emigrant Lake with Uncle Roy. We looked for rocks, saw birds, lichen, mistletoe, breathed fresh air. It was good to be out of the house for a while, and to find some solace in nature.

When Rabbi Marc saw the rocks we'd picked up, he told Dad, "Maybe I'll learn with you about rocks."

Pop said, "This will be my new hobby." I liked hearing him say he has plans for himself.

⤚✦⤙

Yesterday, when I was straightening up, I found an ancient dictionary on Mom's desk. There was a leather bookmark in it. I opened it, and there I saw the word "ark." In Hebrew, *aron* is ark and also coffin. It is the place to keep the Covenant, and also the ship built by Noah for his family and the animals, that is, a place of safety and refuge. That is exactly what Ger built for Mama—a place of safety and refuge. And a ship. I showed the entry to Ger. Strange. I've never known anyone to put a bookmark in a dictionary. I wonder if there are other messages for us on that page. "Armistice," it says, "a temporary cessation of hostilities; a truce." Ger and Lance have been testy with each other lately. Maybe this will help.

⤚✦⤙

My friend Lu sent me an exquisite letter on a beautiful Chinese card. The translation of the calligraphy is, "Together we taste the sweet and the bitter." Her own mother died last year. She wrote: "I know how much you did not want this time to come, and also how deeply you knew it would come, in time, and did all that you could to prepare for your mother's passing. I hold you in my heart as your heart aches. I know how deeply you loved and respected your mother, and I am moved at the memory of your abiding care for her, and for your father. When I look at the night sky tonight (as I do every night), I will think of my mother—and now your mother too. . . " Others have sent sharings from the heart, as well. In all the times I've sent condolence cards and notes, I've never realized how comforting a heartfelt note can be.

Had a sweet time last night at the *shiva minyan*. It wasn't the conversation—just that I sat between Lance and a friend on the couch, and held hands with both of them.

I've learned an important thing about community this week: It's ridiculous to tell myself I don't have time to be a part of it. It is so important to be there for each other that I *must* rearrange my priorities—to have time for family and friends, to go to *shiva min-yanim*, even for people I hardly know. I need to have a personal life again.

One thing I've yearned for these last few years is the way I used to support people, be available for them. I've been saying to myself, "Well, my work is serving the greater community now." But I see there's no substitute for serving the individuals within the community. I hope I'll remember this lesson when I go back to a normal routine.

The last of the relatives left yesterday. It was good to have them here, and I thought I'd feel worse than I do to see them go. I guess I needed my house back. It's good to have a refuge, morning time, a quiet house. It's good to sit with Maya, sharing peace.

Last night Lance brought me a seven-day candle. It's out of sync with sitting *shiva*, but I want it burning here at home. I need the comfort it affords. I feel Mother in the candlelight. Lighting the candle here at home marks the beginning of a transition. I was going to write "to normalcy," but my life has no normalcy. It will never be the same again, and I can't begin to think how it will change, or how I will change.

November 22

Dream

Walking on a road, a country road at the edge of town, with Lance and a young girl-woman.

We continue walking, see other young people. We're in precipitous circumstances. The road has fallen in. The young woman leads the way. Lance assists me so I won't fall. We walk close to buildings, but the surrounding ground has fallen away, and I must hold onto the sides of the buildings and swing myself around corners to follow. It's dangerous, but I don't feel at risk. It's a time of challenges. We wander in old familiar areas that have been radically affected by some kind of disaster, an earthquake perhaps. We are searching, exploring new options, and Lance gives a hand at all the hard places.

How symbolic this is of my life right now. The young woman must be the part of myself which is fresh and new and wise, unaffected by what appears to be.

Yesterday was a little better, but I was irritated when someone set a bare table for dinner. Mom always used place mats or a cloth.

Saturday, November 23

Had a good cry last evening between fixing dinner and going to the table. Was our first *Shabbat* dinner without Mom in the house. I made it all the way through lighting the candles with dry eyes, but I lost it when Ger teared up.

Felt numb at *shul*. We all went at the end of the service to say *Kaddish*.

Had black visions in the night of Mother's body decaying in her casket from the water. I woke myself up exclaiming, but I've lost the words. Helps to know Mom isn't really in there, but grisly thoughts emerge from time to time.

Saturday again. A whole week has passed. Saturday. Hell day. How ever did we make it through those painful early hours of Mom's last day? So much fear, frustration, confusion. What could we do to help? How could we make Mom comfortable? How could we be present for her in the midst of her crisis, assuage her suffering? With prayers, oxygen, loving tenderness. With meds.

Mom was amazingly patient and accepting of her process. Until the last morning, she could still walk to the bathroom. She was coherent until the last afternoon. I wonder what I could have done to make that bathroom scene less of a nightmare? Ger tried to reassure me that I'd handled it properly. I know I made decisions based on best knowledge, based on Mom's weakness, based on circumstance. They must have been the best ones. Too late to change anything, and nothing I could have done would have prolonged her life. I didn't want to prolong her life. I wanted Mom to let go, to stop suffering.

I am so grateful that she called for me, rested with me. I am grateful that Susie came for her when I was there, so I could catch the cue, encourage her to follow. The expression on her face was peaceful, in the midst of her suffering, when she saw Susie, or saw *something* beyond. Who can know what she experienced?

And who can know what she experienced when she threw her head back and stared with such intensity? What feeling, what thought, what vision? Was she trying to convey something? Or was she seeing something so wondrous, or shocking or frightening or unexpected, that she was struck speechless? Well, she already had ceased to speak coherently, except for "Move the pillows," and such.

And the restlessness! Pull the pillows out, place them here, larger, smaller, sit upright, lean back—no physical comfort at all in the hours before passing.

Was she clear at the end? Did the drugs distract her in her

passing? Did they soothe her? I don't *think* they hindered her. I hope not.

I've been reading about mourning. What many people experience is a heaviness I haven't felt yet. My faith has not wavered. I have no sense of rage or abandonment or unresolved issues. Feelings arise like waves, yes. Sadness, but not fear, no guilt I'm aware of at the moment, not even much worry.

I feel peaceful and balanced, yet present when these rolling waves of emotion sweep over me, catch me by surprise, as when, in childhood, I stood with my back to the sea. Sometimes rising over me, sometimes crashing into me. They are not yet sweeping me away. Perhaps I *shall* be ready to move on by Monday. Seems so close—only two days more.

Odd to realize how huge these experiences are in our own lives, and how small they are in terms of the whole world, or even the whole community. Odd that the way our lives will change is so significant to us, yet the changes will hardly be noticed outside our circle of friends.

Whatever shall we do with all the food that's pouring in? Carolyn and Aunt Mick toss stuff when it's been in the fridge awhile. I'm more likely to wait 'til it grows fur. Maybe here's a chance to practice letting go. Or maybe here's the start of a new era, a time to question and make new choices. But not yet.

November 24, 4 a.m.

Maya's just climbed up onto my lap—my comfort kitty. She'll have to move soon, though. I'm going to put the light out and watch Mama's candle burning on the mantlepiece. And I'll listen to an Agatha Christie story on tape. Mom liked mysteries, too.

Shiva is over this morning, and Rabbi Marc will come to take us for a walk, a ritual to mark the end of the first week of mourning and to draw us back into the world. In reality, though, not one of us has sat at home the whole seven days, as is the traditional practice. We've all gone out for a walk at least.

I realized before I finally fell asleep last night that it hasn't hit me yet that Mama is dead. Lance says it's that this whole week has been so odd, and we haven't done everyday things yet. He says that's when it hits you. I'm dreading it. I've been thinking I'm handling things pretty well, but maybe I haven't begun to handle anything at all.

So what will loss be like? "One day at a time," we've always said. I still can't imagine a life without Mother tangibly in it though I've been living it for a week. I can't begin to imagine it.

Rabbi Marc recommended a book, *Mourning and Mitzvah*, by Anne Brener, and we got it. It has some interesting commentary and anecdotes in it, and some exercises I may not do. Well, maybe I'll do some of them. Rabbi Marc says it's the kind of book you open once in a while—you don't have to read it page by page.

November 25

What is a reasonable amount to grieve when one must also be immersed in work? I've noticed that I've managed not to think about any challenges at work, except fleetingly, for a whole week.

Interesting that even in the midst of heavy, intense, exciting change at the mediation center, I am beginning a slow weaning process. With every decision I make now, I must keep in mind that someone else will eventually step in, and that the infrastructure must permit and support the transition. If I can be absent at this critical time, I see that I am not so indispensable there as I had feared. What a gift it is to discover that—the silver lining of a dark cloud in stormy times.

November 26

After Dad and I took Uncle Roy and Aunt Mick to the airport yesterday, we drove up to Union Creek and looked at the gorge and had French fried onion rings and decaf at Becky's Café. Was a peaceful ride, and we were both glad to have gone—a little heart-to-heart, lots of silence, some chatter, even. Came home rested. Made a lot of calls and wrote the rest of the letters to notify people about Mom. I'm glad to have that behind me.

I notice I keep waiting to see what will happen to me now that Mother is no longer with us in the same way. I remember the insight I had while I was floating down the Urubamba River in Peru—that I am living now, in this particular moment. There is nothing to wait for. There is no waiting. This is it. This is what happens when my mother dies. Life happens, same as always. Feelings flow, love is present. I don't see her. I don't hug her. Yet I feel her presence. I needn't try to understand or anticipate. This is the next step.

November 27

Shiva has barely ended, and already I have plunged into my other life. Tough day. I'd worked six hours by noon. Went to the pond with Lance. They're clearing by the creek, maybe to start the Greenway extension, and I suddenly realized we'll lose the privacy of our special place at the pond. My two greatest places of solace and healing, going to see Mom, and sitting by the creek beyond the pond—gone. I found two black and white feathers there. Maybe they were a sign of encouragement.

I feel heavy and sad and weepy today. There's a huge hard rock inside my stomach. And I'm tired. Guess I'll go over and see Dad, maybe take a nap.

November 28 – Thanksgiving

So many things to be thankful for, yet Mama's absence is huge. I know we have many blessings. Even many things about her passing were a blessing. Still, I think it will be a hard day. I was grouchy and depressed and negative all day yesterday.

Dad showed me the *Memoirs* notebook that a friend had given Mom, and we read Mom's only entry together. It was in the section called "My Birth": "On August third, we celebrated my 81st birthday. I love and am loved and count my blessings with abundant gratitude. Life is good!"

How can I ever complain or feel sorry for myself when Mom could write that, knowing her body was full of cancer? Even in the last days she was counting blessings: how lucky we were to be all together, to love so much, to be at home, that there wasn't extreme pain, that we'd shared a good life.

Knowing that doesn't relieve my sadness, or the ache inside, though always my sense of perspective returns after a while. I *do* miss her. I miss her when I have a question, and I know she knows the answer. I don't remember to get quiet and ask. Maybe that's the next big test of faith. Can I remember to get quiet and ask my questions instead of giving in to desolation? Maybe I can get my answers if I'll be still and listen.

I asked Mom for guidance a couple of weeks ago. She said, "Listen." Maybe that's the long-term advice. In order to get past the apparent separation, I need to listen—listen for her presence, listen for her wisdom, listen for her answers. How grateful I shall be if this really works.

In my mind I believe this connection is possible, and in my heart I feel it's true, but doubt rises up and makes me question my certainty. I fear I'm deluding myself because I want to believe it. Maybe tears are Mom's way of getting my attention. Maybe I weep when she's nearby. Maybe the tears are a signal to listen. Maybe the times I miss her most are the times she is most present, and her presence touches me.

I wonder if I should talk with Pop about this. The other day I told him I thought the lamp by their recliners was flickering because Mother was nearby. Uncle Roy said the lamp must have had a short, but Dad agreed it could be Mom.

I've noticed I like wearing black. It helps me remember to check in on my moods, helps me understand when my hormones feel out of control, reminds me to take extra good care of myself. And, especially useful, it reminds other people I'm still fragile.

I went out and bought mourning clothes—three pairs of black pants, a black jacket, and a black skirt. Maybe after a while, I'll brighten them up with accessories. Right now wearing plain black works for me. There must be some point to such a long-standing tradition. Maybe it's as much about mindfulness as about grief.

———————

Dad wants Mother's personal belongings out of the house. Having them there is too painful. It's hard for me to go through Mother's things, and I'm making slow progress. Sometimes I just stuff them in bags and boxes and take them home, where I stick them in my studio, so I can sort them out later. Sometimes I'm ready to let go.

The clothes are the biggest job. I can use some of the cotton blouses for work, and the silk shirts. Some of the dresses will fit, too. I'll take the things I know I'll wear. The rest we can give away to thrift shops—better-quality ones. Weird to think Mama's elegant wardrobe could end up in a thrift shop.

More relatives are coming, this time from Chicago. They'll be here four days. They'd made their reservations for Thanksgiving break so they could come and say goodbye to Mother, but she died before they could get here. I hope they'll be okay with minimal hospitality. I'm not ready to entertain yet. Too bad they're coming at such a hard time. I'd be excited to see them, except for that.

November 29, 3:00 a.m.

The relatives arrived. It's been great to see them, but it's like jumping back into *shiva*. All the bustle is tiring.

I awoke at 3 a.m. in a panic. This is a hard time to trust the Universe that things are unfolding as they should. Everything at work is in turmoil, and in my fragile state after Mom's death, it is hard to feel positive or hopeful or competent. My self-confidence is shattered.

Dad says, "Slow down, make lists, and take things one at a time in order of priority."

November 30 – *Shabbat*

Dad and Ger stayed in the bedroom during candle lighting tonight. I sat with them awhile, then went out and did the *brachot* with the relatives. They joined us for dinner soon after. It was a sad evening.

December ~ A Silver Pathway

December 1, 6 a.m.

December already.

Last night Lance was going to stay here at Dad's with me. We tried, but we barely fit in the double bed. Then, every time he moved, the old bed springs would rock so much I'd get seasick. Lance thought Dad would be upset if I slept on the couch while he slept in the bed, but Lance doesn't fit on the couch. He finally went home. It was easier. It's dumb for him to stay here. It's easier for me when I stay alone.

Woke up around five feeling panicky again. Mom's slippers aren't where I left them. The littlest things can throw me off-balance. I'm amazed. I think I'll take the homeopathic anxiety remedy I got from Elias.

8:45 p.m.

I'm not sure whether to stay with Pop tonight or sleep at home. Hard to know what's best for him and what's best for me. My innards have been twisted all day, and I've been giving myself mixed messages all evening. When I really take a look, I think Dad and I both want me to stay.

Things at work are confusing and frustrating, but I *do* have the courage to hang in there. I know things will be better.

Is that Mom sending messages? I think so. *Calm down. No need to panic.* Dad is right. I need to slow down, take one thing at a time.

December 2, 4 a.m.

Hellish two hours. I can't tell which of my thoughts can be attributed to the Hour of the Wolf, and which thoughts are the ones which must guide my behavior.

Physically, I am exhausted. My heart pounds, throat's tight, forehead is pinched above the bridge of my nose. The only thing that seems real and true is the feeling I have when I clear everything away and watch breath. In. Out. In. Out.

What would happen at the mediation center if I suddenly died or needed to take emergency leave? I was stretched too thin before, and now I see I've lost my elasticity. Since Mother's death, I have no extra resources to draw upon, no desire to draw upon them. With her death, my priorities have changed. I need time and space to grieve. I need to get my life back.

8 a.m.

Just had a important talk with my friend and colleague Alice Phalan. She helped me sort out many things, and most of all she helped me see that mourning Mother's death is important, necessary, expected. It's not appropriate to take one exhausting week off work and jump in again in the way I was threatening to do.

Alice talked to me about grieving and helped me see the need to take time for it. She helped me think through a plan for the next months, helped me see alternatives. She helped me see that the mediation center will be fine.

"A mother's death is the biggest thing that happens in a life," another friend told me yesterday.

It's hard for me to see how my grieving will progress. How much is there to do? Don't people just have to get back to living their lives? I keep wondering what my life *is*.

After Alice and I talked, I spoke with Dad and shared the conversation. "Alice said it's normal to feel exhausted, not to want to do anything, not to know what to do next, and to feel like everything's impossible, even if we're normally optimistic." He recognized those feelings, as I had. "I didn't know those things were a part of grieving," I told him. "I'm glad to know other people experience them."

"I am, too," he said.

I don't think anyone can prepare us for the grief process. We can try to live life in a way that helps us accept change, helps us see challenges as creative opportunities. That leaves room for hope, makes it easier when we vacillate between hope and despair.

But there's no preparation for the immensity of this thing. I still have no grasp of it after two weeks. It's not about loss, exactly. A part of me doesn't even experience Mother's passing as loss, but more as a transition.

Alice said to me, "You need this time to begin to sense what your new relationship with your Mom will look like." How will we be together now that she has no body? Thank God that used-up body no longer hinders her. Thank God. But now what? How do I adjust to this new way of being together? How will we work it out? And I'm afraid I'll hinder Mother's own work, whatever that may be, if I'm too needy.

What happens to a being after the passage? Do we become Everything? Everywhere? Can Mother be with me and still do what she needs to do? I'm only able to think in finite terms, in boxes. I don't yet see how to experience it all without limit, without categories, living/dead, expanded/contracted, present/ absent. Can it truly all happen at once? So some wise ones say, but it's beyond *my* grasp.

December 8

Spent yesterday puttering. Washed four loads of linens, stacked some wood, messed around in the garden, paid some bills. Also made some enquiries about possible venues for a personal retreat. Was good to follow my own rhythm. Healing.

Spent some time with Dad clearing out more stuff, too. I'm still bringing it all home. I can't get rid of stuff any better than Mom could. What is it that makes us hold on so hard to anything with sentimental value? Are we afraid there will be no more memories to collect?

December 9

Went to a work-related gathering and learned it's still hard for me to be around a lot of people. I sat off to the side, and people came to greet me—or they didn't.

I have no interest in most of what goes on around me, am almost completely self-centered, impatient with things that pull me out of myself. Part of me wants to escape and regroup. Part of me wants to stay involved and busy here in town—the ultimate escape, escape from my feelings, from learning who this woman is becoming, this woman who no longer has a living mother.

How melodramatic I can be.

———❧———

I don't know if I ever wrote this down anywhere. This is what I think: That the first day Mama couldn't walk to the bathroom anymore, couldn't take care of her intimate needs, *that* was the day she needed to leave. She didn't want to be bedridden, didn't want us to have to take care of her that way.

One day she felt very weak, and I helped her change her Serenity pad. She said, "You shouldn't have to do this for me." I said, "You've done for me plenty of times," and that made her feel terrible. She didn't want to need that from me. She didn't say another word, but I think that was where she drew the line. That was the limit she set for herself. Living with hardship was worth it 'til then. That's what I think.

———❧———

This is a time of transition with staff at work, as well as in my personal life. Looks like I need to empty out so I can be filled up again. Much loss just now. Much gain, as well. Helen goes, Ginger comes, Sandy and Angeline go, Kate comes, Mom goes—what? I come? That's a hard one.

Detachment is what I need, a sense of rightness that lets me draw away, take care of myself, and know that everything will progress as it must. Felt sad when I realized I'd normally go see Mom at a time like this. She always helped me get things back in perspective, helped me feel better. So, does she guide my pen? Is she the one who brings me the solace that is starting to seep in through the cracks in my confidence?

December 10

What a gift that Mother was able to spare us the pain of watching her deteriorate further. I marvel at how she chose her moment to slip away. Even in dying she considered us, and herself. Perhaps she couldn't bear to see the pain in our eyes any longer. Or maybe that was simply the day she answered the call Home.

———❧———

A friend just called to check on me. I'm grateful for people's kindness these days, for all the love and support that flows my way.

Wednesday, December 11

Tough morning. but now I'm calm again. The sky is clearing and I see icy patches of sunshine on the hills. I've been yearning for sunshine.

So odd, this thing about . . . Lord I get tired of my mind going blank mid-sentence. Think I'll read Madeline L'Engle's first Crosswicks Journal, *A Circle of Quiet*. Mother had it on loan from Catherine, and I brought it home with me.

Oh, I remember what I was thinking. Yesterday I noticed I have hardly any kids in my life. It impoverishes me. I make myself too busy to hang out and meet kids. This is not a good thing.

Was talking with a friend just after my crisis this morning. Much is falling apart right now, disintegrating in order to grow new. She pointed out that a fiftieth birthday can be an exciting, dynamic, life-changing time. I was grateful for the reminder. That's a good reason to have a retreat now, to quiet myself to be ready for this transition which promises to be immense. Would be delicious to follow my own rhythm for about a month. Exciting to think of some real time off without the temptation of getting sucked into everyday stuff, not even pleasant puttering around the house.

Today I coined a new expression: "poisonously conscientious." Lance made me a sign for the bathroom mirror: "Avoid poisonous conscientiousness." All caps. Good, I think. I'm so conscientious I fail to see options for lightening my load. I don't recognize leeway when there is some. Thank God friends are able to point it out to me.

Today I finished reading *A Circle of Quiet*.

Today, for a moment, I wondered if I was having a nervous breakdown.

Today I made a nest for myself upstairs with all the shades open and the light coming in, and I saw the sun on the hills and the wet trees, and I felt peaceful and safe, and Lance and I had a comforting talk.

Today, for the first time that I can remember, Lance brought me a flower from the florist—a single clear red perfect rosebud. He couldn't have touched me more. And he brought me short-bread from the Ashland Bakery Café (my favorite treat) and two beautiful cards. Mostly he brought me love, and I feel safe now, like I have passed another threshold, reached a turning point. As I said to him, a turning point doesn't have to be 180 degrees. Even a few degrees count.

I feel as clear and solid now as I did shattered and split apart this morning. The beginning of feeling better was the decision to stop working on mediation center tasks. Just STOP. I am not capable of handling work right now. I need to follow my heart, move in my own rhythm, and I have not yet learned to do that and do work.

If one afternoon can do me as much good as this one, think what a few days will do. I've decided to go to Bandon, but not until after my birthday. Bandon is special to us, because that's where Lance and I took our last trip with Mom and Dad, the time we all walked on the beach together.

Mother died a month before my fiftieth birthday. I've never had a crisis around a particular birthday before, as some people do. When I asked Mother, not long ago, about her own fiftieth birthday, she said, "Auntie Hort and Aunt Syl gave me a lovely birthday party. But Grandma was already in the sanitarium, and she couldn't come."

I heard the sadness in her voice, and I knew Mother would be gone before my birthday. She was telling me that. I'd have been surprised if she'd stayed this long. I'm glad she didn't. It was too hard at the end. But still, there's that sadness, the one she felt, too.

I haven't felt her as close the last few days. Maybe she is just as present, and I am less attentive. Maybe it's Mother who's helping me heal. I missed her terribly this morning. I've always gone to her when I've felt this blue. She understood me better than anyone else on this planet, except maybe Mary Margaret. So today I was really calling out to Mom, and maybe that's what turned it around.

I've begun reading the second book of L'Engle's Crosswicks Journal, *The Summer of the Great-Grandmother*:

"We must meet the precariousness of the universe without self-pity, and with dignity and courage."

And further on:

"It's a good thing to have all the props pulled out from under us occasionally. It gives us some sense of what is rock under our feet, and what is sand. It stops us from taking anything for granted. It has also taught me a lot about living in the immediate moment. I am somehow managing to live one day, one hour at a time. I have to."

Over and over again I feel like the things Madeline L'Engle writes are things I could have written in my own journal. I wonder, are these thoughts common among women, or have I found a kindred spirit? I'm finding commonality now with other women's experiences around their mother's deaths. The more I read, the more I'd like to write a book about this transition time.

December 12

People keep telling me this is a time to take care of myself, to be good to myself, that losing a mother is the biggest thing in a life. Yet I find myself uncomfortable with this state of self-indulgence. I appreciate the loving support of my dear friends and family, but, still, I have trouble accepting it.

My favorite thing would be to be selfless, giving, supportive to those I love, and instead I'm being self-centered, moody, not there for people in the usual way.

It's like a tango—all the way in this direction, all the way back in the other, a little violent in its abruptness. It disturbs me that I'm incapable of caring much about what's happening outside myself. I have moments of caring, but mostly I'm in a cocoon, and I've spun a web of Teflon around myself—everything slides away.

I don't feel that serenity I felt yesterday—not the devastation either. Just agitated, restless, at a loss.

December 13

Dream

Getting ready to go on some kind of spiritual journey, a retreat. We'll start from a church. It's a pilgrimage, somehow connected with a funeral. Don't know whose. Don't know where we're going. Lance is with me. They've remodeled the church, and they've exchanged the rich teal of the velvet curtains for rose. They've brightened up the whole place, let in more light. This is a sacred and mysterious place which I have loved, and the remodeling has rendered it sterile and unfamiliar though it is pretty. I am fond of the priest, and I'm sorry I can't be enthusiastic about the changes.

There are strange vehicles in the courtyard to carry us. Lance and I are the first to arrive. I leave my big rust-colored leather duffel in one of the vehicles, but when it's almost time to head out, I realize I want to change from travel clothes (jeans) to funeral clothes, something more lovely—my long claret skirt and brown boots.

I go into the vehicle. It has bunks and spaces to store things. Most people have already stashed their stuff, are more organized than I. I only have time to change. I'm concerned we'll be expected to travel in this vehicle. I'm afraid of feeling claustrophobic. Then I realize we'll be riding in a big bus. This vehicle is our closet.

When I think about it, this dream seems to be about my own funeral, of the woman who is 49, who has a mother. It is the ending time of the safe, old familiar sanctuary. I don't know where we're going, but it will never be the same if we come back. I feel the loss. Yet what I choose to wear is festive (hopeful?), and I do not wear my black boots, but brown boots (I don't really own brown boots), and they somehow look like traveling boots.

It appears that the journey will be cramped and uncomfortable, for there are many people along, but then I realize I *will* have the space I need.

I wonder if I can permit myself to lie around and read and sleep and heal without needing to be responsible or take care of things? Why is it so hard to give myself permission to be who I am, where I am?

I think it's my good-girl again. I'm afraid of letting Mother down. Or afraid of not measuring up. If I only follow my heart, will I get enough done? If not, will I be disappointed in myself? Following a Mother who was on a pedestal for lots of people can be tough. I don't put her on a pedestal. Mother and I are much alike. I've seen her foibles. But Dad has given me her slippers saying, "These should be yours. Now you'll walk in her footsteps." Big job.

———

Last evening Lance and I were listening to Nat King Cole on the TV at Dad's. Just the way I was sitting in Mom's recliner with my eyes closed, listening to him croon, I could feel Mother in me—no, it was more than that. I became Mother for an instant. I was having her sensation of enjoyment, having her expressions. Only for an instant, yet it was a powerful affirmation of her presence—as though she'd borrowed my body in order to enjoy the music. It happened twice. The second time I lent it willingly.

———

Sometimes I find myself off somewhere following a wisp of thought, not knowing where, and I come back with a start. I like having the time to do that. It's been a long time since I permitted myself leisure, true leisure. The closest I usually come to it is the sort of follow-my-own-rhythm puttering I do about the house on occasion.

Mama was always warning me to slow down. Is that her legacy to me? Will I finally manage it? That, and standing tall—the two go together. One can't hurry much with regal bearing. There's no elegance in rushing frantically to and fro.

———

Sometimes it makes me sad that I don't hear Mom's voice or see her face or hear her laughter whenever I wish. But I feel her. Perhaps the rest will come in time. I envy people who can hear her laughter. She was a great laugher.

December 14 – Lance's Birthday

Mom was diagnosed one year ago today. I wrote Lance a birthday poem. Haven't written a poem in a long time. It was full of personal allusions, and he liked it a lot. I'm not in a festive mood. What else can I give him, anyway, besides my heart? Maybe a poem is just enough.

For Lance's Birthday

Baby butt soft
Sequoia solid

Steady as a puppy clock
Vast as a wind-swept dune
Jagged as Castle Rocks
Sensual as bare breasts under brushed rayon
Prickery as a cactus apple

Promise of almond buds
Pretty paw upon cheek

Ephemeral as a wisp of smoke
Eternal as sea upon sand
Vulnerable as a lost child
Eye-magic ancient
White Dog dignity

You are new to me
I know you

Pre-dawn Saturday
Whispers of your first beginnings
Walk with me
Forever

Ger says he's doing fine, but I don't think he is. I don't know what to say to him, and I say the wrong things. It would be better to stay silent, to hold him 'til he could cry, but he's tough against me.

Before Mom died, Ger and I helped each other, grieved together, cried together. Now I miss the closeness. He's drawn in and I'm concerned about him.

I showed him the book about grieving that Cheryl brought. "I don't need it," he said. Then he relented, and said he might read part of it, but not now.

December 17 – Uncle Roy's Birthday

Lance reminded me last night that the days I'll be away on retreat provide a good opportunity to look carefully at how I live my life and to think about how I might want to do it differently. I can choose to change whatever I want.

I wonder how to empty myself, to find Silence and sit in it. I feel its presence, but I only manage to be in it for moments at a time, as though Silence and I were existing in parallel realities, as though there were a glass wall keeping me from it. Why do I resist? Maybe this retreat will help.

December 19 – My 50th Birthday

Three-thirty in the morning. Guess I just couldn't wait to get started on my birthday.

Yesterday I didn't cry over Mother, but this morning my mind is on the indignities she suffered at my hand on her last day. I wish we'd known she was dying. I wish I could have helped her more, but I know I did everything I knew to do at the time. And I've been a good daughter. Oh! I'm so sad just now. I was going to write "today," but why assume I shall be sad all day?

What does it mean to have a fiftieth birthday? Not sure this would have even been a special one for me if Mom were still here. But now it is forever cast in the light of Major Transition.

8 a.m.

Heard a train across the field. The rumbling went on such a long time I got up to see it, and I found a "Happy Birthday! I love you" sign from Lance propped up on a kitchen chair.

December 20

Two o'clock in the morning, and I'm awake thinking about the condolence acknowledgments we have to write—over a hundred each.

⟶

Was a pretty nice birthday if you take into consideration that the mother was missing. I spent some time in her room last night, sitting in Dad's big chair, feeling her, seeing her there in the bed, even. Why is it easier for me to find her there than in the rest of the house?

Lance and I had sweet morning time. Then we went to the pond by the creek, and afterward we played with Ben, the little neighbor boy.

Ger and I spent three delightful hours together yesterday. We walked to the upper duck pond in Lithia Park and slid stale *matzoh* across the ice to the ducks, did errands, had delicious Panini Veganini at a new little Mediterranean café called Pilaf.

I had a massage at three, and then we had a family dinner at Macaroni's.

Now the birthday has passed, and I have a sense of emptiness. I was hanging on to make it through my birthday, and now what? The beginning of the Void.

⟶

Suddenly I'm not sure about this retreat. I hope I can feel peaceful and safe in Bandon. Maybe it's crazy. It's a very on-my-own choice I've made. I guess bottom line is I *am* on my own in a way I've never been before. I'm afraid to go, but I'm more afraid to stay here in my present state.

December 21, 8 p.m. – Bandon

Arrived after a six-hour drive and discovered a guesthouse with a comfortable one-bedroom apartment at the edge of the sea. The place belongs to an older woman, Edith. I've already nested and made it my own, and I feel cozy and safe and happy here.

Winter Solstice. Light is coming back to the planet and also, it seems, into my life. In this moment I feel like things won't ever be so hard again. My heart is open, and I'm beginning to realize I can trust that the ups will come, so the downs won't leave me so confused or devastated.

Started reading *The Irrational Season*, the third book of the Crosswicks Journal, and Madeleine L'Engle and I are in tune once again. The book begins just after her birthday when everything is new, as yet unwritten.

I've also been reading the book that Cheryl, the hospice social worker, gave to us, *How to Go on Living When Someone You Love Dies*, by Therese A. Rando. Comments every few pages which are right-on in terms of my feelings and behavior, and it helps to normalize what I'm experiencing. It's easier to accept myself knowing it's "just grieving" that makes me not care about other people right now, for instance. I've become incredibly self-centered. It's not the self I respect or wish to be.

December 22

Awoke before dawn, and I've been watching the light come back. The tide is rising, too. Thought I might have a walk this morning, but I can see I couldn't be out long and still come back dry. The surf crashes in and creeps back. Now I can see as well as feel it, and the horizon has appeared, a subtle shift from gray-green to gray-blue.

I've set up an altar to the east, and I sit before it now. Incense. A votive light in its glass, sea-foam green. My Venetian glass heart. Special rocks. A dime I found on the floor when I arrived (Mother always used to find money—maybe it's a love gift from her). Mom's little brass coal hod for burning sage and juniper. Miscellaneous accouterments—Angel Cards, pendulum, matches, spare candles. A photo of Bartholomew.*

A shelf on the wall above boasts silk flowers that were here when I arrived—bodacious Stargazer lilies without scent, blessedly without scent, and irises and peonies. Mom loved peonies.

---

* A beloved spiritual teacher who has had a profound influence upon my way of being in the world. (See Resources)

I have become slightly acquainted with a gull. She is interested in peanuts. She'll eat them in the shell, but I have agreed, nevertheless, to shell them and put them on the balcony rail. She doesn't want them from the deck.

I wonder if she'll come again, and whether I shall be able to distinguish her from any other gull. Perhaps by her behavior, for we have already begun our dance. I open the door; she withdraws to the corner of the rail. I place the food on the railing and step back. I stand very still and watch as she approaches the food. She sometimes comes with wings spread to keep her balance, or maybe to be ready for flight. She walks slowly and watches me carefully. Then she grabs the food and draws back. It doesn't always seem safe to her that I am standing nearby, especially when the sliding door is open, but sometimes she comes anyway.

The gull had flown away, but a few moments ago she came again to the corner of the rail and called to me and demanded more nuts. Now she is sitting on the rail by the open door, watching me write. Sometimes she speaks in a cooing voice, different from the usual screech I've heard from gulls. Her presence comforts me.

A few moments ago I put out a piece of bread and other gulls came sweeping in to check on us. My friend grabbed the bread and flew off again after a quiet goodbye from the corner of the rail. I hope she returns.

There's a peace and a sadness here. Not sure if I'll ever want to return to my regular life. I guess the point is that I can't. I need a new life that suits the person I'm becoming.

Maybe I don't need to *think* about the changes. Maybe I need to *pray*. Maybe I need to wait and listen, to do nothing until the path is clear. For now, I simply wish to take a shower and get some food into the house.

Had a bracing walk on the beach: brisk wind and a cave. The cave beckons me, yet I went only into the outer chamber. The inner, deeper part is full of treasures, dimly lit, but I could not enter it. It's filled with the roar of the sea.

The sun is shining. I think it's come out to prepare for sunset, though we must have an hour or two to go. It has illuminated one small silver spot of ocean; that must be where it will make its dive. Now the sun has made a silver pathway to the beach. Lovely that it's aimed exactly in my direction.

Rain again, and it makes the sunshine more brilliant. Oh, it was just a shower to spatter my windows. Now the clouds are breaking up and there's glorious blue sky to the north. You miss a lot if you overlook a single moment.

It amazes me that the surf was nearly up to the dunes below the house and now it's miles out. The light has changed again, too. Great clouds and squalls hover along the horizon—here, too, in fact—but the sky is perfectly blue above the western cloud bank. I doubt I ever could tire of looking at the sea and its weather. I feel so . . . what? So connected here.

The sun, the clouds, the sky, the sea all do what they do—without consulting one another—and the result is spectacular. Is it possible I could live my life that way? With pure intent, could I move through my days, doing what I need to do without concern for how I am affecting others? Or do we humans need an intentional collaboration? If I'd simply follow my heart, could it work?

December 23

I lie here this morning and my mind wanders down a long list of concerns, both past and future. Yesterday was fluid, restful. I want to bring that peace into this day. Does lying in bed invite angst? Maybe if I'd arise early to meditate, I could set the rhythm for each day, set an intention of peace, serenity, clarity for my spirit to carry forward.

The gull came again today and sat at the corner of the rail, but when I put out her nuts, she wouldn't approach. She even screeched at me. When I went into the kitchen, she ate the nuts and flew off.

Now she's brought a stunt show back with her—gulls in formation, swooping in pairs. I guess we have a relationship. She'll come every morning, and I'll be glad to have a friend.

⌐◦⌐

I'm reading Rando again. I keep finding sections that are right on target. I'm comforted to know I'm not alone.

For instance: "If you are forced to confront other crises at the same time you are trying to grieve, your grief will be complicated [and] . . . you will tend to have a relatively more difficult time coping with your grief than if these crises were absent. These additional burdens can sap your energy . . . at a time when you are already preoccupied and depleted."

And: "You may be concerned if you're unable to remember the sound of their voice, smell, touch. This can come from trying too hard and later it may become easier—the memories come spontaneously."

I've realized I'm grieving many losses simultaneously—Mother, of course, and my old way of life, but also four people are leaving from work, and, my uncertainty about the challenges there makes it harder still.

December 24

Had an enjoyable visit yesterday afternoon with Edith, the owner of the house. We shared many thoughts and insights. There are things about her I value in myself: independence, love of life, fearlessness (more work needed here), creativity, an open enjoyment of people and of nature. It was nurturing and inspiring to spend time with her.

This morning I saw that I can be okay without Mom. I don't *need* her to be with me anymore, not to be confused with *wanting*. I am grateful for all we shared, and I'm sure a part of me will always wish we had one moment more, or a week, or a year. But today I saw that I'm okay. There are women like Edith, who have walked this path before me and who lead the way with courage.

When Mother died I thought I'd lost my best friend, mentor, healer, provider, nurturer, as well as Mom. Now I see that she is here in a thousand faces. She's part of every woman I meet, because she's not just *my* mom, but The Mother. We women carry her within us, and we inspire each other and guide each other—elders to youth, but also youth to elders.

———

I helped Edith make apple pies today and stacked some wood for her. It feels good to be helpful to someone else, and also to use my body for work. Edith gave me some applesauce she made from the leftover apples.

Cooking with Edith wasn't like cooking with Mom, and I'm glad. I enjoyed it, though. Thing is, I don't want it to be the same with any other person. What I shared with Mother is sacred, and no one will ever fill the space that is left. However, I shall find new ways to enjoy myself, and I shall have new ways of enjoying things we did together, so that my life will be full, and Mother will not be displaced.

I thought about Mother as I helped bake Christmas pies. I remembered the holiday meals we prepared together, and the memories were sweet. I did not cry.

December 25

I started out blue today, but I had a good talk on the phone with Pop and felt better. I worked on the condolence thank you notes and had a nurturing phone call with Shoshana. What a dear friend she is. I hadn't spoken with her since Mother died. We talked a long time. I told my story—in minute detail—for the first time since I'd shared it all with Mary Margaret at the time of the funeral. I cried a lot. It was a good talk. She gave me some good advice: "Do one thing for yourself each day, just because you want to do it, whether you think you have time or not."

———

The gull is sitting on the deck rail in a raging wind and rainstorm, feathers battered, solid as a rock, and not budging in spite of the vicious gusts. I don't think she wants food. She's here more for the company—maybe to reassure me. I wonder why she doesn't at least sit in a sheltered place. Guess she'll do what she needs to. Sometimes I feel as battered as she. Am I also that resilient?

Had a vivifying walk on the beach. The rain had stopped, so I decided to go out. Just as I got all bundled up, it started pouring again, but I decided to go anyway. I walked as far as the rocks, but I didn't go into the cave. I looked at the spire in front of the cave that looks like the wing of a hawk that's crashed into the sand, and I felt anxious. I didn't even want to approach today, didn't go near the cave at all.

Don't know what this cave thing is about. I have the feeling that if I sit in there the sea will follow and swallow me up—totally irrational, yet I have a strong sense of fear, caution, dread—terror, even.

The tide is way out and still has two hours to go 'til its lowest point. I knew that when I was walking, and yet the fear. I knew the tide was going out. Maybe it's my inner cave, some inner part of myself, I'm not yet ready to enter.

I keep feeling like there's more to do than just be here. I sense I've come here to accomplish some important thing, but I don't know what, and I don't know how. In fact, it seems that my life, at least my happiness, depends on accomplishing this thing, yet I can't see what it is.

I'm starting a new journal. This quote from Oliver Wendell Holmes is on the front: "What lies behind us and what lies before us are tiny matters compared to what lies within us."

Blustery day, and I have discovered that, somewhere deep inside, I am hopeful.

December 26

As I'm reading the Rando book, it occurs to me that I have a responsibility to take care of myself and to resolve my personal disharmonies, not only so I will feel better, but in order to help restore balance to the whole family at a time when the balance is pretty delicate.

⤙⤙

Remarkable walk on the beach today. The sun came out awhile and made it warmer. Wasn't long after high tide and the wind was up. Blew little clouds of foam all about. The wind and sand created a thousand textures: little pedestals for each bit of wrack, tufts and ripples, smooths and hollows, hills and layers. Dry, white sand skimmed along the surface, polishing its way across the beach. I found a piece of manzanita burnished to a golden red—a perfect walking stick for a fairy king.

I saw a magical "sculpture" near the end of the dune: a tree stump twisted like a flower, joined by water and wind and sand to make a reflecting pool with many levels, each a different color and texture.

Today the wind taught me about being pliant, suggestible, creative, yielding. The wind has impacted me this week, at least as much as any other thing. It's the wind that has rattled my windows all these stormy days and nights. I sat on the porch in the wind until the sun went away again.

⤙⤙

It's almost time to leave. My fantasy was to do grief in a big way this week and put it behind me. I see it doesn't work that way. Oh well. At least, after reading Rando, I have a better sense of what grief is, what it looks like, how to be okay with it. I can do it. That's a comfort. I shall grieve in a healthy way—and I shall never be the same again. Okay. So be it.

Haven't worn black clothes for four whole days. I haven't needed a reminder to take care of myself. I *am* taking care of myself.

One thing I've enjoyed, one way I've taken care of myself, is helping Edith. "I'm sorry I tend to be so oversolicitous," I told her.

"I like it!" she said.

I'm happy to discover that I'm less inclined to self-absorption. Maybe this is a glimpse of my old self returning.

December 27, 3 a.m.

Awoke with a screaming headache. Reached out to Lance, but he wasn't there. Suddenly, I don't want to be here anymore. I am anxious, and my stomach hurts. I need to remember to be present and breathe. I haven't been silent enough. I've blown my chance for Silence. Maybe I'm not ready for Silence. What now? It's almost time to go back, and I fear I've lost my chance.

—✦—

If I go home today, I can work in Mother's closet tomorrow. That will be a big step. There is something else we need to do, too—the family conference Dad and I spoke about on the phone. "I don't want to be supervised," he told me.

How much help *does* he want? He wants to be self-sufficient, appreciates that we're being supportive. We mustn't make assumptions about what he wants. Just as Mother made her own decisions about her care until the last day, Dad must also be in control of his life.

His confusion and disorientation can surely be a result of grief. It seems likely to me that if he has to take care of himself, he'll pay better attention. He's been distracted by Mom's cancer, and her arthritis before that. He's been distracted for a long time.

—✦—

My gull friend is back. I didn't feed her yesterday, but she came anyway. I went out to give her some peanuts this morning, and then, as I stood gazing at the sea, I was engulfed in sudden tears—no thoughts, no warning. Suddenly they were upon me, like sneaker waves.

Later.

I've moved to another place. Edith had other tenants coming. I'm grateful for this day of transition between Edith's and home. Different feeling from the rest of the week, more quiet. Listened to Bartholomew tapes, sat, drank ginger tea. I'm feeling languid. Much of the time I've just watched the sea or the fire and have hardly even thought.

This time away has served its purpose. I've come back to myself, am feeling more stable. I like who I am here. I've learned I must relax if I'm to heal. That will be the challenge.

I am here in this room gathering courage to go home again.

Tumultuous feelings rise up and then subside. And now I feel listless. And sad.

December 28, 4:30 a.m.

Please God help me get my life back in order—even though it must be a new order, since so much has changed.

10 p.m. – Ashland

Back at home. The drive tonight on Highway 42 was like driving on a long dike. The fields were all flooded and the moonlight gave the water an eerie glow as it lapped against the embankment. The road looked taut, stretched tight like a black rubber band across a silver vastness, and I felt as though, if I made one false move, it would bounce me right off the edge to my death.

January ~ Devastation

January 1

Awoke to news of local flooding. Our yard is soaked, the patio's swamped, water's coming in under the house. Small challenges compared to what else is going on. The town's a mess. People in rural parts of the county are being evacuated. Terrible mudslides. Roads closed. Folks are mobilizing to offer assistance. I helped to carry a friend's belongings to higher ground.

⚊⚊✦⚊⚊

We were at Dad's last night for New Year's Eve. Auntie Mim called, and Dad was actually teasing and laughing with her. His eyes sparkled and his face relaxed. It's the first time I've seen joy in his face since Mother died.

I missed Mom a lot last night. This is the beginning of a year without her in it. I don't sense her near me as much as I did before. Maybe I only wanted to, and I never have. The thought of that makes me cry. There's a part of me that's healing, and another part that's afraid to, for fear I'll lose what's left of her. It's as though I'm afraid of getting past the pain, because the pain is what holds her close.

January 2

Dream

I am standing just inside the front door at Mom and Dad's house, looking down the hall. Mother sticks her head and shoulders out of the bedroom door, raises her right arm for emphasis, and says, "Listen."

This is the first time I have heard Mom's voice since she died. It's a relief, because I've been worried that I'd never be able to recall the sound of her voice again.

January 5

Lance has gone over into California to do some last minute layout work for a client before their publication deadline next week. I hope he won't be gone too long.

It's astonishing how preoccupied one can get with bodily functions without water or sewage services. We've had none since the flood began. The City's set up portable outhouses all over town.

I've rigged up a portable potty in the bathtub, a five-gallon bucket lined with a garbage bag and filled part way with kitty litter. I put the wooden toilet seat on top. It's quite an elegant thing. I've figured out a dishwashing system, too.

I'm hauling water from Ger and Carolyn's house, since they're on a well. This whole experience is an excellent reminder to be grateful for water—and to be frugal with it, even after the crisis is over.

The extent of the flood is mind-boggling. The creek jumped its banks and roared right through the plaza, and Water Street collapsed altogether. The flood plain in our neighborhood is full of water that's lapping over the Nevada Street bridge. The City says we'll have no water or sewage services for two weeks. I hope that's a conservative estimate.

People are panicky, angry, helpless, looking for somewhere to place the blame. The whole town is grieving. It's like a war zone. How do people adjust to these conditions for years at a time?

I've been feeling guilty, or at least uneasy. I've been terribly upset and concerned about the repercussions of the flood and its impact on people, and, at the same time, detached and unable to reach out to help. I've simply withdrawn. Read a mystery book for the first time in months. Haven't offered help to anyone since New Year's Day.

———•———

I'm grateful that my survival systems work. I have electricity and firewood, and a warm, secure home, and an income, and a loving family, and dear, supportive friends. *Many* blessings to count.

I know the flood has exacerbated my grief over Mother's death. Still, after hearing how many challenges everyone else is facing, it's easier for me not to take things quite so personally. And it's easier, too, to think that I just need to flow with it. How many times Mother has said over the years, "This, too, shall pass."

January 6

Saw a striking thing when I opened the wood stove. Gray ash along a fire-orange ridge, then black. Glowing embers below and electric blue flames above. It's a blessing to see beauty amidst the devastation.

———•———

I awoke aching for Lance this morning. I'll be glad when he gets back from California. I miss him—the comfort of reaching out to touch him when fear creeps into my gut in the middle of the night, the possibility of awakening him to talk, even though I rarely do. I had, for the first time, a glimpse of what Pop must feel knowing his dear love will never lie next to him again. Such a terrible, overwhelming loneliness. How can one ever heal from this? How *do* people go on?

———•———

I've been thinking about the last months. I've noticed that benefits have often grown out of loss or pain. And likewise, the good things are sometimes accompanied by challenges. I'm learning some things.

I'm learning that people are willing to help. I'm learning I don't know how to ask. The situation at work right now is similar to when Mom died. Some people would say, "Let me know if you need help with anything," and I knew they were truly reaching out with an open heart. Other people would say, "When can I pick up your laundry?" or "I brought you a pot of soup." And those were the ones who helped the world seem not so upside down.

It's excruciating to my ego, which perceives me as a "good" person, to see that I am not volunteering during the disaster, not reaching out to other people. It's not like me, the "me" I have known. The reality is that the "me" I have become is too needy to feel beyond the edges of my skin. My arms are too short to reach out. I wish I could accept this about myself. I condemn myself. Can grief possibly be an excuse for self-centeredness? How do I live with this? I want to run away from home, but how could I leave everybody else to clean up the mess?

I hope Lance comes home tonight.

January 10

Some interesting things came out of my treatment with Elias yesterday. We worked a lot on a psychic level. He helped me see that (1) some part of me believes I don't deserve to take care of myself and heal if Mother is dead; (2) I have a strong cord binding me to Dad; I am sending much of my life energy to him, but I need it for myself; (3) I do not have a strong wish to continue with my life.

He cleared the erroneous thought and feeling patterns energetically, and he asked for confirmation that I do wish to live a full, healthy life, and that I don't need to hold on to Dad, who has his own life to live. Or not.

I hope Elias doesn't mean it's bad for me to hang out with Dad. I'm sure I can spend time with him without holding on. I like the way Ger and I take turns having dinner with him. One of us is there every night so he doesn't have to eat dinner alone. Sometimes Lance and Carolyn come with us, and sometimes we go alone. Nice family feeling when Lance is there, and I like having time just with Pop, too. We talk or read or play Gin Rummy. And, of course, the five of us still have *Shabbat* dinner together every week.

January 15

I've had an insight about a pattern in my life. I try to please people, and then feel that whatever I do is not enough. Sometimes I feel that Ger is judging me. Maybe he is, but I'm pretty sure I'm really judging myself, because I'm falling short of the way I'd like to be. I am terribly sensitive to the slightest criticism these days. I must remember that Ger has always been my advocate.

When I saw Ger today, he told me he has said goodbye to Mom and is moving on.

January 31

This morning I had an exciting thought: I wonder if I could expand myself into the Vastness to be with Mother instead of wanting her to be here with me.

I sit breathing and I imagine the space between the molecules of my body getting bigger. I am expanding, and the expansion causes relaxation to flood me. What a relief it is. The stress dissipates. I shall remember this and practice it.

February ~ As Though a Dam Broke

February 15

I am happy, as though a dam has broken, and the life force can flow again.

February 18, 4 a.m.

Got to Dad's after a twelve-hour workday. I'd been up since three and was very tired. Ger left in a rush as I came in. Don't know what had passed between them.

Dad met me in the kitchen. "Should we prepare food at home or eat out?"

"I don't feel like cooking," I said.

"Cooking?" he said, glaring at me. "D'you mean heating things up?"

Loneliness for Mom swept through me. She had such a good way of helping things go smoothly. She cooked for Dad, didn't just heat things up. He must miss her terribly.

I went into the bedroom and had a huge sobbing spell—15 minutes, maybe more. I couldn't stop. I cried 'til I was drained. Huge wrenching sobs and tears and a colossal stuffy nose. As though a dam broke.

~

I'm sure my tears and grief came partly from fatigue, but maybe I was crying for all of us. Our family was much nicer when Mother was alive. I don't know how to do her magic. I guess part of what's tough for me is that I believe I *should* be able to do her magic, *should* be able to hold things together, and it isn't working. I know I can't really protect any of us from our own life paths, but I feel I ought to be able to fix everything, wave a wand and bring harmony and well-being. Maybe there just isn't any anymore.

Ger and Lance are impatient with each other again. Therese Rando says, "The stress of a dying or dead parent . . . can put enormous strains on sibling relationships . . . and unresolved issues . . . can erupt." And she says, "You may have a combination of anger and depression, such as irritability, frustration, annoyance, or intolerance." True for relationships with in-laws as well as siblings, I guess.

March ~ Better Balance

Saturday, March 1

Heartening talk with Mary Margaret. She reassured me that when things need to happen, they will. I can't make things happen, but I can be free to let things go and not feel entirely responsible. When it's appropriate that things be done they will be done, by me or by somebody else. Urgencies will bubble up to the top of the list and be taken care of. Everything in its own time. Nothing can be rushed. Life is a huge exercise in letting go.

I'm feeling much better now. I'm ready to trust that what needs to be done will be done. At the moment I am fairly centered and fairly peaceful. Not anxiety-free, but in better balance.

March 4

Yesterday I bailed. I just lay about and read all day. Escaped the pain I was feeling, couldn't face going to work. Wanted to disappear. Now I am just as despairing, just as lost.

Bartholomew says, in this tape I'm hearing, "Go into the pain. Feel it." I'm not sure I am able. I feel like giving up, like never going back to work, like sinking into myself and never coming out to face people or my responsibilities. I am numb. Tears lurk beneath the surface, but they're not coming out.

March 11

Read a good article about voluntary simplicity yesterday—about cleaning out all the extra stuff in life. Dad is doing that, and I'm dragging my feet. I want everything to be the same. I'm refusing to let go of Mom, I'm sure. I don't want Dad's house to change. I don't want to go there and see Mom getting erased, even though I know that things must change, and that the house has to suit Dad's new life.

March 12

Dream

An ancient, formal ceremony. The people are knowledgeable about music, massage, astronomy, and a fourth discipline I don't remember. The setting is stately, reminiscent of Egyptian structures, tall and sharply planed, sandstone colored, honey-yellow.

The ceremony is conducted in the shape of a square, and at each position the participants take their places, stand still and erect. Each has a special talent. It is, perhaps, an initiation.

Though each person's demeanor is formal and ritualistic, there is a sense of love and familiarity about the ceremony, because I know all the participants, and because I have helped to plan it. We are all studying together in this priesthood or mystery school. I am waiting at the side for my turn to enter the procession, but I awake before I have entered and taken my place.

⤙

This was an extraordinary dream. I don't remember many details. Apparently I was moaning and moving a lot, and Lance woke me before it ended.

My sense is that it was some kind of healing ceremony and the patient would enter after all the participants were in place, and then they would each use their own special skills to treat her. The ceremony was stately and elegant, awe-inspiring in its simplicity.

This was a long and powerful dream. I recall no details from the part before the ceremony. One thing that is especially striking is that I didn't feel like I was asleep. I was watching and completely alert, yet I must have been asleep. I didn't hear myself shift and moan. I felt myself to be lying perfectly still on my back in the bed. Absolutely still, yet actively involved in the ceremony. I hope healing *is* happening on some deep level.

March 17

Yesterday was four months since Mom died.

Yesterday I went to the nursing home to visit my friend Annie. Something shifted. I feel for the first time that I have glimpsed her suffering, her loss. Before, I only could be in my mind and emotions about it, but I could never really sense her experience. What a complex life she has, and all of it lived in a bed and a wheelchair, in a body debilitated by M.S. What does that feel like?

I think our relationship has deepened because I have deepened. I want to learn from her. I think I have, in my arrogance, thought I had something to teach—about spirituality. Now I see we have much to learn from each other.

March 26

Huge realization yesterday that I do so much to *understand* my feelings when they arise—write, talk, think—that I am drawn away from simply experiencing them.

⤙

Today I sat to meditate. I used a Bartholomew tape as a focus. It got my mind out of the way so I could feel the Vastness, and I felt a tremendous sense of relief that it is still accessible to me. My mind doesn't have to be empty. I can sense the Vastness behind the busyness. Thank God. I've come home again.

April ~ Playing Dress-Up

April 21

Tonight is *Erev Pesach*, our first *seder* without Mom. Usually cooking holiday meals is a joyful experience, but this has not been a fun day. Carolyn and I worked nicely together, and Dad was a great help. He chopped all the apples and pecans for the *charoses*. But I missed Mother terribly, even though I felt her with us on some level. Pop took a nap in Mom's recliner. I wished I could have curled up on her lap.

Aunt Mick called and asked what to do with her cake that had fallen—said she would have asked Mother, so now she's asking me. I had no clue. Auntie Es says now I am her confidante.

I don't know how to walk in my mother's slippers. Well, maybe I can walk in them, but I don't fill them. It feels like playing dress-up. People look to me as though I were Mom. I can never be anything but myself. I can't take her place. Anyway, I wouldn't want to.

April 25

Went to the Jacksonville Cemetery yesterday to visit Mother's grave for the first time. Mary Margaret is in town to give a workshop, and she came with me. I like it there. It's peaceful. I think Mom is everywhere, though.

May ~ Where My Comfort Lies

May 1

I talked with Mary Margaret about the despair I sometimes feel. All that is really left to me is Silence, and that is where my comfort lies. In every moment, I can simply turn my awareness there and be comforted.

Saturday, May 3

Lance has been upset with me because I don't take good enough care of myself. He blames it on my work at the mediation center. Today I said I'd quit my job. I just don't care anymore. I've felt the change coming. It's not time yet, but I can see I'm moving in that direction. Things are falling into place there.

I'm not sad to think of leaving, only relieved. I want to strip down my life, simplify again. I'm sick of being around people all the time, and I need time to grieve. I don't know how to be moderate. I don't want another job—maybe ever. It will be interesting to see if I create another stressor in my life. I don't really know if I'm capable of a leisurely pace anymore. God willing, I am.

———

Outside my window, a huge bumblebee alights on a small red flower. Too heavy, and the bloom tips sideways. I hope I have the resiliency to right myself, as the blossom did, once the weight's been lifted.

When I told Ginger I'm getting ready to leave the mediation center, she said, "You're still needed there." I wanted to shout, "No!" I don't want to feel I'm needed there, don't want to be indispensable. I must believe the right person will come.

May 4

Woke up today realizing it would be very hard for me to leave the mediation center under these circumstances. If I leave before this job is done, then I shall just be stuck in another place to learn these lessons. My task is to learn moderation, to be able to work without sacrificing my personal life.

Lance and I need to work out something he can live with. I have to create a work style now that satisfies Lance's demands for me to take care of myself. And they do feel like demands, however well-meaning they may be.

———

I feel turmoil and resentment and more loss. Do I have to lose the whole job on top of losing everything else?

May 10 – Mother's Day

Lance and I went for a drive in the mountains with Pop and visited five lakes. Stopped for a picnic at Fish Lake and when I went to spread out Mom's old green tablecloth, I found a quarter on the ground by the table, kind of scuffed over with dirt. Felt like Mom planted it.

At the end of the day, when it was too late to do anything about it, Dad very casually mentioned that Ger had gone to the cemetery today and had taken flowers.

"Are you sorry you didn't go?" I asked.

"Yes."

Why couldn't he have said something to me earlier? He and I were planning to go next Saturday. I told him I'd gone, and he'd asked if I wanted to go with him sometime. He'd never mentioned it before. Maybe he'd rather have gone with Ger today than come with us, but he didn't want to say so and risk hurting my feelings. So hard to work our way through all this.

May 25

Dream

Elias does something to "uncord" me from Dad. Says it is important. Then I am in a student union with Dad. We are on the way to a lecture. I am somehow separated from him. I wait for him in the lecture hall, and when he doesn't arrive, I go to look for him. I find him lying on a bench with his head on somebody's balled-up jacket, holding a cup of water. Lance is massaging his feet. I know without being told that he's fainted. Lance says he hasn't drunk enough water and has collapsed from dehydration. I feel responsible, because I haven't kept close enough track of him.

There was Lance showing up to help me through yet another crisis. This dream reflects a lot of anxiety about whether Dad will be okay if we detach ourselves from him. A lot of emotions are connected with this detachment thing.

In the last couple of weeks, three different people have expressed surprise that we spend so much time with Pop. I wondered recently whether we are somehow getting in the way of his healing by being there every night. I've thought of it as helpful. He's told us, "I don't know how I'd have managed without you kids." I've liked having the family feeling, and so has Lance, yet I know I'd have more time to myself if we didn't go over so often.

In a traditional family there wouldn't have been an issue about whether he'd have to eat alone after his wife died. He would have lived with his children. Sometimes I let other people's attitudes get in the way of what is healthy and right for us. Then I wonder whether we are doing the wrong thing. Maybe Dad's too polite to tell us that he doesn't want/need us to be there so much. I surely don't want to keep him from being self-sufficient.

Okay. So when I look at this on a larger scale, I have to trust that we have been doing just what is needed, because that's what we've been moved to do. I need to trust that circumstances will change when it's time for them to change. I sometimes have this magical belief that if only I can take good enough care of Dad, he'll be fine, and he'll want to live a long time. Can I let go of him and still be a helpful, loving daughter without the hooks? I need him as much as he needs me. Maybe the question is, am *I* ready to be okay on my own? Maybe I am, if the question is even coming up.

———

I've been judging myself for all the things I never get around to doing, for not dispersing Mother's stuff, for not answering the condolences, making the memorial contributions, gardening. I have the notion that I can't be okay until my surroundings are in order. All this self-criticism sounds like grief talking. The lesson here is that I can choose to be okay no matter what is going on (or not going on) around me. Okay-ness is inside. Order isn't necessary to a peaceful heart.

May 26

Pop's 85th birthday—happy/sad day. Dad and I went through Mother's jewelry together and had lots of memories. Then we all went to dinner at *Il Giardino* with friends. Then more jewelry with Carolyn. I finally sorted through some of Mom's things in my studio, too. It was a relief to get it done.

June ~ An Occasion for Gratitude

June 2

Today's our sixth wedding anniversary. This is a beginning time, the beginning of a year of spontaneity and willingness. I shall be the hollow reed, the willing channel, the implement of God's will. This is the year to follow my heart, and to trust that every day the necessary things will be done.

June 8

I realized last night that when I doubt myself, it's always when I am focusing on my mistakes and overlooking the dozens of things every day that go well.

Here are some things I can do to help myself:

1. Refrain from worrying. When worry is present, shift attention to breath.

2. Listen to inner promptings. Even when I am involved with another task, stop and do what I am prompted to do. Trust that this will not cause important things to be left undone.

3. Express gratitude. Write thank you notes, offer prayers of thanksgiving, notice beauty and harmony around me. Let each breath be an occasion for gratitude.

June 16

I'm scattered and feeling anxious about things. I sit here at my altar, and I can't even remember what things. I know I need to. . . to. . . . My mind is so cluttered, I just go vague.

June 22

Dream

Mom is volunteering for a social service agency. I'm working with a kid who is disturbed, and I find out that the agency is planning to send someone to take him away to a shelter because they don't think I can help him enough. I realize that Mom, as part of her work, is setting it up to have the kid picked up. I feel betrayed, but also glad she is helping in the community.

Dad's in the dream, too. He's wrapping a poster-sized picture for mailing. It has glass on it. I say, "Dad, you can't send this through the mail without more protection. The glass is exposed. It'll shatter and get slivers of glass all over everyone's stuff." Then I see he has a big cardboard box on the upstairs windowsill. No problem.

Then I'm out in front of the house, and I see some unusual flowers. I pick them, but I leave one special one that is an exquisite blue-gray—an other-worldly color—and hairy inside like an iris, but a different shape. It's furled inside itself. I know it has a lot more unfurling to do, and I don't want to shorten its life.

The people come for the boy.

⟿

I'm feeling betrayed by Mom, and I'm fearful that Dad isn't competent to do what he needs to do. But there is hope. The flower is still unfurling.

June 23, 6 a.m.

Lance and I spent the weekend at the coast with Ben and Julia. It was healing to get away. Yesterday we all went to the beach. I was walking by myself on the seaward side of some big jagged rocks. Sometimes the water was out, sometimes in, but I felt safe, because there was plenty of room to step between the boulders.

Then, while the water was in, I stepped into a narrow place, and suddenly there was no sand. My foot went down and down, and I was thrown face forward into a huge boulder. I must have braced myself with my hands, because both palms are scraped. My nose hit the rock with the gentlest sensation, and then my fall was arrested. Not even a scrape on my nose. It was as though

I'd fallen into a cushion of air. I went in up to my thigh, and so quickly I didn't know what had happened.

My right leg was bruised and scraped, and my left ankle twisted. The bruise on the inside of my knee is pretty tender, but the rest of the injuries are just abrasions.

9 p.m.

Been thinking a lot about my fall. One thing I noticed is that the abrasions on my legs are in the same place where Elias has been needling me. Also, it's miraculous that I didn't smash my face into the rock when I fell. Maybe my guardian angel caught me. Mom used to talk with me about guardian angels. I didn't catch myself with my arms and shoulders, I'm sure, because they weren't sore afterwards, and the scrapes on my hands were practically non-existent. I fell heavily. Maybe the Powers That Be were trying to get my attention. My thanks to whatever saved me. I am feeling protected and loved.

July ~ Ready to Move On

July 7, 5 a.m.

I'm ready to move on from the mediation center. Yesterday I found out one of our board members is seriously ill, and I couldn't spare even an hour to go and see her. This is not the person I want to be.

I hope people accept that this is what I need to do and are graceful with it. If not, so be it. I want time for myself in my bereavement, and I want to follow my heart for a while. I haven't felt free to do that since I started working full-time.

Lance felt conflicted when I told him I'm ready to leave. First he said, "I'm glad you'll be out of that poisonous environment." Then he felt anxious about how we'll get on without the income. I set him up in a terrible way, and I deeply regret it. I asked him to share his thoughts about the change, and then I didn't listen. I was trying to edit, trying to convince him to see it from my perspective, instead of hearing what he had to say. I'm sorry to have done that. It hurt him a lot. He didn't even want to talk to me before we went to sleep—just said he felt badly, and it wasn't time to talk about it yet.

I asked him whether he likes that I talk with him in the early stages of contemplating a change, and he looked surprised and hurt that I might consider *not* talking with him about it. Yet sometimes talking things over is hard, because we see things differently, and I find myself feeling defensive. Yuck.

July 12

Aunt Mick and Uncle Roy are visiting. It's been a pretty nice visit, but last night I was furious with Uncle Roy. He called someone stupid on our way out to Emigrant Lake, and I lashed out at him. My anger upset him, and he said he wouldn't sleep all night because of it. What is it with all this anger lately?

July 18

Lance and Ger had a good talk yesterday. They both seemed cheerful and relieved afterwards. I am moved that they both love me so much they are willing to stretch to make things more comfortable between them. Had lots of insights, looked at some agree-to-disagree stuff, noticed commonalities and ways they differ, acknowledged how much they do share and enjoy in each other. I hope the tension has dissipated. God willing. Best of all, they figured out new ways to deal with hard stuff in the future and ways to avoid some of the pitfalls. I am grateful.

July 22

A realization: this foray into the world of conflict management has given me useful insights into human nature. This is the poison that makes people ill: the unresolved anger and hurt, the pain we carry.

Someone pointed out to me at work the other day that mediation is a lot harder than other kinds of dispute resolution, because you have to face each other with an open heart. You have to be honest with one another—and with yourself. Interesting insight.

Finally spoke with Helen Wallace, the board president, about a possible transition out of the mediation center. She was absolutely supportive. As we sat planning in Hawthorne Park, the reality started to sink in, and I wound up saying, "Give me until the September board meeting to make a final decision." She was fine with that.

Well, the news is out, and I'll see what develops. I must admit I'm afraid as well as excited. And grateful.

July 24

Really enjoying work. Maybe this let-go is what I needed. I dreaded getting up today, though. I'm not at all looking forward to doing the mediation training in the church social hall where I spent most of Mom's Last Good Day.

I've been tired all week. Lance and Lu have both spoken to me about grief fatigue. I suspect they're right. I surely did have a tough weekend with the relatives, and I've been weepy and tired since then.

July 25

Dream

I am having an autopsy. It's to be a learning experience, so I am going to stay alive as long as possible so I can see what it is like. They do very fine, gentle cuts, and I can't feel any of them. They will have to kill me before they do the belly. I say I want to take a shower first to wash off the blood.

＊

This is a lot like losing someone to cancer.

July 27

An amazing, hopeful dream

A starry night sky, and I am traveling through it, and the path is shown to me by an exquisite electric-blue light. This glorious light illuminates a vast sweep of stars. As the stars turn blue, they show me the path I am to take. The path curves off to the left, and I follow it as it extends deeper and deeper into the vastness. It's exhilarating, like riding a motorcycle on a mountain road, only way better.

August ~ I Begin to Realize

Monday, August 4

We all went to the cemetery for Mom's birthday yesterday. Tearful day. I felt sad, and it was painful to watch Dad's sadness. Planted mums at the grave, and then the five of us had brunch at Bella Union.

—✦—

Yesterday afternoon I talked on the phone with a lot of people I love, and it was comforting. Then Lance and I had dinner with a friend.

The call with Auntie Mim was especially nice. She'd called Saturday night, but everyone was on the phone, and we couldn't really talk. She said she'd called the night before so she wouldn't impose on Mom's birthday. Impose! I was amazed. She could never be an imposition on me, and I told her so. We've always shared a special closeness, and I love to talk with her.

Auntie's having some kind of heart problems, and the doctor is urging her to have surgery.

"It won't prolong your life," he told her, "but it will improve the quality of your life."

"I already like the quality of my life," she said.

So many people I love are getting old.

August 6

Had a horrendous confrontation with a young colleague yesterday. She projected a whole lot of her anger toward her dead mother onto me. In a meeting. In front of the whole staff. I was pissed.

This feels like her stuff, but all the same, I need to look and see what part of me it's poking. I want to be a loving person. How do I find Love in my heart in the moment I'm being attacked? I responded to her attack with hurt and anger, and no healing was possible.

I need to be with that, to see what's here for me to learn. Can there be unconditional love when we place limits on who receives our love? We either love, or we do not. If I can love thirty persons but not the thirty-first, then am I a "loving person"? I think not.

This is a test. Loving and hurting have come up against each other. Yesterday, loving lost. I can find compassion, but I can't find open-hearted loving. I don't think I know what it feels like to be totally open-hearted. In moments I glimpse it, maybe, but not often enough.

August 7

I feel like I'm stuck in a cage, going round and round like a gerbil in an exercise wheel. My mind is cluttered. Interesting. I'm not repulsed by the clutter. Rather, I'm excited about creating order. Somehow, in my mind, order plus creativity yields balance, and that is what I yearn for with all my heart.

August 17

Spent yesterday morning crafting my resignation letter. I want input from Lance before I submit it.

———

Was reading Dorothy Gilman's autobiographical work, *A New Kind of Country*: "We lose parents, wives, husbands, marriages, friends, children, illusions, but there is this to be added: nothing ever ends without something new beginning."

Wonder what I'll do next. Might be fun to have a part-time job at the synagogue.

August 20

Helen and I drove up to Salem for a meeting with colleagues. I announced my resignation and said I was taking time to heal after Mom's death. Many people came up to me afterwards to say how important that is, and that too many people don't do it. One woman said she had waited seven years to grieve her mother. I saw yearning in their eyes, and tears. A few mentioned my good fortune in being able to take the time off.

I have the feeling I'm doing this, not only for myself, but also for all the people who haven't yet grieved. I was surprised by their response, and I begin to realize the pain that people must be carrying around with them every day. Maybe this is why our society is falling apart. Too much pain to bear, and we don't attend to it. No wonder people walk around with haunted eyes.

August 21 – Mother and Dad's 59th Wedding Anniversary

Ger and Pop and I went to the cemetery. We took red and white carnations, and I took a pinkish heart-shaped stone. Then we went to the Oregon Granite Company to look at gravestones. We chose a light gray stone, and it will have a sailboat on it, sailing towards a setting sun. The words will say something like, "Together forever, sailing into the sunset," and it will be big enough for Dad as well as Mom.

Dad wants his own boat in the picture. We have to figure out how to get it rendered into a likeness that can be transferred to the stone. This evening, Lance and I took some clipart boats over to show Pop, thinking that one might be close enough, but no.

While we were there, Dad told me he didn't want to have breakfast with me in the morning, as we'd planned. He said he wanted to go to bed late and sleep late, and he'd just see me Friday night. I felt a little surprised and hurt, but I knew it had been a tough day for him, so I let it go. Then he called back later to say, "Do come for breakfast. Come at eight."

I don't know if he changed his mind because my hurt showed in my face, or whether he'd been irritated about something or what. Was kind of unusual, but he has every right to be a little inconsistent. He probably feels wrenched to pieces inside at a time like this, the first anniversary since Mom's death.

August 22

Had breakfast with Dad and a good talk. He hadn't realized that my main motivation for resigning is to deal with my grief.

"I wonder when it will stop hurting so much," he said.

September ~ Change We Must

September 11

I realized my primary identity has been "Fayegail Mandell Bisaccia, Executive Director." Now I must again become "Fayegail."

September 12

Auntie Mim told me she has taught herself not to cry. She's been having heart trouble, and I wondered if her heart is breaking because Mother and Uncle Mac have died. I phoned to ask her that.

"Yes," she said. "It's true."

September 13

I asked Dad on the way home from the *Shabbat* service last night if he's interested in seeing a grief counselor. He said talking doesn't help him. But he said he *was* thinking of going to see Jeff Elder, his GP. He hasn't been there in a long time.

I think I said too much about counseling. I should have broached it when I could see his face instead of in the car at night. "I wonder how long it will take to feel better," he said.

—◆—

Carolyn was installed as president of the synagogue last night. I got all the way to the *Misheberach*, the healing prayer near the end of the service, before I started crying. Leona, our cantorial soloist, looked at me full-on as she sang it, and the tears flowed. I still can't be in that building without missing Mom though I did enjoy myself at the gathering after the service.

September 21

I am reading *Change We Must: My Spiritual Journey* by Nana Veary. Here is a part I like: Her grandmother said, upon feeding a stranger, "I was not feeding the man; I was entertaining the spirit of God within him." Mother used to tell me about the men who would come to Grandma's back door during the Great Depression to ask for food. She gave them whatever she could spare and spoke kindly to them. And it makes me remember the way our friends were always welcome in *our* mother's home, in her kitchen, in her refrigerator. She'd feed them, and she'd listen while they talked about tough times at home.

October ~ Might As Well Get Used to It

Friday, October 3

Our friend Peter's mother has been diagnosed with pancreatic cancer. It's one of the fast ones. Maybe two more months. It's already in her liver.

We spoke a lot with Peter about our experiences with Mom, and he felt like it was useful. I hope it can help him. No matter how much you try to prepare yourself, you're never really ready.

We found out about his mom's diagnosis on Monday, then spoke with him at length on Tuesday night. Wednesday, *Erev Rosh Hashanah*, I felt like a basket case most of the day. Holidays are hard.

I was crying Wednesday when I got to work and bemoaning the fact that I didn't seem to be able to pull myself together. My assistant, Nancy, said, "I'll say to you what you once said to me: You don't *have* to pull yourself together." Wise of her to mention that. I felt better soon after, and functioned fairly well until I went home to help cook the holiday dinner.

Thursday was much better. Dad and I had decided to keep each other company at home instead of going to the *Rosh Hashanah* service. Neither of us was up for it. Too soon.

Carolyn and I went through Mom's Judaica books, and we're donating a big box of them to the synagogue library. There are some we want to save and read, too, and we can donate them at another time. I found books with Grandma's name in them, and books from Mother's youth. I like having this chance to know Mother and Gram better through their books.

Much sadness these days. I want to go to L.A. soon to see Auntie Mim. I want to spend time with her, just be with her— talk and laugh and cry together. Right now I feel like never coming back, but of course that's my fatigue and sorrow talking.

—✦—

I find myself day-dreaming of things I'll enjoy once I'm no longer working—walking, meeting friends for lunch, gardening, reading, writing, dancing. Being quiet. Long, lazy mornings with Lance.

Then I think about work I might do—write a book about losing mothers, work with Lance in our desktop publishing business, bring mediation to families of terminal patients who have issues to resolve.

Who can know? I'm impatient to see, like a child who wakes up on her birthday and can't wait to open the presents. I wonder if I'll create another thing in my life to be stressed over, instead of regaining my balance. Maybe I'll just sit around and read mystery novels.

Funny, I haven't thought much about the financial impact of my decision to resign. Yesterday Dad offered help, in case we need it, but I'm not worried. Lance and I have some savings, and a lot of expenses we have now, such as gas and eating out, will decrease when I stop working. Lance and I have both lived frugally before.

Saturday, October 4

Ginger and I met for lunch on the Plaza. We talked about general stuff for a while, then she asked me about my plans.

"I don't know yet. I have lots of ideas."

"More walks with me," she said with a smile.

"I've been thinking about writing a book about losing mothers," I told her. "This year has been so hard, and other women must be going through this, too. I've looked at Bloomsbury Books, and at the library, and I can't find anything written for middle-aged women about how to survive the first year. There's a lot of other stuff about grief, but nobody is saying, 'You'll make it. This is how I did it,' and that's what I've been craving."

"I guess I need to talk with my aunts," I said. "I want to know what it was like for them when Grandma died. Mother never talked about it much."

October 10

Things are finally falling into place at the mediation center. We've found my replacement.

October 11 – *Yom Kippur*

Dream

Ger tells me he feels like something is wrong, and suddenly I realize I am hurt that Mother and Dad gave him and Carolyn the mahogany breakfront when they moved to Ashland. I start to tell Ger and Carolyn about my feelings. I'm not trying to get them to give it to me. I just want to get my hurt out in the open, because it is Yom Kippur, and because Ger had sensed that something was awry. As I am speaking Dad walks up, but before I can finish my thought, I awake.

I think the breakfront, with its little drawers and cubbyholes with secret things inside, the old-fashioned fountain pens and airmail labels, the red and golden sticky stars, is symbolic of all the things I love in Mother and Dad's home—the brass *chanukiah*, the mahogany card table, Grandma's sideboard and the silk embroidery of the fruit bowl, the *challah* plate, the chair in the bedroom where Mother died. The memories.

I brought home Grandma's favorite novel, the three volumes of *Daniel Daronda* by George Eliot. I was with Mom when she bought it, secondhand, from a bookseller in Ojai. Mother said reading it taught her a lot about Grandma. Maybe that's another thing I have in common with my mother—that yearning to know more of a mother who was very private, and the sense of loss that comes from not being able to do much of anything about it.

I didn't go to services this year on *Rosh Hashanah*, and I'm not fasting for *Yom Kippur*. I will go to *Yizkor*, to the memorial service, with Dad and Ger though I dread sitting there crying. I haven't made it through a service dry-eyed since Mom died. I don't even want to go, but I'll go to be with Dad.

This is the first year in eight that Ger and I won't go off to the woods together for *Yom Kippur.* We've done it every year we've been in town together since he was in college. I love that tradition. We don't, either of us, want to leave Dad alone today. It's stuff like this that's so hard, the little things you don't think about that creep up on you. Well, the reality is that things will never be the same again, so we might as well get used to it.

October 12

I feel so close to Mom just sitting in the big chair in Dad's bedroom, the one in the corner where she was sitting when she died. Daddy's easy chair. I love to be there, quietly, by myself. I can see her best from there.

Yesterday was tough. I went to *Yizkor* with Dad, then we picked up Ger at the house and went to the cemetery. Odd. I never thought I'd be a person who visited a grave, but I like to go to the cemetery. I like to take flowers though the traditional thing to take is a stone. I probably get the flower thing from Dad.

⎯⎯⤙⎯

Strange. I've often wished Mom hadn't been so private, yet I'm the same way. There's much about myself I don't share, things I never speak about, or even write. One can't really know another person though we'd like to think we do. I wonder if one can even know oneself completely.

October 25

One more week. I'm so excited about becoming an unemployed person that I can hardly stand it. Guess I'm not being very present if I'm counting days, but that is exactly what I am doing.

Wednesday, October 29

I was supposed to be out of the center by Friday, but I think I'll need the weekend to be able to walk away with closure. I need to gather back together all the pieces of myself hidden in nooks and crannies, snip the tendrils that have entwined me, say my farewells to my work, privately, quietly. I can't do that when people are around and needing my attention. I want to clean out old files and see for myself what we've accomplished these past years. That is my gift to myself.

Thursday, October 30

Staff put on a surprise goodbye party for me during the Leadership Team meeting yesterday. This is starting to feel real. My life is going upside-down this weekend—in the nicest way, of course!

Friday, October 31, 5:50 a.m.

Last official day of work at the mediation center. I'll be unemployed twelve hours from now.

At our volunteer in-service last evening, Ginger presented me with a beautiful bouquet in a glass vase. She talked about our friendship, and she said, "I am so happy to be working in the office environment Fayegail has created." Then she invited the rest of the people to speak.

People were kind. Helen and Art, as the presidents during my tenure, gave me a certificate thanking me for my dedication and the qualities of my leadership. Many others spoke. I was unprepared for this outpouring of love and respect and appreciation. Yet I could see, in the midst of my discomfort, that what these people said to me was a reflection of the special relationship I have with each of them. It warmed my heart to think of what we have shared, and to know that I could say to each of them something equally appreciative.

I really don't think I've taken time to notice just how well regarded I am by my community. It's a good feeling.

First Yahrzeit

November ~ Free to Emerge

Saturday, November 1

The first of November. Nearly a year since Mother's death. My first day as the former Executive Director of the Community Dispute Resolution Center.

Dad and Ger got back from a visit to Los Angeles yesterday morning, and Carolyn orchestrated a family celebration for me at *Shabbos* dinner last night to mark this transition: a gorgeous bouquet of carnations and a sweet noodle *kugel* and salad and an almond torte from the Apple Cellar, my favorite dessert, and Chardonnay. She's a dear to have surprised me with such a special dinner. She knew just how I was feeling.

Driving to work yesterday, I was really missing Mom. I know she was there in the car with me. I felt her. But I'd like to have seen her face, would like to have had a hug when I told her about all the nice things people said to me on Thursday night. And last night, too, I missed seeing her at the table, sharing in the celebration though I know she's always with us. I miss the part of her I'm used to knowing.

November 3

I've been thinking about the weeks just before Mom died. Every time she had visitors, afterwards she'd have those terrible vomiting attacks. I asked her about it. She saw the pattern, too, and I see now that it was saying goodbye that upset her, tore her guts out. Each of us had to say goodbye to her, but she had to say goodbye to everyone. She lost every person she ever loved or cared about. It's unimaginable.

I guess I knew that before on an intellectual level, but the immensity of her loss has just now overtaken me. How ever did she find it within herself to walk this path so courageously? I realize now that she has shown me—is showing me—the way, and perhaps without many words, it is more profound.

I haven't known until the last months how blessed I am, how much of Mother I carry inside of me. More and more of her emerges as I move through my days. Her wisdom speaks through my lips and her knowledge flashes into my mind. I know things I didn't know I knew. Simple things, even, like using oil instead of butter to grease the potato *kugel* pan.

—✦—

I didn't know what to expect in these days without structure. I thought about making a list of things I want to do, but it occurs to me that everything will happen in its own time. This is interesting: I have no need to rush. I can just putter my way through my days, and when needs arise, I can take care of them.

November 10

Days are too full lately. Things fill my mind, if not my calendar. I have trouble being inward. Are there things I want to do this week to prepare for Mama's *yahrzeit*, for this first anniversary of her death? If I could get quiet enough, I'd know.

—✦—

I drew Angel Cards today: Truth, Delight, Spontaneity. Am I supposed to be light-hearted now? It's a year since Mom died, and shouldn't this be a sorrowful time? How can I dare move on in life when Mom is gone? Maybe—I think *yes*—she is showing me the way. The truth is that she has made her transition, and for me to live in delight, to live spontaneously, is the best way I can honor her. God willing, I shall always honor her in the choices I make.

Can it really be time to move on? Not away from Mother, but into a new way of being with her, out of the twilight and into the sunshine again?

November 11

Was so tired yesterday. Dad and I had gone out for errands and lunch, and I came home exhausted. Wound up sleeping on the couch until dinner—a three-hour nap. Then I barely held myself upright long enough to eat my soup, and I slept again 'til nearly two-thirty this morning. Today I'm drowsy again. Therese Rando says, "Frequently, physical symptoms are the only indication that grief still remains unresolved." I wonder if it is the approach of Mom's *yahrzeit* that makes me feel this deep physical and emotional exhaustion.

November 12

When I woke up this morning, I found Mom's memorial candle glass cracked and a huge shard sticking out of the side of it imbedded in the spilled paraffin that had puddled in the dish.

I noticed the room was dark when I came downstairs, and then I found the glass. Relief that there was no fire, and sadness. It felt like a sign not to burn the candles anymore. It will be a year on Sunday since Mother died. I've always felt her in that flame. I stood near it to talk with her. I greeted her when I saw the flame, and felt her in its light.

It's time to release my dependence on the candle, time to know that Mother's in all places. I've known that, yet I haven't wanted to let her go, and that ominous vision of the broken glass was a warning: Don't hold on too tight. And yet was it a sign, too, that she protects me. The house didn't catch fire, right?

⟶

Maya climbs onto my lap to comfort me. My dear friend.

⟶

I am full of self-pity. Why do I have the luxury to grieve this way when in so many parts of the world, loss and death hit people over and over again, bam, bam, bam? No time to grieve. Must get on with life. Must escape the atrocities, the natural disasters, the hunger, the disease, the war that is taking all the others. What a luxury to have this time to do my grief work. I wonder if my friends from other lands could see my situation as anything but self-indulgent. Would friends from Ethiopia or Mexico or Israel possibly understand me if I said, "I'm taking some time off from work, just to rest, to find out who I am now without my mother." It would have to be a foreign concept—or would it? How universal are these feelings?

Sometimes I feel so out of control, a pebble in the river, being washed this way and that. Can we claim order? I have come to the limit of my understanding.

November 13

Last night, Eileen, our hospice nurse, came to Pop's house for dinner. We've seen her socially a few times since Mother died. The evening was filled with light-hearted conversation. Then Eileen mentioned Trudy, and suddenly it was awful.

"Who's that?" Dad asked.

Eileen said, "She's been to the house," and left it at that, but Dad persisted.

"When?"

I said, "On Mom's last day, when she fell." I felt like I'd driven a knife into Dad's heart—and into my own.

On the way home all the memories of that dreadful day came flooding back. It was the worst day of Mother's illness, with the fall and the suppositories and Trudy, the nurse, walking in, a total stranger, trying to assess the situation while we were trying to get our poor limp Mother up off the floor.

I was mortified that the pain had intruded, had insinuated itself into our delightful evening. But maybe that is the way it needs to be. Mother is always with us. Why should we forget the hard stuff? Why should we forget any of it?

The worst part was finding myself trapped into telling Dad Trudy had come *that* day. I didn't have any warning. If I had, maybe I would have found a way around it. Did he need to know that?

Dad doesn't seem affected by the approach of Mom's *yahrzeit* and the unveiling of the headstone. I am, though. I'm expecting a big change. Don't know what to do with myself. I feel anxious, agitated, feel like I'm making too big a deal out of it. I need to be careful not to suffer over my suffering.

⚬⚬⚬

I'm reading mystery novels—my addiction. As long as the books are here from the library, I am compelled to read them, just as when there are sweets or chips or bread in the house, I am compelled to eat them. The books are engaging, but they're clearly vehicles of escape. I've decided not to check out any more for a while, but I see I'm not willing to return this last one without finishing it.

November 16, 5:15 a.m. – 1st Anniversary of Mother's Death

Sitting in front of the fire bundled up in Mom's hot pink chenille robe. It's a year since she died. A whole year. How did we survive it? The *yahrzeit* candle is flickering on the mantle, and the flames are roaring in the stove. I'm blasting out the creosote so we don't have a chimney fire. Odd blend of the eternal and the mundane. Maybe fire is the bridge.

I've been nervous about this day for weeks, even months. Will there be a change? Our tradition tells us to mourn for a year. It's forbidden to grieve too much. So, if I've had to work hard on my job this past year, if I haven't had a chance to grieve properly, do I get an extension?

I do notice something: I don't feel different today from other days—not yet, at least.

I cried when I lighted the *yahrzeit* candle with Dad and Lance last evening. We read a prayer from a traditional prayer book. It talked about honoring Mother by our right living. I do try to do that.

Darkness every morning this week as I came into the living room, and no seven-day memorial candle glass glowing on the mantle. Now this morning again, there is a tiny, comforting light, this little twenty-four-hour candle in its aluminum container. We're unveiling Mom's gravestone today. The forecast is for rain. That's fitting.

—✦—

I haven't yet remembered how to live with fluidity. I move awkwardly through my days. I resist my natural rhythm. Maybe this day is a boundary, a gateway to the rest of my life—life without Mother, in her body, hugable, available for conversation. More drama. Even as I write this, I know she is still available for conversation—in a sense.

I wish I could just be present, not want to know so much, not think or predict or worry. I think too much these days. Maybe I'll go away for a while and just *be*.

November 17

Made it past the sixteenth. Was an odd day. We had the unveiling, and I partly like the headstone—the concept at least. I'll get used to the art.

The service Rabbi Marc conducted was just right for Mom. Main thing I got out of the ceremony is that just because the formal period of mourning is over, I'm not necessarily expected to stop grieving. It's not a thing you just turn off. And also, that the best way to honor Mother is to live a good life, according to her loving example. I can do that.

Talked to the aunts. Auntie Es said she wishes I lived closer. She said she's sad nearly all the time.

The unveiling opened a lot of pain. One of our friends was saying it's been five years since his dad died. He said the first year is the worst. "After a while," he said, "you can look at pictures and have warm memories." I look forward to that.

—✦—

I'm reading Barry Neil Kaufman's, *To Love Is to Be Happy With*. I'm learning that I do things based on assumptions. For instance, now that I'm not working, I have time to resume a regular meditation practice, therefore I assume that I will (should) resume a regular meditation practice. Hidden message: If I don't resume a regular meditation practice, it's appropriate to feel bad about it. This way of thinking is not good for me.

The point of this time off is to remember how to be fluid in my life. I'm carrying a lot of notions about appropriate next steps. I'm afraid I won't be productive enough, won't help people enough, will feel critical of myself. So many expectations.

I like examining these things. It's more how I used to be. I'm in peeling-the-onion mode. Lots of good stuff farther in if I can shed the old dried-up layers.

November 18

Inspiring visit with Lu this afternoon. She talked about a friend's passing, and we shared some insights we've had. I cherish our times together. Lu seems to understand more about death and loss than any of my other friends here, except maybe Ginger.

Lu asked me if I felt my mother knew me well. Yes, she did, and if I ever went to see her sad, anxious, depressed, I always came away feeling better. It was the love, always there, and it brought everything else into balance. It was the harmony *between* my parents, too. They made magic together.

So now what happens? Does Dad still make magic? Does he find a new balance without Mother?

December ~ Too Many Feelings

December 3

Was reading Kaufman again, and he caught my attention. He says some folks believe they need to be unhappy now in order to be happy later. I say to myself, *As soon as I get my studio cleaned up, I'll take better care of myself.*

I fear I'll come to the end of my R&R allotment and not be rested, not be ready to go on. Again I have forgotten that one is always going on. Going on is what we do. If you're not going on, you're dead, and it doesn't matter anymore.

I waited to start living again until we passed the one-year mark with Mom. Then I realized, not surprisingly, that I didn't feel any different. Still miss her, still know I need to live life, still feel her around.

December 4

Saw Elias yesterday. He says much of my physical discomfort is connected with holding onto Mom, instead of recognizing the Mother part within me.

If I can use thoughts of Mother to remind me to drop into Center, into Love, into Silence, then I will be with her in the way I want to be. It would be a good practice to hold her essence and release my sense of loss. Time passes, healing comes. Today I am not fragile.

Nothing on my calendar for today. Good opportunity to follow my heart.

December 19 – My 51st Birthday–Los Angeles

Aunt Estyr is in critical condition in a Cardiac Care Unit in Sacramento. She had a heart attack. She's off the ventilator now, but she's still terribly weak. They'll know more after the first seventy-two hours. I'm sorry for her suffering.

Lance and I are in California visiting family. We stopped in Sacramento on our way to Los Angeles and had a good visit with Auntie Es and Uncle Joe. Then, three hours after we left, she had the attack. It reminds me of the way Mother would get terribly ill after she'd say goodbye to visiting relatives.

December 25

I'm feeling unsettled. Lance is driving home alone tomorrow, and I'm to fly home in two weeks. I miss Pop. I hope it's okay to be gone that long. I've seen most of the family, but I want more time with Auntie Mim and Beth, and I want to see friends in Ventura. I want to remember Mom with them.

December 29

I'm feeling like a pariah. I went to Sacramento to visit Aunt Estyr, and hours after I left she had a heart attack. I wanted to talk with Auntie Mim about how she dealt with Grandma's death, but she said dredging up all those feelings now would be too hard. She's finally more herself after losing Uncle Mac. I surely respect her decision, but of course I am disappointed.

I think that being with me right now is hard for the aunts, that it makes them miss Mom too much. I didn't realize how difficult it would be for people to dig into their feelings about loss. I'm learning that many are able to put their feelings behind them and move on. They want to get beyond the grief, not think about it, analyze it, revisit it, as I am inclined to do.

The other day Beth said she admired the way I really felt my sadness on my birthday and then just moved past it and was fine the next day. It's a thing I take for granted. I haven't really thought about how other people handle sadness.

⌐•⌐

Sweet afternoon with Beth. We walked on the beach at sunset, and I did a little Tai Chi for the first time since Mother died, there on the shore as the sun sank into the sea. Felt like sacred ceremony, even though I've forgotten most of the moves.

December 30 – At Auntie Mim's in Los Angeles

Auntie Mim has come down with a terrible flu—high fever and a heavy cough. I'm afraid my presence here is hard on her, but I'm not sure what to do about it. My flight's not for a few days, and I couldn't get a better reservation.

January ~ I Have Made It Down This Road

January 13 – Ashland

Once in a while I ask myself what kind of job I would like to have when I go back to work. One day last summer, out of the blue came, *I'd like to work at the synagogue.* This morning I met Carolyn for lattés at Starbucks. She mentioned casually that Karen, the temple secretary, is expecting a baby. Without thinking I blurted, "I'd be happy to cover for her while she's on maternity leave." I surprised myself. I surprised Carolyn, too.

I hadn't planned to start back to work so soon, but this would just be for six weeks or so, and it's part time. I think I have a good chance of getting the job. I have perfectly appropriate skills. So strange the way this came up.

January 20

Mary Margaret said that if I would write a book about what I know, she'd read it. We made a deal. I can't tell if my stuff is worth reading, but I trust her judgment. I guess she has enough confidence in me to invest the time.

⤙✦⤚

Yesterday I caught myself thinking: *As soon as I get rid of the clutter in my studio, I will be happy (peaceful, clear, okay, able to get on with things)*. Not that again! It's taking me awhile to recognize this pattern, but when I do see it, I can shift right away from it now.

January 21

I got the job as Karen's substitute at the synagogue. I'll start in early February. I'm a bit concerned about going back to work so soon, but maybe some structure in my life will be helpful. My primary motive in working there is to have a chance to spend time around Rabbi Marc. I think I can learn a lot from him. But if that doesn't work out, at least I'll have a little income.

January 22

Mood swings lately, and I'm not sure what to do about it. My studio is almost cleared of Mom's stuff, and it's a relief, although what is left to do—sorting out the correspondence—is daunting.

I used these sorting and purging criteria I learned from my dear friend Jimmie when I was down in Ventura: Keep whatever is valuable sentimentally, monetarily, aesthetically, or practically. Get rid of the rest.

Saturday, January 24

I've decided to stop seeing Elias regularly. I have taken back the responsibility for my health, both physical and emotional.

⤙✦⤚

Peter's mom died Thursday. Helping him through this has brought up a lot of stuff for me about Mother's death, but one thing I notice is that it's given me the gift of distance. Talking with Peter about our experiences, about things that happened over a year ago, helped me realize that I am healing, that I have made it past twenty-five months since Mother's diagnosis when everything turned upside down. As we take Peter through each step, I realize that I've made it down this road before him. That's why I can be helpful to him—because I've made it this far, and I'm no longer in it in the most immediate sense.

January 27

I just finished reading *A Sacred Dying* by Barry and Samharia Kaufman. I wish I'd been able to talk with Mother more candidly about her death. I once overheard her remark to a friend who is a cancer survivor, "People who haven't been diagnosed with cancer can't possibly understand what it's like." It's no wonder she didn't want to talk with me about it much.

February ~ The Love Was There

February 5

Two days into this job at Temple Emek Shalom and I'm delighted. I already like working with Rabbi Marc, and with Judy, who is the head of the religious school.

February 12

Today is the day to forgive myself for the things I'd like to have done differently when Mother was dying. And today I realize that I've been blessed to talk with Mom on a deeper level than most people have done. I realize I've known her very well. She'd throw out a sentence here or there that said a lot, that told me exactly what I needed to know. She said what she needed to say, and there never was any question that the Love was there.

These last few days have brought an intense up-welling of emotion. I miss Mom terribly. Memories are pouring in. Little snatches: how she looked in her black crepe floor-length cocktail gown with the deep square neckline, or that certain expression, impish and delighted, she used to get on her face when she was being a little naughty. Dear but tearful memories, and I hurt inside as I haven't in weeks. My mood can soar like an osprey and plunge beneath the surface of the lake in an instant. The transitions are that quick, still, after more than a year.

Dad and I had a good talk about grieving yesterday, and we shared stories about Mom. I love to hear him talk about her and to look at photos with him. I wonder how one could possibly go through this kind of bereavement without loving family around to share it with. God willing, I shall never know.

March ~ Background Person

March 9

I've noticed I am sinking into depression. I've fallen into a habit of doubting myself again, my emotions are close to the surface, and I have other symptoms of grieving. Perhaps I am partly grieving a loss of stature in the community, or at least in my own eyes. I don't feel like a temple secretary though I'm glad to be doing the work. Perhaps it is not, as Lance sometimes wonders, the best use of myself.

But maybe there is no better use of myself than helping people through life, being kind and loving. I may not be a public helper, after all. This morning I realized I have a sense of shame that I am no longer a Big Impact Person. I felt good about myself when I was director of the mediation center, felt that I was helping the community.

Many of my friends contribute to this planet in a huge, public way. Do I squander my talents? Or am I most gifted in loving and supporting those who do that public work? Maybe I'm more comfortable as a background person. We each have our own jobs to do.

It's that plummeting osprey thing again. I value myself and find my activities useful in one moment, and in the next I am disappointed in myself for not doing more to heal this world. My opinion of myself is shaky, and this is all a big wallow in self-pity. Getting down to it, what difference does it make? I'll lead the life I'm led to lead, and I'll do it, usually, in good cheer.

Saturday, April 18

Delightful walk around our Greenway pond with Dad yesterday—saw two kinds of ducks and some insects and a few wild flowers. The blackberry leaves are in their bright-green-just-leafing-out stage and look like fans for elfin ladies. We had great fun. Afterwards, we stopped at the nursery to buy primroses for the planter by Dad's front door, and a couple of artichoke plants for the back garden. Dad enjoyed himself so much he said, "Well, maybe I *will* make it to my hundredth birthday after all!"

April 22

Davida, the coordinator of the Mavens seniors' group, came to the office to help with phones yesterday, and we talked while I had lunch. She showed me a part of Mom I hadn't known before. She said it was Mom who helped the Mavens get off to such a good start. Mother hadn't wanted to be on the organizing committee, but she told Davida she'd be happy to consult based on her experience with the seniors' group in Ventura. She'd go to meetings, then discuss them with Davida afterward. They talked about what went well and what could be improved and how to do it.

I don't think I've ever thought of Mother as a mentor in the formal sense. Of course she was *my* mentor, always, but I loved hearing what she did for Davida and for the temple community. She brought such wisdom and clarity to everyday things.

It occurs to me that this way of serving I find comfortable for myself is the way I learned from Mom. She was there for people but never cared much about being in the limelight. She cared a lot about *tikkun olam* though, about repairing the world.

April 27 – Ger's 57th Birthday

I'm looking at the little garden outside my studio window, and I am filled with peace and joy. The tulips are blooming, and the irises are coming on. I love taking time to notice.

I see myself slowly reclaiming my serenity. I am returning to the self I was before I came back to America from Jerusalem, rediscovering the harmony which has been buried under the busyness of my life these past years.

April 28

We had a birthday party for Ger last night. We all toasted him and expressed the ways we appreciate his presence in our lives. It was moving. Dad started off his toast by remembering Mother and all the years she has been with us on such occasions. I missed her a lot. Then in the living room after dinner, I sat for a long time leaning up against Pop's chair, and he played with my hair. I didn't see his face, but it was a tender time.

I'm glad we've revived our tradition of cooking at home for birthdays, instead of assuming we'll go out. Cooking for birthdays brings Mom close, because that was a special thing she always did for us. We'd choose our birthday menu, and Mom would cook dinner.

April 29

I want Silence. I want the . . . the what? The Light from the underside of things, the part that doesn't usually show. Except I think it really does show all the time, and our vision is adjusted to another wavelength.

May ~ Emptiness without a Name

May 1

I tried going to a service again, and I made it almost to the end of the *Misheberach*, the healing prayer, before the tears came. All this crying makes me want to avoid services. At least I don't cry much at work.

Saturday, May 2

Today I hit bottom—deeply painful, even physical, feelings of grief. I felt sad this morning, and I realized I was feeling crowded by our heavy weekend schedule. We canceled our plans. Then I sobbed on Lance's shoulder and felt better. Odd, though, that while I cried, I was also watching, and the tears weren't accompanied by the usual feelings one would expect—self-pity, mourning, missing Mom. It was an emptiness without a name.

Had some good insights during my walk with Lance today. He pointed out how well I feel when I spend time each morning in my studio doing respiration exercises, yoga, writing, meditating. I come out shiny and peaceful, he says.

We also noticed that some things I hold dear, like gardening and visiting my friend Annie, have become *shoulds,* and now the thought of them produces stress instead of pleasure. If I let go of the shoulds, I could have my peaceful life with no strings attached. No need to give up the activities I care about, only the accompanying stress. I'm giving myself permission to bring spontaneity back into my life, to surrender to my heart promptings.

Another insight: I saw, with Lance's help, that if I watch myself, and ask, *Am I willing to come to this (challenging situation) off-center?* I will never—or almost never—choose to do that. I think just noticing will help.

May 5

Told Dad I'd hit golf balls with him today, but it's raining again. I think the Universe is supporting my lack of interest in golf. I love to hang out with him, though. We were going to see the rhododendrons in the park today, too. Oh, well. Maybe it'll clear later.

I'm starting to see a pattern emerge. I notice Dad is vague, forgetful, unfocused; I'm not sleeping well, and feel blue for days on end. I realize we're approaching a holiday.

The grieving intensifies whether or not I am consciously anticipating a special occasion. Something inside me simply knows, and it seems to happen for Dad, too. We're on the same schedule.

I'm concerned about Pop. Don't know how many of these plunges into despair he can stand. This time of year there are a lot of family occasions—Ger's birthday, Passover, Carolyn's birthday, Mother's Day, Pop's birthday all in a month—not much respite.

I wonder how long this continues, this feeling of guts ripped out and things upside-down.

May 9

Every time I go to a service, it gets a little easier, and I'm a little more willing to be part of the community. I feel welcome. People have made a point of saying how pleased they are to have me in the office. I'm glad I can make a difference, even in my depleted state. It's nice to know that taking time for my own healing can help other people, too.

My left hip has been bothering me. I read in *Heal Your Body*, by Louise Hay, that hips symbolize keeping perfectly balanced. My grief is keeping me off-balance. I need to balance grief with joy, loss with creativity.

I've been thinking that this job is just what I am doing until I can move forward in my life again. But now I see I *am* moving forward. I was worried that I might need hip surgery, as Mother did, but now I see that what I need is more joy in my life.

May 10 – Mother's Day

Apparently *last* week was the week to be devastated about Mother's Day. Today I feel pretty regular—good, in fact. Ben and Julia are here, and they've been warm and attentive. It's good to have them home.

May 12

I've noticed that during my quiet morning time, I'm much more centered if I haven't encountered any work projects, people, kitchen chores on the way. Just out of bed, into the shower, into my studio, and I can be deep into Silence in a flash. Interesting.

May 16

Dad and I had a good visit after dinner. We talked about work and fixing up our house, and Auntie Es, and grieving. And I shared my insight about needing to balance grief with everyday joy. Then I hugged him and said, "I love you, Dad," and the way I did it made him think of Mom.

"You sounded just like your mother," he told me. "At the end, I would be lying next to her in the bed, and she would say, 'Hold me, Dan.' She knew she was going fast, and I would hold her, and we would be there together."

We were sitting in the darkened living room, and I couldn't see his face. I could hear the pain in his voice, though. We didn't talk much after that.

May 27

Dad's birthday yesterday, and we made a special dinner at his place. Happy/sad occasion, as always. He was disoriented all day, and I cried all the way home.

May 30 – *Erev Shavuot* / Memorial Day

It's nice to be back in the rhythm of the Jewish calendar. In Jerusalem, holy days are so central to the way of life that one is always aware of them. Being in tune with the Jewish cycles gives me a chance to prepare myself, inside and out.

June ~ Navy Blue Silk

June 3

Yesterday was our seventh wedding anniversary, and last evening we had a most marvelous celebration. Lance and I went to dinner at Gen Kai, all dressed up. I wore my navy blue silk dress. After dinner, we walked in the park, and watched the swans and ducklings at the pond, and browsed on Main Street. Then we visited with Dad.

Pop had forgotten the date, but we reminded him he's giving us a great anniversary present—an awning for the sun room. I wondered whether he might feel embarrassed if we showed up in our dress-up clothes, but I wanted to be with him, and we all had a good time.

I missed Mother a lot yesterday. I do every day, actually. Tears are close to the surface lately. I wonder if I'm holding on to my grief in an unhealthy way. I certainly am functioning in my daily life. I guess if I couldn't, I'd have reason for concern.

Today I'm feeling exasperated with Lance. I project my own inadequacies onto him, and then I'm impatient with myself. At least underneath it all is Love.

Next Saturday, Lance and I are going to the coast with Pop, weather permitting.

June 4

Dad and I have been helping an immigrant couple from Mexico with their English as a nice way to spend time together. Yesterday, they canceled our lesson, so Pop and I drove up to the Grizzly Peak trail head and watched a spectacular sunset, instead. We sang off key all the way home. It was grand.

July ~ Needing to Go On

July 1

Had a poignant experience on my way to work this morning. A city workman crossed Mountain Avenue with a dead cat in his hand. Looked like a cartoon cat. Stiff. He carried it by its front legs, slung it up into the back of his pickup like an old tennis racquet. Flung it in, as though it had never been a precious, living thing. Do workers with dead people develop this off-hand attitude? Do they see our empty bodies only as something to be dealt with? Discarded? These vessels are sacred. That they held Life is sacred. I want my body regarded with respect and tenderness after Life has passed out of it, even when it starts to decay and returns to earth.

July 3

Went to the *Shabbat* service tonight. Felt sad, but this might be the first time I've made it through the whole thing without crying.

July 5

I awoke in the night with nausea, and I've been thinking about Mom, how she felt queasy all the time before she died. How ever did she stay so cheery, feeling like this?

July 16

Had a huge cry this morning, and a long talk with Lance. I noticed that I am attributing my every emotional response to losing Mother, but surely I had feelings before she became ill. If I would look deeper, not be satisfied with the most ready explanation, I could probably learn a lot about myself.

Lance says this is a big insight which could significantly affect my healing. He's helped me see I *am* healing. I know it's true, although in the middle of this storm of emotion, as he called it, it was hard to recognize that. And it *was* like a storm blowing through—laughter and tears, confusion, swaying and eddying, flowing and swirling. Then it passed and left me with a greater sense of peace and clarity than I've had in days though I feel a bit drained.

July 21, 5 a.m.

Shocking dream

I go to a meeting. On the way out I see Dad, and I catch up with him so we can walk out together. As we are walking Dad says he feels ill and dizzy. I am supporting him and am astonished at how light he is. Then he feels worse, and we head toward a concrete picnic table to rest and get help.

Next I know, I am awakening from slumber. Dad is lying on the floor. There is a huge bloody stain on the gray carpet near him. I look at the woman who is watching over me and ask if it is Dad's blood. She nods.

Then I go to kneel by him and cradle him, and he has a lot of blood rising up in his mouth. He says, "No matter what you think of me, know that I love you." I say, "I love you, Dad." He doesn't say anything more.

I can't tell whether or not he has died.

When I awoke I was numb. I lay still a long time. I wanted to call Dad right away, but of course I wouldn't at this hour. My stomach is full of knots. This dream doesn't seem literal. I wasn't terrified, in spite of the blood. The dream was filled with love and a bewildered feeling. Very strange. Dad was walking and fine, and suddenly he was terribly weak. I know I still carry a deep-down fear of needing to go on without him someday.

August ~ Not in Control

August 2

I've been thinking about control. The more we feel out of control in some areas of our life, the more we want to control what we still can. I saw that in Mom as she became sicker. I see it in myself at work. I say to myself, *If only I could get things in order, I wouldn't feel so out of control.* Bottom line is, we are not in control, no matter how we would love to be. Life flows as it will, and I must remember this.

I am frustrated that I can't simply move through my life without resistance. I do believe Life is unfolding as it should. I fear I'm not doing enough. Self-criticism and self-doubt rise up. Here is the grieving pattern again. Tomorrow would have been Mother's 83rd birthday, but I don't want to blame Mother's passing for my lack of clarity.

Sometimes I look at the big picture and realize it doesn't matter at all what I do, what choices I make. My part in this world is infinitesimally small. How could any one decision of mine have an impact on the vastness of the world we inhabit? Yet, from another point of view, one kind word can save a life. How does one come to terms with the largeness and smallness of things?

And I do feel so terribly small sometimes, when I look at these old hills, or at a mountain, or at the night sky full of stars. How could any of these worries, how could *I*, matter? I do not understand this. Every day I do my little jobs, somehow find meaning in my day-to-day relationships, think myself important, think it matters whether the files are straightened up or not. What a joke.

I wonder what *does* matter.

August 4

Yesterday was hard. We went to the cemetery for Mother's birthday. Was going to be just Dad and Ger and I, but Carolyn came too. Lance was at work.

We found a penny on the headstone. Mom used to find coins wherever she went, and Dad and I think she leaves coins for us in odd places, as a sign.

I said to Dad, "Maybe Mom left it." Ger overheard me, and rolled his eyes. Then he apologized, and when I tried to talk about it, he cut me off. That hurt.

August 5

Dad has treated us to an air conditioning and heating system. What a generous thing. He says he wants to see us enjoying his gifts instead of leaving everything for us to inherit.

It's been a hundred and five degrees for days, and it was great to have a cool place to escape to after the heat yesterday.

August 8

Carolyn and Ger have moved to a new house two doors up from Dad's, and we had *Shabbat* dinner there for the first time. Dad made a blessing. After dinner, he and Ger were speaking together about how fortunate they are to be living two doors away from each other now. They embraced, and I was moved to tears to see them so happy.

As always when we reach a milestone, I'm feeling Mother's presence, and also her absence. She's so much *here* with us, yet still I yearn to hold her.

Dad found an autobiography that Mother wrote when she was in college, and he gave it to us to read. It's a gift to have a glimpse of who she was as a young woman. Again, I see how much we are alike.

August 9

Beautiful, beautiful, peaceful time with Lance at the waterfall pond above the irrigation ditch. No one else was there. It was quiet, restful, healing, and we both came back renewed. What a perfect *Shabbat*. Mother left another quarter by the creek.

August 13

Turning point at work this week. I feel lighter, and many of my biggest challenges are coming to resolution. Something has ripened. I shall get my hair cut short tomorrow. It's timely; I'll continue fresh inside and out. It feels like a rebirth—to a new and healthier, less cluttered, more fluid life.

August 16

I wrote to three friends yesterday. Maybe I'm writing letters again. Haven't done that since Mother died. Not many.

———

A new bridge is being constructed on the Greenway, and people crossing it will be able to see the special sitting place by the creek where Lance and I go to talk. I'm sorry we'll lose our privacy.

August 21 – Mom and Dad's 60th Wedding Anniversary

I'm sitting before my altar, and I see something I've never noticed before about the candles. On the left, five votive lights. Two clear fluted ones; one in the shape of a *Magen David*, a six-pointed star; one in the shape of a bird; and one with straight sides, cobalt blue. On the right, one tall taper with no enclosure. The fluted ones, Lance and Ger; the star, Carolyn; the bird, me; the blue, Pop. And the one that stands apart? Mother.

As I write, the blue glass cracks violently and splits apart. I hope Pop is all right. It's left my heart pounding. *His* heart is broken.

Thursday, August 27

Pop and I are flying to L.A. for Aunt Mick's 75th birthday party. We're leaving this afternoon. It's important for Dad and Uncle

Roy, and for Aunt Mick, to have us come for a happy occasion after all their challenges. Uncle Roy has been terribly ill.

September ~ Ask Me Any Question

September 3 – Ashland

Had occasion to be at the Rogue Valley Medical Center yesterday, and it brought up a memory from the time of Mother's cancer surgery. Lance and I were with her in her room the night before her surgery. Everyone else had gone home. Mother had to drink a whole gallon of this disgusting cherry-flavored Kool-Aid-looking stuff as part of her prep. We all got to laughing—I don't even remember what we were talking about—but we laughed 'til we held our bellies, some of the best laughing ever. Nice to have that memory along with the pain.

September 18

Just heard that Mary Margaret and Justin are going to move here. It will be glorious to have Mary Margaret close enough for a weekly lunch or a cup of tea.

September 21 – *Rosh Hashanah*

Today Dad and I walked out at the lake, and made our own little *tashlich*, our own ceremony to cast away the mistakes and heaviness we are ready to surrender to prepare for the new year.

Dad told me his kids make a good reason for him to keep living. He really does want to stick around awhile. I'm blessed to have this time with him. Today he told me, "You can talk with me about anything you like, ask me any question." I'm grateful for that.

September 25

Ger sent me a gorgeous bouquet at work with a card: "You are very dear to me." What a bro I've got.

September 30 – *Yom Kippur*

I'm feeling a lot of sadness today. I have absolutely no desire to go to *shul*. Didn't go last night for *Kol Nidre*, either. I'll go to *Yizkor*, to the memorial service, with Dad and Ger this afternoon. I don't feel like fasting. I don't even feel like *being*.

   Ger sounds sad today, too. Maybe it's that kind of a day. We're going to spend some time together before *Yizkor.*

Maya wants to come into my studio, but I want to be alone.

October ~ A Thing I Can Do

October 1

Spent some lovely *Yom Kippur* time with Ger yesterday. We had a good catch-up. And we talked about ethical wills, and how it would be worthwhile to write one, even if we don't have our own kids to pass our values on to. Then Ger said, "This is the kind of stuff we should be talking about now, instead of writing it down to be read after we're gone."

October 9

Had a realization early this morning. I remembered the time I was in Italy a few years ago, the time I felt a sudden terror that Dad was dying. I called home from Assisi, and he was fine. It never occurred to me then that it was Mom who was dying. She probably already had the cancer by then. She seemed so indomitable to me, so strong and indestructible. I couldn't have imagined life without her. She was my pillar of strength. I guess she still is. How I would love a good laugh together, or a walk on the beach.

October 11

About dying: I yearn to keep in mind that Death takes us all, and is not a thing to fear. Why do we avoid it? Maybe because we always have that feeling that we haven't done enough. We think, *If only I could have one more chance to do it right.*

Or maybe some folks are afraid of what happens afterwards. I don't think that's my issue. I think of the vastness, of the emptiness I've experienced in meditation. I think of the bliss. Death isn't a scary thing to me. Not *being* dead. But it's scary to think of suffering and pain on the way to being dead. I wonder if, as with many things, the fear is worse than the experience itself. Fear goes on and on. Experiences end.

October 14

Lance and I just came back from a trip to the coast to see Ben and Julia, and to meet Julia's parents. Was great. We spent about an hour over breakfast with Julia and her folks, Jeff and Deb, who are visiting from Colorado. They're delightful. They surely are fond of Ben. Was nice to see. We had lots of laughing together, and some raw sadness, too, about losing parents.

The rest of the time we were alone with Ben. All day Sunday we hiked in Fern Canyon. We went off trail and jumped the creek, balanced on precarious stones and branches all the way up. Found luscious little grottos among the roots of giant redwoods. Traversed a landslide. Straddled fallen trees as thick as my waist is high. Root-walked our way up a muddy crevice.

Ben inspires us to do things we don't usually do. We crept down into low places, got our shoes wet, ate food from muddy fingers. We abandoned ourselves to the joy of it, and as Lance said later, "Everything else went away."

It was a joy to share the day, a total, total pleasure for us all. At one point, when we had just managed the most challenging climb, Ben looked directly into my eyes and said, "I didn't know it would be like this."

———

Carolyn has been feeling overwhelmed lately, and I wonder if my wish to "help" tires her. As Lance says, "You never know where help will strike next." I wish I could learn to shut up and listen, to be there for her without offering to do anything. I need practice.

Sometimes I wonder how Ger and Carolyn can be so fond of me when I'm so different from them. Sometimes when I'm with them,

I feel like a galumphing, exuberant puppy, and I don't know how to tone it down. I wish there were something useful I could do. Maybe I'll make them some soup.

Second Yahrzeit

November ~ Seasons of Joy, Seasons of Pain

November 1

November. So many feelings going through. I think this is a black-garment month. Odd that for months I've just *missed* Mom, but now I'm thinking of her death a lot more—I guess because the two-year mark is almost here.

I know I'm healing. I can make love with my husband without my sorrow for Dad's loneliness getting in the middle. I can go days without crying though lately tears are just below the surface again. Maybe this is how it will be for the rest of my life. Seasons of joy, seasons of pain—and all of it worth it. What a blessing to have Mom in my life, present in body, or not.

Only two weeks until Mary Margaret and Justin come to live in Ashland. I'm excited.

November 9

I feel peaceful mourning Mom. I'm simply feeling what comes up, don't really want to get rid of it.

Finished reading *Tuesdays with Morrie* by Mitch Albom last night. Poignant. Much of it reminded me of Mother, especially of her dignity and courage.

This morning Carolyn loaned me a book of contemporary psalms by Debbie Perlman called *Flames to Heaven, New Psalms for Healing and Praise*. Debbie Perlman is a cancer survivor, and many of the psalms she has written for herself and her friends are uplifting windows into the soul of a person experiencing the courage, pain, confusion, surrender that are part of living with cancer and its treatment. I am grateful for the insights that reading it has given me, and for the comfort.

It's what I've yearned for—to glimpse the inexpressible. And it gives me a better sense of what Mother meant when she told her friend that someone who has never been diagnosed with cancer couldn't possibly understand what it is like.

Debbie Perlman has opened a place of empathy inside me I had no way of reaching on my own.

November 11

Lance and I have been especially joyful together lately. I hadn't been meditating regularly until the last few days, and now I am. There's a direct connection between that and our sense of well-being. When I get too far off center, Lance absorbs my moods like a sponge on spilled milk. When I meditate, it's good for both of us. I am finally able again to drop into Silence when I sit. It's comforting to know it isn't lost to me.

November 14

Thoughts of Mother's *yahrzeit* hover, but I don't feel dismal. Dad's off center, but not as much as in earlier years. I think I see healing there, as well. I don't feel great, but okay is good enough for now.

November 16

Two years since Mom died. I'm functioning, and way better than I did a year ago. I drew Angel Cards today: Compassion, Faith, Strength. A perfect description of Mother. I lit a seven-day candle, my own little ritual. I'll wait to light the *yahrzeit* candle until the date on the Jewish calendar—six *Kislev*.

Mary Margaret and Justin have arrived. Mary Margaret called this morning. What a perfect day for her to come. I see I am looking to her for a kind of comfort I haven't had in a long time—Mother comfort. She understands me so well. I don't want to have expectations that she will fill that empty space. Or maybe that's why we will be together again—to nurture that part of each other that yearns for the Mother Love that I miss, and that she has hardly known.

I've been weepy the last few days. I don't know what's going on inside of Dad. He seems pretty centered. We're going to the cemetery today. Just Pop and I. Ger and Carolyn are in Washington, D.C., and Lance is working.

November 17

I don't like my birthdays much anymore. Three years ago: Mother's diagnosis (age 49). Two years ago: Mother had just died, and the mediation center seemed to be falling apart (age 50). Last year: Aunt Estyr's heart attack, and I felt stranded in Southern California in an awkward situation (age 51). I dread to see what this December will bring.

I'm being foolish. These associations all bring up fear. Maybe it's some childlike effort on my part to explain the inexplicable. *Well, it is December. Of course something crummy will happen.*

I need to stop this right now. I don't need to carry these expectations around with me. I think I'll just plan to have a great birthday this year. It falls on a Saturday night. Maybe we'll have a party for all the friends I've been wanting to introduce to each other. That's a terrific idea. We have a month to plan it.

November 20

Anguish all around us these days. The week's been full of people's ill health, sadness, and loss. Rabbi Marc says we're moving into the darkening time of the yearly cycle, and it's painful. The Light from the High Holy Days is fading (even if only in our perception), and we're trying in vain to hold onto it.

November 26 – Thanksgiving

Well, we have a lot to be thankful for, as always. Ate Thanksgiving dinner at Pop's. The food was good, but next year I want to cook there at Pop's instead of bringing stuff over from home in time for dinner. It's more like a holiday when we cook together.

December ~ Down, Deeper

December 1

Twelfth Month. Birthday Month. Sorrow Month. What will *this* December bring? This is the Dark Time. If I immerse myself in the blackness of my spirit, will I arrive at the Light in the Center?

I need to let go my chatter, let go my busyness, let go the angst. I need to settle down, down, deeper and deeper, to rest in the quiet, in Silence.

December 2

Maybe I was too cocky. For many weeks I was able to ask myself, *Is it worth it to be off center because of this situation?* and I've always been able to say, *No, it's not,* and drop back into Center. But the last days, maybe even weeks, it hasn't been working well. There's an underlying heaviness, a sadness, a forlorn feeling that I haven't experienced in a long time. Sadness. Do I hold onto it? I'm not required to have a hard time during this season.

I'd been feeling almost euphoric with Lance for some time, and now the high has subsided again. What an obvious state of ego this is, that my emotions can see-saw this way. I need to drop to the ground *beneath* the see-saw, into the stillness that never changes. It's fun to feel euphoric, not so much fun to feel this intense melancholy just under the pleasantness of the moment. Must drop.

I feel unstable right now, at risk. At risk that the satisfying feeling of well-being I've enjoyed these last months won't come back. I wonder how much of this is taking on other people's stuff, and how much is my own. None of it is Source. Of that, I am sure. Or, maybe all of it is Source, and at the moment, Source is doing "melancholy."

December 3

There is so much suffering around me right now. I yearn to be of some comfort, but I don't know how. Maybe I just need to be centered. Maybe that helps in some way I don't understand. Instead of sinking with it, maybe I can be the barge. Or maybe I can be the beacon.

December 17

Rabbi Marc left a note on my desk: "In appreciation for the light you bring to the community," and a gift. I was moved. What a precious thing to be able to work with him, who truly is a Light Bringer.

December 19, 3:30 a.m. – My Birthday

Fifty-two today. I picked up the Angel Cards and these fell out: Communication, Blank, Healing, Simplicity, Tenderness. These are my cards for the coming year. The Blank card stands for "infinite possibilities."

I'm going with Ginger to hear Mary Margaret speak this morning at nine-thirty, and Justin is coming at one this afternoon to do a numerology reading. Tonight Lance and I are having fifteen people over for a joint birthday party.

It's turned into a busy day, full of warm and nurturing activities. I was hoping for a delightful birthday. Maybe it will snap me out of this lingering heaviness I've been feeling.

December 27

Aunt Estyr died at nine o'clock last night. She felt ill and took some nitro and fell unconscious, and that was that. She was ill so often and survived it. Seemed like she'd go on forever. She had a tremendous will to live, even with all her suffering. Thank God it was fast in the end.

It's strange to think Aunt Estyr is gone. It feels like she's still there at the other end of the telephone wire. I'm glad we had that good visit before her heart attack last December. It sounds like she passed her last year fairly happily. I'm glad of that, too. I've been sending prayers for her. God willing she's found peace at last. Maybe Mom can help her find the peace she needs. Or maybe we *are* peace once the body is gone.

December 30

It feels as though Aunt Estyr isn't really gone. Well, maybe that's the point. Maybe in some sense, she isn't. I still don't see her every day. I continue to think of her warmly. The realization will come, I suppose, when I want to phone her, and she won't be there.

Just realized something. I always relied on Auntie Es to keep me in touch with what Cousin Lynne is up to. I need to take responsibility for that myself now. I've been relying on Dad to get reports from Uncle Roy and Aunt Syl about their families, too. Would I lose track of the family if I had to take the initiative to keep in touch? I wonder which of them would want to keep in touch with me.

January ~ A Fitting Thing

January 9

Had a shock when I walked into Ger and Carolyn's house last night for dinner. The Big Chair was in the living room, Daddy's easy chair, the one Mother was sitting in when she died. The other day, Ger told Dad he was buying himself an easy chair, and Dad gave him the one that has always been his.

It was a fitting thing—to pass it down from father to son. I am terribly sorry to have reacted the way I did. I started crying. I absolutely don't begrudge Ger the chair. It looks great in their new living room. But seeing it there without warning was tough. I would have liked someone to tell me first, or even to ask how I felt about it.

A good thing came out of the pain, though. Ger and I have agreed to talk before taking stuff from Dad from now on. If we'd had that process in place, the hurt feelings would have been avoided. On the other hand, Ger and Dad might have missed the delight of Dad's spontaneous gesture.

Ger and I talked afterward. I realized it's good for me to express my feelings, and he said it's a good reminder for him to be sensitive to other people. The two of us had a good cry together, and now we all have to go on from here, more sensitive to this emotion-filled issue of dispersing Mother and Dad's household.

That chair was an anchor. As long as I could sit there and feel Mom in it, or see her in the bed, I didn't have to let her go. The wrenching shock last night was that now I have to face the reality yet again that she is gone. There's no magic chair at Dad's where I can sit and pretend she's there beside me.

January 10

I dreamed about Mom the other night. I don't remember the dream, only that I'd had it, and that it left me feeling happy.

February ~ Unhealed Grief

February 3

Lance was driving over to Dad's for dinner and saw the commotion of a fire. As he continued, he realized the fire was in Mary Margaret and Justin's apartment. They're in New Mexico on business. We called to let them know, and they spoke with the fire chief. Almost everything was lost.

February 15

It's been days since I've written in my journal, or even approached my altar. I've experienced a barrenness and a fatigue that verges on depression. I look in the mirror and see an exhausted face, empty of animation. I think these last weeks with the fire and other people's troubles have gotten to me.

It's not that I'm going through my days without pleasure or laughter. It's just that sadness washes over me sometimes, and I can do nothing to fend it off. Maybe I don't want to. As Lance says, it's part of The Procession. I think the loss that Mary Margaret and Justin have suffered is triggering my own unhealed grief.

I haven't had a period in many weeks, maybe seven. I suppose I'm beginning menopause. I keep waiting. I guess there's no point in it. Perhaps it's the waiting that makes me irritable and exhausted.

February 20

I've been leaving our bed in the night. I'm restless lying there, and I rarely fall back asleep once my mind gets going. I come downstairs to the couch and listen to Bartholomew tapes until I fall asleep. If that doesn't work, I write, or iron. Lance isn't thrilled about this new pattern, and neither am I.

February 24, 4:15 a.m.

Mary Margaret and Justin are home from New Mexico. They've decided to go back to there to live. I feel like Mary Margaret is the only person alive who understands me as well as Mother did, and having her leave now feels a little like losing Mom all over again. I was so happy to have her near me at last after so many years apart.

March ~ Companion of Forty Years

March 18

I went to see a new acupuncturist, Kevin Laird, and the herbs he gave me for menopause are helping. I think it's the psychological adjustment to menopause I still have to make. A companion of forty years is gone. New way of life coming. More let-go. Another era. I miss Mom especially at times like this. I have questions.

Sat for a deep meditation today for the first time in ages. Felt good to be back in that space.

April ~ Five Precious Days

April 1

I have several days off from work because of Passover, and I want to go on retreat. I've been wanting to go for a long time, but now

I fear I won't let myself be quiet. I see myself planning, planning what to take: belt loom, underwear to mend, letters to answer, recorder, sketch book, legal pads, journal. With all these plans, how will I ever find Silence? It's what I crave, yet somehow, I've come to fear it, too.

Do I want time alone in an empty room? Do I want to fill my senses with the complexities of nature? What *do* I want? Here are five precious days. What do I *want*?

April 2 – Port Orford

Splurging on a B&B called Home by the Sea. Was an easy drive over. My mind kept dancing. Then I'd think, *Silence*, and I'd drop into the moment and that deep restful energy would flood my body. It's nice to have the time and space to re-create the Silence habit. I'd strayed.

Saturday, April 3

This is exactly what I needed. I spent the morning at the beach near the B&B. Walked down toward the mouth of the creek, and it hailed. Turned a corner, and the whole beach was white. I love being here this time of year. The weather is harsh, but not discouraging, not harsh enough to keep me inside.

The light has been spectacular, and I watched sun patches out at sea while it stormed on the beach. Interesting that precipitation doesn't impede the visibility.

This afternoon, my host drove me up to Port Orford Head, and showed me how to find a bench right out on the headlands. Wind ripped through hail and drizzle and sunshine, but it was never bitter cold, and I stayed fairly dry.

Saw two distinct ecosystems up there: one, a fern and cedar forest, moist and intimate; the other, scrubby trees and brush, windswept, open. Stark. And from the headlands: blue-green coves and rocks offshore. Huge swells, spectacular surf. Looking to the north, I could see all the way to Cape Blanco.

I felt some fear when my host left me in a stretch of open, intensely windy terrain. "Just follow this trail all the way out to the end," he told me. "You'll be fine." I took a big breath and went for it, and my reward was an exhilarating adventure.

I've been watching thoughts a lot today. Sometimes they're about the moment, what I'm experiencing exactly then. But sometimes they go to future or past, and then I remind myself to come back. I can't feel Silence in my body when I'm in the past or future.

April 4

Drove over to Cape Blanco today. The surf pounded in, set upon set of enormous waves, crashing through the offshore rocks, three or four sets breaking at a time.

Spent most of my time at the river instead of the beach. Played with a critter, an otter, I think. He'd pop his head out of the water, snort at me, and ride the current downstream. He'd snort; I'd snort; he'd snort again. He'd float down until he was almost out of sight, then dive under and swim upstream to where a submerged branch poked its tip up out of the water. Then we'd start the whole game again. We played together a long time. I gave up first. I hoped he'd follow me down river, but no, he stayed put. Maybe that was his territory. Maybe he wasn't *really* playing with me. Maybe that's the way he foraged.

I'll think of it as a game. It was fun, and he was good company.

An extraordinary thing happened over breakfast. I was chatting with my hosts, and we realized that the tulips in the center of the table had opened while we were talking. We were all so sorry to have missed the show that they brought in another pot from the deck, and we sat and watched the blooms. I could actually see the petals move, sometimes smoothly, sometimes in tiny jerks. In the end, each tulip boasted a different, striking center design.

Afterwards, when the pots were returned to the deck, the tulips folded up again.

May ~ Asking for Her Light

May 6 – Ashland

My energy is back after an exhausting menstrual period. I thought I was menopausal, but I guess it's only slowed down. Well, I *am* meno-*pause*-al, but not meno-*terminal*! Lost a lot of blood. Felt terribly weak, but better yesterday, and even better today.

I have decided to have a woman's exam. It's been seven years, and I want to set minds at ease. I'm talking about Lance's and Carolyn's. They have both been encouraging me to do it. Maybe my own, too. It is a hard decision for me to make. I'm not inclined toward a Western medical perspective. I get afraid that if I ever had a Western diagnosis, like cancer, it would cause conflict in the family if I didn't choose a Western treatment. Lance doesn't think this is true. At least, he thinks we could deal with it, so I've agreed to go. I haven't made an appointment yet, but soon.

May 20

Dream

I'm with Mom. She's wearing a purple sun dress and her skin is tanned. She doesn't feel well. We're outside, and it's dark. I say I'll try to find the car and come and pick her up. Does she have a flashlight I can take?

This is one of the few times I've seen Mom in a dream. I was asking for her light.

May 24

I've been doing lots of gardening. I enjoy the work, and I don't think of anything else when I'm out there.

I'm embarrassed to be so jealously guarding my free time these past weeks, but I feel like healing is taking place on some deep level when I take time to garden, to be alone, to be less compulsive about my job, and about spending time with other people. I almost dread an invitation to socialize. I'd rather spend my social time with family, or be alone to replenish myself.

May 25

I realize I haven't had as much down time as I've needed since I left the mediation center. Taking this job at the synagogue has postponed my healing further. Mary Margaret warned me. "It's easy to clear space in our lives," she said, "but then we allow something else to rush in and fill the vacuum." I need to guard this space I am creating.

⟶

Pop's 87ᵗʰ birthday is tomorrow.

June ~ Case of the Blues

June 26

I have a case of the blues that surfaces every time there's a *bar* or *bat mitzvah* celebration in the synagogue. I need to look at my ambivalence about my Jewishness. On the one hand, I identify deeply with this tradition. On the other, I resist the daily practices. I resist the intellectual unraveling of text, yet I am sometimes curiously moved by the insights that come from these exercises.

I also resist throwing myself whole-heartedly into the community, yet I have chosen to work there, for heaven's sake. And I feel comfortable there, and safe, and engaged. I care about these people, and I support them in their endeavors, yet I am writing "them" and "their," not "us" and "our." I am holding myself apart, defending myself against this immersion. I tell myself the reason is that Lance is not Jewish. Ironically, as I write this, he has gone off to a friend's *bar mitzvah* in the park, and here I sit, confused and sorry for myself.

Lance has attended several other activities at the synagogue lately, a conservation committee meeting, a meeting for intermarried couples, I forget what else. I love that he's been going. He's drawn to the feeling of community, and he likes a bunch of the people involved. Sometimes he helps out with computer stuff, too.

I'm like a teenager with an identity crisis. Part of me wants to support the families, to celebrate their *simchas*, their happy occasions, to make them mine, too. Another part holds back, threatened, fearful of being sucked into the warmth and commonality.

I'd like to talk with Rabbi Marc about this, but I'm reluctant. He's my rabbi, but he is also my work partner. Do I want to be so vulnerable with him?

June 28

I'm tired of trying to shape my life. What would happen if I only did what I was drawn to do in the moment? Yesterday I read a novel, made love with Lance, took a walk. Then we went to Dad's for dinner and a sunset ride up to Mount Ashland. Was relaxing not to do any "shoulds."

July ~ Riveted

Friday, July 2

Home from work. My new gynecologist, Holly Granger, did a biopsy on me Monday to follow up on an abnormal Pap smear. Since then, I've been ill. My temperature's been fluctuating between 97 degrees and 101.5. I'm seeing Kevin for acupuncture today. My attention is riveted on my body.

Thursday, July 8

I've started a series of improvisational dance classes with Robin Bryant. I realized that I need to expand my boundaries, to spend more time in creative expression.

Holly Granger got the reports back from the biopsy, and they don't know what caused the abnormalities. She's never seen this condition before, and neither has anyone in the lab. She called it plaque on my cervix. She wants to track it. I've agreed to another Pap test in four months, but I'm afraid of getting sucked into this mainstream medical model.

I have the feeling that the plaque is a physical and psychic response to some inner work I've been doing. I cleared out a lot of old garbage about sexuality from the sixties recently.

July 31

Jim and David, dear, dear friends, came to visit from California. They wanted to go out to the cemetery in Jacksonville to pay their respects to Mom. We went and straightened up the area around

Mother's grave, and Davey held me while I had a good cry.

Tears have been near the surface these last weeks. Mom's birthday is in a few days. But also, our neighbor Ruth died of a stroke last Tuesday. Last time I saw her, she was cheery and optimistic. But she took my hand as I was leaving, and we were quiet together for a few moments. Maybe that was her way of saying goodbye.

August ~ Kinda Shiny

August 2

I'd left my wallet at Dad's, and I went over to pick it up on my way to work this morning. I had the feeling Dad wanted me to stick around awhile, so I stayed for breakfast. Sometimes he seems so lonely. Mom's birthday is tomorrow.

August 10

I've been overeating. I think I'll model my portions after Dad's. He does a good job of maintaining his weight and good health. He makes me take a second look at the current theories about healthy diet. I tease him that the reason he's lived so long is that all the preservatives he's eaten over the years in hot dogs and salami have preserved *him*!

I am concerned, though. He's been feeling short of breath lately, and even though he rides his stationary bike every day, I wish he'd walk more. He doesn't like to go alone, and I don't make time to go with him.

August 16

Special time with Lu today. We bought lunch at Bento Express and ate by the stream in Lithia Park. Then we sat and talked, didn't talk, wandered, rested, wandered some more. Went to visit all our favorite rocks and trees, and browsed in the sycamore grove, and visited a tree that was special to Lu's dear friend who died. Was a day to cherish, all the way to the end.

August 23

Ger is worried about Dad's driving. I'm less worried. I read a Pacific Northwest Extension publication this weekend called *Driving Decisions in Later Life* about when older people's driving skills become impaired or when they become unsafe drivers. It's a good guide for families, as well as elders.

The booklet makes some good points. One is that people drive differently, depending on who is in the car with them. We need to talk with Pop about paying attention, about staying focused. I don't think he knows how vague he gets. I don't know if he is trying to be focused and can't, or if somebody just needs to point it out. One thing for sure. I don't want him to suffer any more loss if there's any way around it.

August 26

I once tried to get Mom to keep a journal. I remember the day I asked her. We were on a picnic out at Emigrant Lake. She said it would bring up too much hard stuff. She made it clear she didn't want to go there.

But then she did start a journal not long before she died. I remember looking at it with Dad afterwards. I found it again today. This is what she wrote: "We celebrated my 81st birthday on August third. I love and am loved, and I count my blessings with abundant gratitude. Life is good!"

That was the only entry, and when I think back on Mother's life, I can't really imagine anything more appropriate. She didn't speak much about her feelings, but that *was* the way she lived. What more inspiring teaching could she have left us?

September ~ Fragile Shelter

September 6

It was ten years ago today that Lance and I met. Amazing. Mother and Dad were together fifty-eight years—almost six times as many. Pop says we're beginners.

September 17

I am totally back in my grief—inept, fragile, off-balance, self-criti-cal, weepy. I've been working all week on the *Yizkor* list, the list of loved ones we read on *Yom Kippur* afternoon during the memorial service. I feel as though I have a deep, deep puncture wound that must be repeatedly opened on the surface to allow healing from the inside out.

Had a good talk with Judy at work. She's such a comfort. She told me that grieving time is not linear. I see this.

"Time is meaningless in grief," she said, "as it is on *Shabbat*. There is no time. There is wholeness."

Maybe time is meaningless in general. Perhaps that is why it is inconceivable to me that I shall ever become an old woman. I don't believe my mother ever did. Only her body became old.

September 18 – *Shabbat*

Perhaps grief is the thing that allows us to go deeper than we ever have done before. Perhaps grief opens us in a way that is not possible in everyday life. Perhaps one cannot really enter into the spirit of *Yom Kippur* without having experienced grief. That is what opens the gate, what enables us to ascend. With grief comes an amazing capacity for appreciation and gratitude, an amazing capacity for clarity. In grief, one knows what is important.

I went to Rabbi Marc's meditation class yesterday. I'd like to go every Friday. It's a perfect way to prepare for *Shabbat*.

September 25

Last evening we had *Shabbat* dinner in the *sukkah* at Ger and Carolyn's house. I love the tradition of building this fragile shelter each year to remind us of the times we were vulnerable, wander-ing in the desert. We are still vulnerable. The *sukkah* is homey and peaceful, decorated with rugs and hangings from the house. I could see myself spending time in there, studying and eating, even sleeping. I enjoyed the view out over the garden and beyond, and we sat until the stars came out.

⤙⤙⤙⤙⤙⤙

I'm going to a seminar called "The Sacred Art of Dying—Diagnosing and Addressing Spiritual Pain." Richard Groves is the presenter.

At the moment I don't work with the dying though many people I encounter are in spiritual pain. Rabbi Marc says this seminar is relevant to my work, and he generously paid for my tuition and gave me time off from work to attend.

Someday I'll share with him my dream of mediating with families of terminal patients to help them address their unresolved conflicts.

September 28

I feel withdrawn. The seminar has ended. I can't exactly say I'm disappointed, but I didn't realize how much of the material would already be familiar to me. I saw some neat film footage and heard some good stories, but the pace was often hurried. The time available for this seminar was less than Groves usually has for it, and he tried to cram in too much.

I had trouble fully immersing myself in the experience. I wanted to feel peaceful and intimate with this work, but I felt a lot of resistance, and when I explored it with friends on a break, I realized what was bothering me. There we were, in a huge church social hall with a hundred and ten people, trying to learn about things that are personal and intimate. Too hard for Richard Groves. Too hard for me.

I did enquire about Groves' longer course, though. He and his team are good presenters. The topics interest me, and I can see myself getting more involved with end-of-life issues. Or, maybe I already know *things*. Maybe it's more experience that I want.

⤙⤙⤙⤙⤙⤙

I walked home from the seminar via Helman Street, and I stopped at the farm to see the animals. The mare was right by the gate, and I fed her grass for a while. Then I walked down by the pasture and stopped to watch a woodpecker. A little boy stopped to watch it too, and afterwards we walked a ways together and chatted about everyday things.

Now I am sitting on a log across the stream from the Ashland Greenhouse, listening to the water and the wind. The sun throws dappled shadows on my journal as the wind blows through the trees, and the shushing of the creek washes over me. Cattle bellow, and I hear the muted roar of trucks up on the freeway. I am grateful for this peaceful place.

~

Last night Marc and Judy and I talked at dinner about training a core group of volunteers who could help organize a family's support team to cope with end-of-life challenges. The committee wouldn't *be* the support team, but would arrange for help with caregiving, food, respite, whatever was needed. I like the idea. Something to serve in the space between the *bikkur holim* committee, the people who visit the sick, and the *chevra kadisha*, the burial society.

October ~ An Old Friend

October 2, Midnight

Lance is angry with the noisy teenagers down the street, and I don't know how to support him. Well, I guess I do, actually. That is, feel my feelings, watch my thoughts, take no action, do not try to understand or fix anything. Breathe and watch. And love. Is that what's best in this situation? If I can do that, breathe and watch and love, maybe my steadiness can be helpful to Lance.

October 10

Yesterday we had a family conference. Ger and Carolyn and Lance and I got together to talk about strategies for anticipating and dealing with Dad's needs—without Dad. It's hard to have a conversation like that, hard to deal with the issues and challenges of Dad's aging. We talked again about his driving, but nobody thinks it's time to ask him to stop. Ger's managing Dad's bank accounts, and is having Dad's bills sent to him, so he can remind Dad to pay them.

I pray that Dad doesn't become ill and suffer at his ending time. God willing, we'll all handle his aging with grace, and he'll pass through it easily. He yearns be with Mom again though he's content to be with us, for now. I find myself resisting this whole process though I know it's a part of life I must accept. I wonder why we pretend that things don't change.

My self-absorption makes me wonder how I'll ever manage with both parents gone. I've been thrown so far off-center losing Mother. Yes, they'll be here, guiding me from inside. But what about the dinners and the hugs and the laughter?

Then I say to myself, *Don't project yourself into the future. Don't lose this precious time worrying about something that hasn't happened yet.* It's a greater challenge than ever to stay present.

October 11

I'm having a hard time with Dad's diminishing capacity. It's hard for me to talk about it, and it's hard for me to consider choices about his lifestyle without his involvement. Perhaps I'm afraid to acknowledge the reality, but I'm concerned that our fear is inclining us to be overprotective. We want Dad to have as much help as he needs without compromising his dignity or his feelings of self-reliance.

The rest of the family is seeing the driving situation differently from the way I do, and it's hard when we all have different comfort levels. Ger doesn't want to be in the car with Dad when he drives anymore. He says he'll do the driving when they're together. I want Dad to keep driving, and arrange for me or someone else to monitor the way he drives. Maybe I'll talk with Rabbi Marc about this. I'm sure he's helped other families deal with it. It must come up a lot.

October 27

Dream

I'm in a big theater after a film. People all dressed up in King of Hearts *sorts of costumes are thronging the aisles. I spot Mother and Dad in the crowd leaving. Pop is wheeling Mom on a brown metal cart. She looks emaciated. She doesn't even look like Mom, but I feel her joy and recognize her. They look happy to be at the festivities. I marvel that they have come with Mom in that condition, marvel that they have the strength to do that. We don't say much. It's hard to stay together with the crowd pressing.*

———

This is my mourning season—between the High Holy Days and Mom's *yahrzeit*. Odd. I suppose the whole year is my mourning season, yet now my emotions are particularly strong and raw, and the memories, both sweet and painful, are especially poignant.

I'm blessed to have been with Mother at her ending time though her gradual drawing away was sad and confusing. How many times Mom seemed ready to go, then strengthened again. I remember some days thinking, *Go ahead now*, and then I would be shocked that I could think such a thing. I wanted her to be with me as long as she could—forever, really. Hard when those conflicting emotions flooded in. Hard not to feel disloyal. Hard to know things ripen in their own time, yet wonder, some days, if I really believe that.

Will I be processing this all the rest of my life? It was comforting to hear Judy say that mourning time is like *Shabbat* time—not linear. Whole. Folding back on itself. Circular. One doesn't get over things. They cycle back, curve around, jump across again, and again, and again, without end. At any moment, grief can present itself and fade just as quickly. There's a comfort in that, somehow. Grief has become an old friend.

Third Yahrzeit

November ~ Feel the Loss

November 1

November. The month of Mother's death. My body knows the time's approaching, whether I'm thinking of Mom or not. I've felt it coming on for weeks, have been absent-minded, have been making foolish mistakes.

November 8

Angel Cards: Simplicity, Purification, Trust. There it is, let go and trust the One. I wish I could live permanently in that place.

I feel an underlying dread—of loss, of a world without Pop. He seems well, and I am grateful for each moment we're together. Still, the dread is there, has been there for a long time. Mother's illness and death took me by surprise, in a way. There was no dread. I thought she would live forever.

I wonder why this fear about Pop. Is it that I have put my faith in him to take care of me, and in the end, I shall have to turn to Source? With all of Life's intricacies, I surely do need help from something vaster than I know myself to be. One part of me is the Vastness, and another part questions its very existence. And anyway, how shall I say goodbye to my dear friend and companion? I know my life will change profoundly with his passing. Another unknown. How shall I go on?

I don't want to dwell on this, yet I am fearful as we approach the third anniversary of Mother's death. I am crowded with feelings of loss—and self-pity, perhaps.

Mother and Dad have always held the peace for me. No matter how troubled I have felt, I could go to them and come away restored. It's still like that with Pop. Is this what I shall learn with his passing: That I don't need to go anywhere? That it is inside of me, that peaceful place? Like knowing what to say when someone else is hurting, or how to cook the *matzoh* meal pancakes? The things I learned from Mother and Dad without knowing that I did?

November 15

Took Catherine and Marc and Zoey to the airport at five this morning. They'll be gone for three weeks. I'm glad I went.

I liked being out at that early morning hour. I felt an intimacy with the morning that is different from what I feel at home—some secret sharing among the beings abroad in the time before morning light: The street sweeper on North Main. People with dogs. A deer walking down Siskiyou Boulevard. A lone giant leaf, brown and tumbling in the middle of the street.

Mother's third *yahrzeit* is tomorrow, but I don't feel fragile this morning. Only pensive.

November 16 – Third Anniversary of Mother's Death

All kinds of feelings going through me. Memories of Mother's last day, and memories of loving, happier times, and feelings of inadequacy and failure because I couldn't help her be more comfortable in the last hours. Sadness. Love. Overwhelming gratitude that she was who she was, and that she was my mom.

November 21

I talked with Auntie Mim this morning. It was a hard conversation. Kept going to difficult, depressing things. We'd pull ourselves out, and back we'd go again. It's not like us.

It's been a heavy week, several losses in our community, but no need to despair. I need to drop into Center and let the temptations of panic and self-pity slide by. I must remember I have choices—even about fatigue, perhaps.

November 25 – Thanksgiving

Thanksgiving has turned sour for me. I used to anticipate it with pleasure until Uncle Mac died, and it's been hard every year since. But, this is also a time to feel the loss and turn to the light, to count blessings. We're still supporting each other through the losses. Our homes are standing, we have food to eat, love, and a caring family and community.

—✦—

I asked Dad if it's easier to hear about death as one gets older.
    "No," he said.
    "How do you make peace with it?" I asked.
    "It's part of life," he said.

—✦—

I've been thinking about Carolyn a lot. She's a wonderful role model, such a substantial person. I was thinking how poised she has become, with a depth and elegance that makes me think of our mothers. When she talks about her mother, I see how much like her she is—more than I ever knew before. You can see our moms' influence in the way she leads the community, too. We've both been influenced by our moms.

November 28

Pretty normal Saturday. Woke up full of energy and started some chores. Then Lance and I had a walk on the Greenway with a friend.

    By evening I felt irritable and blue. Wasn't sure why. Everything Lance did was annoying, and then I realized I'd fallen into grieving mode again. These moods wash over me and catch me unawares—like sneaker waves.

November 30

Dad and I had a great "date" last night. Went to Macaroni's for dinner. He was in good spirits all day (he'd gone to *Mavens*) and all evening. We were talking about packing for our upcoming trip to see relatives in Southern California. Then I teased him about Mom sitting on his shoulder and reminding him to take a sport jacket and slacks. His face fell, and so did his spirits. The light went out. At the mention of her name, he was totally in grief.

Maybe Ger and I should stop talking about Mom unless Dad mentions her first. I've seen this happen to him before. I felt so sorry. He's finally able to have a day without feeling devastated, but only because he's finally able to think of other things. Or, maybe he's been more fully in the moment lately, and mention of Mom flashes him back into his memories and out of the present.

Dad said he doesn't want to go on this trip. He said there's too much to do to get ready. I thought he meant packing at the time, but maybe it's the psychic preparation that's hard.

December ~ Put the Word Out

December 2

I came home to a phone message from Ben: "I am going to marry Julia Baker and I love you *sooo* much." I phoned him back, and we had the best talk we've ever had.

I am thrilled for them, and I am thrilled that Julia will continue to be part of our family. They're good together, and she's a doll. Lance and I are both delighted at the news.

———✦———

So much change. I look back on the last weeks and see that I have become more centered, more at peace within myself. The recognition of death as change, as a thing to accept, as an opportunity to meet challenges, expand, grow, has affected me deeply. It helps to dissipate the fear of loss and replaces it with anticipation and an awareness of the flow of Life. Pop told me death is a part of life, and we must accept it. What simple and profound words those are.

December 8

Lance and Pop and I saw the film *Tuesdays with Morrie*—excellent and moving. Jack Lemmon was Morrie. I mentioned Mom. Dad had to leave the room. I need to talk more with Ger about how to handle this. Should we never mention Mom when Dad's around? Should we leave it to him to initiate a conversation about her? I want to talk about her, but I don't want to rub Dad's face in his loss.

December 17

I've lost my wedding ring. I noticed when we got to Nancy's this evening that it wasn't on my hand. Ben and Julia showed us their handmade engagement rings. I held out my hand to show them my ring, also handmade, and it wasn't there. Dad made it for us. That makes it doubly precious. I hope we find it. I have no idea when it fell off—sometime in the last two days, I'm sure. I've been many places since I last noticed it.

I'm not willing to assume yet that it is gone for good. I need to retrace my steps and put the word out. If it is gone, my inclination is not to replace it. It wouldn't be the same.

December 19 – My 53rd Birthday

A birthday prayer: God, help me be conscious. Help me reflect the light which is so ready at hand. Help me bring peace and light to those around me—and especially to myself.

—◆—

Another birthday. I'm not enthusiastic. I want a quiet day. I miss Mom.

December 20

Had a fine birthday yesterday. Woke up and spent morning time at my altar. Then I did some yoga, and had a walk and breakfast with Lance. Carolyn and I did errands. Then we had lunch and a good heart connection. Later I went to the cemetery and hung out for a while by myself. I sat behind Mom's gravestone and spaced out—didn't even think much. It was pretty up there at dusk. After that, I stopped to see friends in Jacksonville. Had a good catch-up visit.

We went out for a family dinner at Gen Kai, then back to Dad's for awhile. Was a warm, loving evening. Lance gave me Jane Goodall's memoir, *Reason for Hope*. Dad's going to have my car detailed, and Ger and Carolyn gave me a gift certificate for a massage.

I am happy to have found my center again. Lance is more peaceful, too. It's a good time for us.

Saturday, December 25

Today we had no commitments, and Lance and I decided to have a Joy Day. It's been a long time since we had an unencumbered *Shabbat*. We had a deliciously sensuous time in bed, and then he made me scrumptious rye waffles.

After breakfast, we hiked up Table Rock. The trail head was obscured by heavy mist—fog, or a maybe huge cloud. But we decided to hike anyway, because it looked like it was lighter up top. Well, it was. The whole hike was a metamorphosis—of us, and of our surroundings. On the way back we sat on a bench facing Mount McLaughlin and witnessed an extraordinary sunset, ethereal, powerful, perfect.

Then we stopped for a Chinese dinner in Medford—at the one restaurant we could find open—and came home for a lazy read.

Tuesday, December 28

I realize it's time to shift my priorities. I've been keeping Sundays open for myself for some months, taking the day to flow at my own pace. But I saw on Saturday that spending such a day with Lance is equally healing. It is a loving and tender and sustaining part of our relationship which has been left undernourished.

We do take time to be together each week, but too often it is crammed between other activities, and without this luxurious feeling of flow. So we have declared Sundays Joy Days again. Saturdays are too unpredictable. It's been a long time since we took a whole day so consciously. We won't be rigid, but we'll be respectful of it. It's a high priority. If last *Shabbat* is any measure, then we will thrive.

January ~ Turning toward Life

January 1 – *Shabbat*

First day of the year. This is my prayer: that people will value peace and integrity over being right, and over avenging past wrongs. It has to stop sometime. Why not now? The new year is a good time for a new beginning—for going "cold turkey" on violence.

Lance woke me up before midnight so we could bring in the new year together.

———✦———

Last night at dinner, Carolyn asked Dad to share some thoughts about his life, and about his feelings as we pass into a new year.

"I've never questioned that I'd live so many years," he said. "There have been times I might not have wanted to continue, but they didn't last long.

"The new term at SOLIR* will begin soon, and I'm going to sign up for some classes. I realize how much more I still want to learn. The other retired people who study there have lived through many of the things that I've lived through. I'm looking forward to the pleasure of getting involved with people and having interesting new experiences."

I can't remember all that he said, but as he spoke, we were filled with joy to hear his optimism. This feels to me like a turning toward Life, like he's no longer biding time until he can be with Mom again. I saw Ger's face. He looked quietly happy, and his face reflected what I felt in my heart.

———✦———

I asked Carolyn about *Torah* study on the way home from the service. She said that over the centuries, the nature of *Torah* study has reflected the concerns of the people of the times. When Reform Jews were most concerned with social action, they looked to *Torah* for support for social action: How does *Torah* encourage us to care for our fellow human beings, our planet, our political health? Now there is also an impulse to look inward, toward a more spiritual consciousness, toward the light, and self-awareness. Current *Torah* study reflects that trend, as well. She told me, "That is why it is

---

* Southern Oregon Learning in Retirement

called a 'Living *Torah*.' It offers truth and guidance and wisdom to every generation."

———

Two weeks until Zoey's *bat mitzvah*. It must be terribly challenging for Catherine to be in the midst of preparing for this *simcha*, one of the most important times of her life, and at the same time preparing for her mother's impending death. Elizabeth is in hospice care and has been failing steadily. How wrenching it must be for Catherine to move back and forth between those two realities.

The family has asked me to participate in the *Torah* service, to open the *Aron*, the Ark where the *Torah* scrolls are kept. I am honored that Zoey wants to include me.

I've been trying to think of just the right gift for her. I want it to be something artistic, something meaningful. I thought of weaving her a belt, or giving her a piece of art by one of my Israeli friends. Then, today, as I was sitting here by my altar, I looked up, and there were the little pieces of wood and silver—my *Chai* Dancers, my Life Dancers. I designed them, Dad cast them for me in silver, and Ger mounted them. Now, it's time to pass them on. I'll write Zoey a letter about them.

———

I've been enjoying the handmade candles that Catherine and Marc and Zoey brought me from Israel. I've been burning them on my altar—to bring light, especially, for the many who have died recently, and for those who survive them.

———

Maya, loyal friend, sits curled up under my blanket as I write.

January 18

Marvelous *Shabbat*. Zoey played her flute with her teacher, Dennis Freese, during *Kabbalat Shabbat*, the late-afternoon service of song and psalms that welcomes *Shabbat*. Then after dinner, Dad and I went to a chamber music concert to hear the Colorado Quartet. It's the first time we've gone since Mother died. Perhaps another hurdle passed. Bless Milt Goldman for his insight. He's the friend who gave Dad the tickets, saying, "I know it was too hard for you to go after Johanna died. Maybe it's time."

Dad and I are talking about going again. He spoke of turning toward life again, but he seems terribly sad now, too. Is that his struggle? Does he feel like he's forsaking Mother when he enjoys life? I hope he concludes that he isn't. I know she'd cheer him on in this. Mom was so full of vitality herself.

I really never dreamed he'd survive her—odd, that. He was healthier than Mom, with her rheumatoid arthritis. But her will was so strong. I guess Dad's is, too.

Back to *Shabbat*. Zoey's *bat mitzvah* was inspiring. Her *haftorah*, a reading relating to her *Torah* portion, was from the writings of modern-day prophets, rather than Biblical ones—the reverend Martin Luther King, Jr. (it was his birthday) and Rabbi Abraham Joshua Heschel. And in the *Amidah*, during the recitation of our ancestors, she chanted Rachel and Leah separately, instead of listing them together as Jacob's wives, as is usually done. I'm glad she did that. After all, they each did have their own relationship with God, as do we all. They were more than just appendages of the husband they shared.

The honor of opening the *Aron* had a surprising effect on me. I felt as though Zoey were my own niece as I followed the *Torah* around the room wishing people good *Shabbos* and smiling—no, beaming—at everyone. I felt so much a part of everything, as I never have felt before. It truly has been one of the most profound experiences of my life—to share this *simcha* with Zoey and her family.

Catherine chanted *Torah*—her first time—and it was clear, and beautiful, and inspiring. And now, I, myself, am considering learning to chant *Torah*. I've never been drawn to prepare for my own *bat mitzvah*, but sharing this with Zoey has made me ask myself, *Would I like to read Torah?* And my answer is, *Yes. I would. I would like to study and to chant.*

⟶

I've been enjoying the *Torah* study at the beginning of our Friday meditation class. Rabbi Marc teaches with a spiritual sensitivity to *Torah*, rather than with the hard, intellectual flavor I experienced in my classes in Israel years ago. I like the way he teaches us to consider the text on many different levels, from the most literal to the most esoteric. All of these aspects can be present whenever one studies *Torah*. One is not more important than another. As Judy said in class this week, the temptation is to value the mysterious above the more basic understandings, but they must all be considered and valued.

⸺

I wonder if I truly will chant *Torah* someday. Working with Rabbi Marc and Judy at the synagogue is no accident. I am opening to *Torah* as I haven't done before. It is provoking me to deepen myself, and I have many opportunities to find wisdom in *Torah*. This impulse to chant feels like one of those little hints that come along, and then looking back, one says, "Ah yes, that was the beginning."

January 20

I've noticed I have actually been doing more of the *gimilut chasadim*, the acts of lovingkindness, that I think about. So often I have great impulses in the shower in the morning—to call someone who's ill, or to write a thinking-of-you note—and I don't get around to things. One effect of all the illness and death in our lives is that I realize it might be too late if I don't act when I think of it.

January 24

Painful memory. One day, while Mom was still alive, during the months she was taking Essiac, we were joking about Dad's 100th birthday party. Sometimes we used to plan it, just for fun. I said to Mother, "I hope you'll still be with us, Mom," or some other clumsy thing. She looked at me, one of those still, hold-your-breath kinds of looks, and I knew I'd hurt her. I would have sucked those words right back inside myself if I could. I would have choked on them—anything to erase that moment of insensitivity.

Sometimes my thoughts go more readily to that comment than to all the tender, loving times we spent together those last months. Perhaps someday the self-criticism will fade. Things do ease with time. I know that. But still, these three years later, the memory is raw. Even some of those last painful hours have receded so they're rarely in my thoughts. But not that one. Not yet.

I used to say I felt no regret about the way I'd lived my life. Maybe I could say that because I hadn't lived long enough, or maybe I was simply more insensitive in those days to the ways one can hurt, inadvertently, deeply—a stab like a knife or a punch in the gut, one thoughtless word that takes the breath away and leaves one raw and hurting. God willing, I shall learn to think before I speak, or better yet, learn not to chatter, not to fill with words the space that is better left to silence.

January 25

A friend asked me if I'd consider being in a writers' group with her. She's thinking of starting one. I've never done that before, but I've often thought about it. I'm not even sure how they're conducted, but going regularly, and needing to share something I'd written, would make me write more actively—write for others more, in addition to the journaling I do as part of my inner process.

January 28

Saw Kevin for acupuncture today. He said I'm stuck in the earth element. I didn't fully understand his diagnosis, but he said it would be good to dance anger, that I am holding in anger, which is affecting my health. I don't feel angry now. Maybe I'll see what comes out in dance class next Thursday. Or maybe I'll find time to dance by myself at home.

February ~ Slug a Pillow

February 5

Yesterday a neighbor was walking her dog past our house and stopped to talk. Her dog bit me. I approached him respectfully, and when I presented my hand for inspection, he bit my knuckle. No growl. No warning. The woman admitted he'd bitten before.

Fury obscured the pain: "You should have warned me your dog bites! How could you let me close to him, knowing that?"

February 6

Awoke in the night, and I couldn't get back to sleep, so I soaked in the spa. Stars shone down from the blackest sky, and the wind was up. An impulse made me bundle up and spend the rest of the night under the stars. I was meditating—sleeping, maybe, but I had the sensation of coming back, not waking up. I knew I had gone to "the other place," into the Vastness. It was comforting. Hopeful. A reassurance that I am not alone.

February 7

One Hundred Fifty-Four

Gather my scattered thoughts, Holy One,
Open my tight held fist.
Loosen my tension, leaning on You,
Dreams calming, days again bright
As I wake to behold the land's splendor.

Shutter my fears with sweet recall,
Heal wounds of witnessed terrors.
Invent me again for Your blessing:
Renewal and strength, comfort and peace
As I rise to affirm Your glory.

I read this psalm by Debbie Perlman yesterday, and it all came together in the night. I finally saw a pattern about the anger. Now maybe I can heal. It *is* about anger, my anger as well as other people's. Old memories have come up.

It's the pointing finger, the blaming finger, that is infected from the dog bite. How symbolic. Memories of betrayal, memories of shrinking away from neighbors' anger in my childhood, feelings of being disregarded, feelings of ice cold withdrawal that came up in dance class, constriction in my throat, hoarse voice. Robin observed that I stuff my anger—she can see it in my body, in my movements, when I dance. I resisted it when she told me that, but now I see it's true.

I've never learned to express anger very well. It wasn't done in our family. I need to learn to express it, to release the fear that if I do so, I will topple some delicate balance and throw us all into chaos.

I need to do a ritual. I need to slug a pillow. I don't want to hurt my hand worse, but I feel the tears, the fullness in my chest. I need to push it out.

Lance reminded me of *The Dance of Anger*, written by Harriet Goldhor Lerner. I saw it on my shelf Saturday. Now I remember how hard it was, years ago, for me to read that book. I couldn't even sit straight through it. I'd have to get up and pace. I guess I need to read it again today.

I think this infection in my hand is spilling over onto my middle finger—the "fuck you" finger.

Mother and Dad were proud of never expressing anger in front of me and Gerry when we were little. Now I wonder. Maybe there *was* anger, and it got turned into agonizing joint pain, rigidity, diverticulitis, ulcers, cancer. God help Ger and me get it out in healthy ways. There must be a healthy, balanced way to deal with it. Humans feel anger. It's part of who we are.

February 16

The tension between Ger and Lance has surfaced again. Yesterday Carolyn and I met with them and Rabbi Marc to bring some harmony to the situation. Rabbi Marc was masterful, helping where help was needed, letting us do much of the work ourselves. He started the session with this great quote by Rabbi Rami Shapiro: "Peace is not the absence of conflict. It is the handling of conflict without the loss of balance."

It wasn't easy, but we found our way through the obstacles with courage and a strong commitment to heal the breach. We've all come out of it relieved and lighter and hopeful for a brighter future—no more walking on eggshells. We've created strategies for handling hard feelings as they arise. No more stuffing complaints. We've agreed to bring them into the open with kindness and humor, and thankfully, I've been extricated from the middle.

February 22

It's a relief to see Lance and Ger really using the tools and systems they set up to get past awkward moments. I feel such a shift in the energy. We mustn't let things deteriorate again. Something awkward happened the other day between them. Lance and I discussed how to handle it, he took care of it, and it was finished. I felt much more able to say my stuff, and to let it go, because there wasn't any charge on it.

February 25

The other night I found out Uncle Joe is in the hospital and Ger and Dad both forgot to tell me. I felt angry, and have been feeling weepy and fragile ever since. I wish feeling anger didn't throw me off center this way.

I'm annoyed by my impatience with Dad. He didn't really disregard me. He just forgot to tell me. He and Ger both apologized.

I can see this is partly a reaction to the frailty I see in Dad these days. Sometimes he seems less present than at other times. It's as though his spirit is with Mom, and his body is here. I'm afraid Dad is starting to slip away. That's what the weeping is about.

All day at work, I was off-balance and close to tears; everything was out of sync. Then I went to the nursing home to see Annie. As I was leaving Annie smiled at me. "Look, Fayegail, you're feeling better!" And it was true. I'd been transformed. She's magic. Simply being in her presence is healing for me. That's how it is when I'm with Dad, too, and how it used to be with Mom.

The tears that were welling up inside of me subsided after I was with Annie, without ever being shed. Maybe they would come now, though, if I'd invite them, sitting here at two in the morning, sleepless and restless and not really all the way back to myself. Something is still going on in there.

March ~ The Procession

March 6

Many deaths have occurred in our circle of acquaintance in the last months, and three more in the last two weeks. I know it's partly because I work at the synagogue that I am aware of every death that touches our community. But it's striking to me that there are so many. I've never experienced so many deaths in such a short time. Is there a particular thing I need to learn from this? Acceptance? A celebration of Life? I've been dreaming of Death.

Thursday, March 30

Had an amazing conversation with Lance this evening. We ate dinner at Mihama's, and afterwards, we sat and talked in the restaurant for a long time.

I realized that grief has two parts. There's the familiar, painful, almost debilitating grief, but there's also another lighter, more celebratory grief, with memories of the good times.

"I didn't know I could remember without getting stuck in my sorrow," I said, and he asked me to explain.

"You could have a birthday dinner and be sad that Mom isn't with us, but at the same time you could think about the way she always used to let us choose our own birthday menus, and you'd smile at the memory."

There was another thing I saw about grief, too, a surprising thing. There's a benefit to heavy grieving. It gives you permission to drop out for a while, to be slow and quiet.

We talked about how Dad and I have gotten even closer since Mother died. I just wish we could spend more time in celebratory mode.

"I can see you're healing," Lance told me. "You're less self-critical lately, and more relaxed. Think of The Procession: the fatigue, the sorrow, the elation, the depression—the peace. You're leveling out."

I felt transformed by our conversation. I rarely share my inner process with him. I'm more likely to write in my journal. It was wondrous to feel so open. Things have shifted since our Joy Day on Table Rock. We have come to a new level of intimacy.

Friday, March 31

During meditation class today we were talking about *Yetziat Mitzraim*—the exodus from Egypt—coming through, bursting forth from a narrow place. Surely, the insights from my talk with Lance about grieving come under this category.

This morning was gorgeous, and Lance and I were walking down by the greenhouses.

"Swallows," he said. "These are the first of the year."

"Let's say a *Shehekianu*," I said. "Mom loved that prayer." I chanted the Hebrew, "You abound in blessings, Eternal One our God, Sovereign of all time and space, who has kept us in life, sustained us, and allowed us to reach this moment," and Lance said, "Amen."

"I just realized that every time we say the *Shehekianu*, we're inviting Mom into the moment to celebrate with us. I love that."

I was thinking about that moment again on the way to work, and tears sprang to my eyes. I was startled, thinking that somehow my revelations of Thursday evening had put an end to the tears. Then I noticed the quality of the tears. They weren't the stark, desolate tears of grieving, but more the gentle tears that come when one is moved, full of emotion, even joy—the kind of tears one sheds at a wedding or a *bat mitzvah*.

Another revelation: Grieving brings tears, yes, but there can be a sweetness in them, and a clarity. It came to me as a great surprise. Something has shifted, and I am awed by the possibilities.

———

I'm taking an energetics class on Wednesdays from a man named Paul Richards. We talked about resolution sickness. This is the need for everything to come out okay, for everything to have the closure that makes us say, "Ah, now I can get on with my life." But, as Paul says, often no closure is forthcoming, and we still need to get on with our lives.

In nature, in spite of its cyclical quality, there often is no apparent closure, no completion. A flood comes, or an earthquake, or a wildfire. Everything stops mid-cycle. I suppose there is some kind of closure in the big picture, but every living thing does not reach old age, and sometimes trees are uprooted in their prime.

I saw Wednesday night that resolution sickness has been affecting my feelings about Mother. I've been filled with regret that I didn't know how to ask the right questions, didn't know how to draw her out. I wanted to tap her wisdom, feel her sorrow, understand my own pain. I wanted her to teach me how to do this, how to do this horrendous, poignant, wrenching thing of watching my mother die. For the first time she couldn't help me, and I couldn't help myself.

We did make one resolution together. We went to the coast. We walked on the beach at Bandon and filled ourselves up with the sea and the sand and the exhilaration that Mother could once again walk on the shore. How her face shone with the pleasure of it. She finally could walk again, after all the pain and all the surgeries and all the rehab. What a triumphant day that was.

I can permit myself to move on without resolution of *all* the issues. I can learn to accept the reality that some things get resolved, and some things don't. Paul Richards says, in *Energetic Empowerment: Level One: Path, Practice, and State of Being,* "Always be prepared to abandon your own desire for resolution when it is destructive, or impossible to attain." There's an important lesson here for me.

April ~ Inner Promptings

April 9

Interesting. I've been looking forward to creating a vegetable garden. Our neighbor Steve came and rototilled a plot at the back of the yard, and Lance and I began to prepare it for planting. Suddenly, I'm immobilized. What am I afraid of? That I'll screw up. That I'll forget to water, lose control of it, hurt the plants I meant to love and care for.

This is symbolic of deeper issues. I'm afraid of being out of control and overwhelmed by too much to do and too little time. It's not a gardening issue, but a life issue.

Here is one of those times when we crave an illusion of security, of order, because it's scary to think of what will happen if there is no security or order. In fact, there is not. There is only the impression of order, and it lives alongside chaos, and we really never know which will prevail in any given moment.

It rained again—lots of thunder and lightning. The ground is moist and receptive.

Monday, April 10

Yesterday Lance and I went shopping with Dad. Ger tried to call him, and when Dad didn't answer, he was worried. We hadn't told Ger where we were going. And the day before, Dad was asleep when I called, and he didn't hear the phone. He'd left it in the bathroom. I called Ger's to see if Pop was there, and he wasn't, so Ger went down to check on him. And sometimes Dad gets worried if he can't find any of us. We need to work out a communication system. And we probably don't need to worry so much.

The thought had occurred to me that I should call Gerry to say we were going out with Dad, but I dismissed it. I figured Dad would have mentioned it to Ger, so I didn't bother. Now I see, yet again, that it's smart to follow my inner promptings. Saves a lot of trouble. I just have to pay attention, and things go more smoothly. It's hard to learn this new dance. I don't always get it right.

April 11

We started the garden yesterday—actually planting. We put in lettuce. Today we're planting strawberries, and tomorrow peas.

It was fun to work with Lance. I love having something to do together outside in the fresh air, something creative.

Now that the weather is mild, I am rediscovering the simple joy of early mornings in the garden. Even watering for fifteen minutes brings peace to my heart. The longer days energize me remarkably. I clearly respond to the light.

Saturday, April 29

Dad's giving stuff away, and I'm feeling panic, overwhelm, turmoil, resistance, fear. I'm not handling it well at all.

I sense he's preparing for his 88th birthday next month, that he's thinking, *I'd better take care of this business. I really can't expect to be around much longer.*

Actually, he's setting us a good example. We all ought to have our affairs in order, no matter what our age. But his busyness is jumping me into too many scary what-ifs.

The thought of losing Dad is dreadful, and then there will be all the decisions to be made. I know I take a long time to work through things, and I'm afraid that Ger and Carolyn will want to hurry things up. That's a big one—not feeling free to go at my own pace. I need to talk with Ger.

And I worry about Ger losing his best friend. What will happen to him? So many thoughts churning—I don't have the courage to write them all yet, let alone say them aloud.

Fear comes and goes. It's always nearby. I guess opening my heart to it, and trusting the One to guide me, is what I must continue to do. But the hole is so great from Mother's passing. Can I deal with this times two?

May ~ Feel the Joy

Monday, May 1

Lance was doing what-ifs about something that happened this morning, wondering whether we were entering a new phase, and so on. At first I felt impatient, but then I could see a parallel with my own drama about Dad on Saturday. That was just as much a what-if situation. I saw it was okay, maybe even helpful, if it helped me prepare for the actual loss which is, of course, inevitable—unless I die first.

Thursday, May 4

Had my first private session with Paul Richards last Monday, and I felt truly seen. He gets who I am inside. Since then, I've started shifting my life to reflect what I love: to live more in the delicate, quiet part of myself, and less in the problem-solving, "out there" part, to be more in the present, less in the past and future.

I have turned a corner. My quiet self is urging me to recognize and nurture it more. We will see what evolves. Paul said maybe it will be a year before I see a new direction, but things are already shifting, moving into place, ripening.

I'm always so curious when I'm in a transition like this. What will my new life be like? But really, there is no waiting. Life is happening always—no in-between times.

May 6

Ger and I took a ride up toward Hyatt Lake and had a great talk about this thing of rushing through the process of settling Dad's affairs and my fears about it. He was so kind and understanding. Said he wanted it to be as comfortable for me as he could make it, and that he would take as much time as I needed. I'm relieved. I love my bro.

May 7

Had a sweet, tender dream last night. I dreamed I was nursing Lance through cancer. The idea frightens me, but the flavor of the dream was peaceful. God willing it will never be necessary.

⟶

Experiences I'm having now, especially with Paul Richards and Rabbi Marc and Judy, are filling in gaps in my learning. From Paul I am learning to be more true to my essential self. Rabbi Marc is showing me a depth and relevance of Jewish spirituality I'd rarely known before. And Judy teaches me to be steady. These are three faces of Wholeness. I'm grateful they're in my life.

May 8

I was bemoaning the fact that my day had gone so differently from my plans and expectations. I'd meant to garden, do chores, and take a hike with Lance. Instead, Lance and I had a frustrating computer session. Then we had lunch and a ride with Dad, but I was so tired, I slept through half of the gorgeous scenery. Late in the day, and after another nap, Lance and I took a glorious walk on the Talent Greenway. The gray sky made the colors vivid, and every detail stood out.

As soon as I got out of my own way, and stopped feeling guilty for what I hadn't accomplished, I felt much better about what *had* transpired. The rest of the day unfolded in a delightful way. And no, I didn't get much work done.

I'm beginning, finally, to understand the value of leisure time. Until recently, I assumed I needed always to be accomplishing something, always to be busy, to be puttering. I adore puttering, getting things off my list, the sense of completion. The problem is that chores hover endlessly.

Saturday, May 13

I realized this morning that my relationship with community has grown and changed a lot since I've worked at the *shul*. For much of my life, I've felt a huge resistance to praying in community. My spiritual time was solitary time. Now, I am finding spiritual nourishment within the Jewish community, and I am grateful to Carolyn and Rabbi Marc and Judy for their wisdom and their support. I feel an opening in myself, a thawing of my resistance, a transformation of my ambivalence.

Today we celebrated another *bar mitzvah*. How precious it is that we provide this guidance and love and spiritual education to our young people, and especially so when much of our national culture falls short in providing this kind of sustenance. They need the loving support of the whole community, not just their close circle of friends and family. I love attending the services. It's powerful to see the depth and wisdom of these young people who will be inheriting, and I hope continuing to preserve and enrich, our traditions and our community.

I see it doesn't matter to me anymore whether I know the child's family well or not. Of course it is all the more sweet when I attend the *bar* or *bat mitzvah* service of someone who is dear to my heart. But still I feel the joy, and I am often moved to tears by the young people's teachings and by the poignant things that family members say to each other during the service. We are all at our best.

Listening to the mother of the *bar mitzvah* chant *Torah* today made me think again about doing it myself. Maybe I will one day. Maybe I'll make it part of my private journey, the journey that leads from Mother's death to healing.

I would love to chant *Torah* on the *Shabbat* of her *yahrzeit*. Six *Kislev* is the Hebrew date. It falls in December this year. Maybe I'll talk with Rabbi Marc and find out which portion that is. I'd like one that's meaningful to me. Mom would love for me to further my Jewish education in her honor. Maybe she herself would have chanted *Torah*, had she been born at a different time. Maybe I can chant *Torah* for both of us.

May 18

Dream

I'm wandering around somewhere with my dear friend Rabbi Joe, maybe in another country. We are near a tree covered with ripe fruit. The leaves are like a plum, but the fruit looks like a green avocado. We're eating a lot of this fruit, and I am messy and looking for a place to wash my hands.

We see a big white building. Rabbi Joe says, "Here's an Orthodox shul. There will surely be a place to wash inside." We go through a narrow door into a hallway. There, against the wall, is a little sink, so I go to wash my hands. But a man is walking down the hall toward us, and here I am, wearing pants, which he would likely consider immodest. Rabbi Joe stands behind me, shielding me from the man while I wash my hands and say the Hebrew prayer for hand washing.

―――――

I told Lance about my dream.

"There's a lot of religious imagery here," he said. "Look at the symbolism. You're with a rabbi: That's pretty religious. You're eating from a tree that is two kinds superimposed on one another: You have a foot in two worlds—the spiritual and the religious. You get too dirty and need to clean yourself: This lack of integration is messy, maybe even "wrong." You go to an Orthodox synagogue where you fear you'll encounter disapproval. Rabbi Joe stands by you: He is sheltering you from the censure of the traditional man. He's encouraging you to be who you are."

I can see Lance's point. I haven't told him yet that I've decided to chant *Torah*, but isn't this symbolism interesting? Is there some part of me that feels I am unclean, unworthy of going into men's sacred territory?

———

I've been thinking of the first time I had an *aliyah*, the first time I was called to chant the blessings before the *Torah* reading. The *shul* in Ventura held a service and a luncheon in Mother and Dad's honor before they moved to Oregon. It was during that service that I chanted the blessings. Without warning I was called for an *aliyah*. I had no time to prepare, and no opportunity to refuse, and to do so would have been an embarrassment to my parents and myself. So I went forward, and I sang the blessings.

Something incredible happened to me up there. My voice was exquisite as I chanted. Afterwards, the cantor came up to me and startled me by asking if I were a singer. I know my voice that day was divinely empowered.

In some way, that experience was my *bat mitzvah*, my coming to *Torah*. What a gift that my voice should be so clear and true that day, of all days. Until then I did not know how much I had yearned to approach *Torah*, and had never found the way.

When I was a girl, I didn't study to prepare myself as a *bat mitzvah*, although a few girls in our community at that time were already doing it. I thought they mostly did it for the presents. I don't remember that anyone particularly encouraged me to do it.

On some level, I must have gotten a message that being involved with *Torah* wasn't for girls. In any event, for most of my life I have felt a shyness and resistance to approaching the *Torah*—almost to the point of aversion.

Once, when I lived in Jerusalem, I went as my friend Shoshana's guest to the Reform synagogue in Emek Rafa'im. They offered me an *aliyah,* but I couldn't let myself accept it. Then I felt ashamed that I'd refused.

Now here's this startling impulse to honor Mother by chanting *Torah* on the *Shabbat* closest to her *yahrzeit* at age fifty-three, forty years from the time I'd have celebrated my *bat mitzvah* in Ventura, if I'd chosen to do so.

Rabbi Marc is delighted. He says he'll study the *Torah* portion with me.

May 21

Spoke more with Rabbi Marc on Friday about reading *Torah*. *Vayatze* is the reading for the *Shabbat* nearest Mom's *yahrzeit*. Marc's giving me a book about that portion, *God Is in This Place and I, i Did Not Know,* by Rabbi Lawrence Kushner.

I like talking with Rabbi Marc about spirituality. He always seems to know what I'm experiencing inside. Anytime I mention a practice of my own, his response makes me think it's familiar to him, too. I'm grateful he's in my life. I've been having the sense that these two powerful paths—Judaism and my personal spirituality—are at last converging.

May 26 – Dad's Birthday

Our congregation has purchased a new *Torah*, and it arrived at the synagogue today. We made a ceremony. Soon I shall read from it to honor Mother.

I'm missing Mother a lot today. I felt her there as we stood in awe of this beautiful *Sefer Torah*. I felt so aware today that the *Sefer Torah*, the scroll, is one part of *Torah*, and doing *Torah* is another part. There is a fullness in the way we live as Jews which I took into myself today. The doing is a profound path of the spirit. We do *mitzvot*, not just think about them. We serve the world to heal it, not just pray for it—yet thoughts and prayers are also important. I love the way Judaism calls us to do the *mitzvot*, to accept certain obligations, certain challenges, and to do good deeds.

This afternoon I'm preparing for Dad's party. I shall set a formal table for the hot dogs, his favorite birthday meal. I'm grateful to be able to do this for him. Mother won't be singing "Happy Birthday" with us, but she is surely here in the vastness of her spirit. Normally, we'd be cooking together today to make this celebration for Pop. Makes me wonder what "normal" is. Probably there's no such thing—only flow, only change. I feel blessed when I can surrender to that.

So today Mother is here in spirit. I see that I am not wrenched apart when I think of her. Only the sweetness is here. A new era.

May 27

Dad's birthday party was a big success. He liked the hot dogs, of course. We had tofu dogs for the vegetarians among us, and we had some side dishes. Zoey couldn't come, but she sent a gorgeous fruit salad with Marc and Catherine. The most wonderful part was that Dad got up and spoke.

"Thank you all for coming to help me celebrate my birthday," he said. "A short time ago I couldn't have imagined looking forward with hope. But now, we are here together, and I am surrounded and supported by loving family and friends. It is time to face the future with optimism and hope and enjoyment. It's time to move forward again."

I wish I could remember everything he said. I love that he would share those feelings when we were all together. He was so eloquent, so open. It was a blessing for us all, and we were moved. What a fine role model he is for us as we grow older.

June ~ On Retreat

June 3 – Mount Angel

I'm on vacation from work, and I've come to the Shalom Prayer Center of the Queen of Angels Monastery on retreat. Drove many hours today, and all the while I was chanting, searching out old hurts and angers and forgiving them, releasing them, blessing the people involved. The common theme: They didn't ask me, didn't discuss it with me, didn't give me a choice. I felt powerless.

I realized that the tension in my jaw is connected with this wordlessness, this need to speak for myself. I hate it when people talk about me when I'm present, when they speak for me. I need to speak for myself. I need to feel heard.

Somehow this is connected with chanting *Torah* to honor Mother. *I* will do it, not wait for others to read *Torah* for me. In a sense it is a ritual for taking back my voice. I wonder if I am doing that for Mother, too.

My host, Sister Dorothy, is a dear. I feel so welcome. This is clearly meant to be.

The room is simple and clean, and there is a little chest where I can set up my altar. There is even a meditation stool here, in case I need a switch from my cushion. I'll use my navy blue shawl as an altar cloth.

I am comfortable here. There are several nice lounge areas. My favorite one is all windows and full of light with a view of the trees.

I brought the Kushner book Rabbi Marc gave me. The first sentence he showed me in it resonated on such a deep level that I want more. On the other hand, perhaps that one sentence can get me through the whole week: "Self-reflection . . . prohibits awareness of God."

June 4

I danced and chanted my anger, hurt, shame, forgiveness, guilt, release in a grove beyond the orchard—and my gratitude. So much poison has accumulated in my spirit over the years, and I did not know until this day how serious was the effect. The issue is respect. Respect of self. Respect for others. Respect from others.

The flip side of this is the many times in my life I have pitied someone, or have been arrogant enough to believe they needed my help or special understanding, or that I was in any way better than they, more blessed, more gifted, more intelligent, quicker to understand. A humility lesson. Rabbi Marc wished me humility on my journey.

This is what I saw while I was dancing this morning and cleansing the poison out of my body with the sunlight: My only job is to reflect God's light to others. My only job is to honor the sacredness of each being—mine, as well as others—so that we can remember who we are—a sacred, holy part of the One that is All.

Yes, I see I can serve in whatever way I am called to serve, but the essence of all service is to be a reflective pool—deep in myself, yet reflecting to others the Light, their part of the Light. It is my job to see the Light within every other being—and within myself—and to be mindful of it, and to accept the myriad ways in which the Light presents itself.

So often, I have thought someone needed my help. Who am I to assume that I know what is "wrong" with someone, what kind of help she needs, what to do about it? Perhaps the very challenge a person faces is the one which will lead to a final breakthrough, a knowing of the One, a complete healing. What if giving unsolicited help only distracts people from their best course?

———

This matter of silence. I sat in my room, and the quieter I got, the more I heard outside myself. Perhaps there are places, like the chapels, where there is less going on. But that is the paradox: the only silent place is deep within—or deep without—in that sacred holiness, in the vastness beyond time and space.

June 5

More about silence. I have been silent much of the day. Sitting, walking, eating in silence—sleeping. No reading. No writing for the last several hours. I've learned that the more I speak, the more I fill my mind with unnecessary thoughts. I see I don't need absolute silence. It's a certain *kind* of quiet that I'm after. Quietness within.

There is no silence without. Everywhere outside is the sound of equipment and people going about their work. I went to meditate in the monastery cemetery this afternoon, and a man was pruning my favorite tree there with a chainsaw.

Going to the Silent Place seems rather a matter of grace—an opportunity by invitation only. I don't believe one can rest there more than a moment strictly by intention or practice. Perhaps one can, and I have not prepared myself well enough. But this I know: Having once experienced the vastness of Silence, I know it. I shall never forget the safety there, the absolute certainty that all is well. No matter what is blowing across the surface of my life, that I know.

June 6

This trip is about endings. It is time to end the chaos in my life that ensued from Mother's death. I have passed into a state of sweetness with my grieving, and it's time for my external life to reflect that.

———

Here I am in the presence of Sister Dorothy, and I have heard she is an excellent grief counselor. This is a perfect opportunity for me to talk with her about the Mother Book. Maybe she'll have some reflections to share with me, or draw out of me, that would be helpful to my process. This is clearly the time to start writing. I have no notes with me, no journals. I can begin by writing an introduction, at least, to set my intention.

———

This matter of self-reflection that Rabbi Kushner talks about that keeps us from experiencing Nothingness seems to me closely related to self-consciousness. I watched myself dancing today. From time to time I would wonder how a certain movement would look to an observer, or whether anyone could see me through the glass doors to the lounge, or through the windows. Most of me hoped not, but a little part thought, *Cool move,* and *Somebody'd like seeing that—maybe they'd think I'm a good dancer.* And then there was the part of me that felt embarrassed to have had such thoughts. So all of this together caused a self-consciousness within me that really did keep me from immersing myself totally in the dance, in the One.

June 7, 2 a.m.

I have been writing introductory remarks for the Mother Book in preparation for my meeting with Sister Dorothy today. This won't be an easy process. It'll mean opening wounds, delving into stuff that I have safely tucked away. It's probably a good thing to do in the presence of an excellent grief counselor. When I made the appointment, I didn't consider what would be required of me. Maybe this is why I came here instead of going to the coast for this retreat.

———

> Hear me, Eternal One, and be gracious;
> Eternal One, be a help for me.
> You turned my mourning into dancing,
> You undid my sackcloth and girded me with joy,
> That I might sing your praise and not be silent.
> Eternal my God, I shall praise you for ever.
>   — Psalm 30

Just had a most marvelous visit with Sister Dorothy. We talked mostly about the Mother Book, but about lots of other things as well.

She shared many suggestions and observations based on her work as a grief counselor. She thought using the journals, the actual experiences, was a good idea. She asked me if I could integrate faith into the story, and write about how I found hope. She said hope gives people the ability to go on. She also said hope is tied in with what the grieving person believes about the person who has died, and how they were connected with them. She asked about my perception of what happened with Mother after she died.

We talked about how there is no separation between us and the people we love in the spirit world, but that the connection is intangible. She suggested that I normalize the idea that there is communication between us and our deceased loved ones. She also said that grief has no time line, and that the nature of the relationship determines the depth and length of grief.

Sister Dorothy said the most personal story is the strongest. She suggested that I share the feelings I experienced and minimize the intellectualizing. (She's got me pegged!)

I thoroughly enjoyed my time with her. She was supportive of my project, and I was encouraged to hear her say a book like this could be a useful addition to the literature about death and bereavement.

June 8

I have deepened my relationship with Hebrew prayer these past days, and I've enjoyed a growing intimacy with my prayer book. Having time to read the Hebrew has enhanced my enjoyment of praying in Hebrew. At services it all goes by so quickly. When I read the prayers, especially aloud, I see the roots and hear derivations of words that are familiar to me from modern Hebrew, and so it brings a kind of unity and integration. Rabbi Marc's suggestion to bring my prayer book was a good one.

This has been a good week. When I spoke with Lance last evening, he said I sounded languid. I *feel* languid. I thought I wanted to spend time in silence, but I haven't craved it. I've enjoyed the companionship of women, time in nature and in prayer. I'm excited about working on the Mother Book, too.

June 12 – Ashland

Just got home from Los Angeles. After my retreat, the whole family flew down for Beth and Eddie's wedding. It was held in a beautiful hotel garden. The service was moving, the reception was exuberant, and the food was scrumptious. It was a blessing to see Dad and Uncle Roy and Aunt Sylvia—the three siblings—enjoying the celebration together. And Uncle Roy felt well enough to dance with Beth. That was the highlight of the whole weekend.

June 16

I'm enjoying my time off. I shall do more of this vacationing at home. I like being this relaxed, puttering, moving at my own pace, doing what I want to do. I finally found the top of my desk.

It occurs to me that, except for the five or six hours a day I work at the synagogue, I could arrange my whole life to feel as though I were on vacation, with this delightful sense of relaxation. What gets done gets done, and why worry about the rest? Everything in its own time. It's a pleasure, and I could probably work a part-time job indefinitely if only I could keep this attitude. I wonder what's stopping me. I'm going back to work on Tuesday, and hopefully the whole summer will have this puttery, catching-up flavor.

I'm learning to use a program called Dragon NaturallySpeaking. It lets me dictate my journal entries for the Mother Book directly into my new laptop. Seems promising. Supposedly, it will get to be extremely accurate as I train the software. I dictated one paragraph three times, and the last time it was perfect.

I've already started transcribing the first journal. I'm only entering some of the material—entries about Mom and my grieving process, and about the family when they're relevant. Interesting insights, even if they aren't related to grief *per se*. Entries about the ways I am healing.

June 17

Mary Margaret and Justin are in town to do a seminar. They came for dinner last night, and we had pasta with salad from our own garden. Was a good visit.

Here's something she said during the intensive today: "The space around things defines the shape—not the other way around." That was worth hearing. It was my favorite part of a good workshop.

June 18

I've been thinking about the growth on my cervix. I looked in an anatomy book. The cervix is associated with blood vessels called the arbor vitae. Tree of Life. Interesting. We've been studying the Kabbalistic Tree of Life in Rabbi Marc's meditation class.

We're also studying about the exodus from Egypt, the journey from constriction to freedom, a time of healing, of coming into new knowledge, of receiving *Torah* at Mount Sinai. Surely this health issue reflects a constricted place for me—my sadness about never having borne children.

Part of me, deep inside, believes that when a couple marries, they should produce progeny. I'm grateful for the free life I have lived, but I also regret that I haven't carried on the family line, haven't produced grandchildren for my parents to teach and enjoy.

I sense that this constriction in my cervix is connected with bound up creativity that I must release. Instead of producing something tangible in the external world, I have created this new tissue inside.

Creativity must express itself. I need to do a ritual. I need to release this lingering desire to bear a child. I shall make time daily to write the Mother Book, transcribe the journals, pull together this work that needs to be borne into the material world. I can make this practice the widening of the narrow place.

Later

I arose from my journaling knowing this was a big moment and knowing I wanted to begin right away on the next phase of the book, the book written with new understanding. I made a cleansing ritual as close to a *mikvah,* a ritual bath, as I could do here at home, without actually immersing myself—an extremely mindful shower and shampoo.

I was standing in the shower stall, still wrapped in my towel, and I heard this conversation going on in my mind—well, really more one side of a conversation. I was talking to Mother.

I'm done grieving, Imah. I will always remember you and love you and talk with you, and ask your advice, and feel you near me, but I am finished grieving, and I am ready to write this book.

The knowing was complete, solid, clear. No question. A page had turned. I looked down and noticed a little heart-shaped puddle of water on the bottom of the tub.

It's a startling thing to know, but I *do* know it. The grieving is over, and I shall go on honoring and cherishing Mother until the day I die. And here is my ending ritual—the shower, and the writing.

June 20

Yesterday I transcribed the journal entry about the image Carolyn shared with us the evening Mother died—that God is an ocean and each person's life is a wave that rises up from it, but is not separate from it, and then goes back to it. A little while later, I opened the Kushner book Rabbi Marc gave me before my retreat, and there was the passage about the wave.

I typed the whole entry from the day of Mother's death, and I didn't cry. I never thought I would come to a day when I could do that.

June 21

I was typing the journal entry from the day Dad gave me Mother's slippers, and a title for the Mother Book popped into my mind—*In My Mother's Slippers: A Journey of Grief and Healing.*

June 24

I am so engaged by the work on *Slippers* that I find it hard to do anything else, especially the morning work at my altar and my *Torah* chanting practice. But now Paul Perper, the dear man who is helping me learn to chant, has made me a cassette so I'll be able to listen to my *Torah* portion and practice it in the car.

June 26

I'm being sharp with Lance. I'm frustrated at not being able to do all the things I want to do today, and I'm taking it out on him. Time I want to spend writing *Slippers* is spent instead on preparations for Ben and Julia's wedding and on housework. I need to stay centered and remember, everything in its own time.

June 28

I wrote a letter to Benjamin, a stepmother-to-son-before-you-marry kind of letter, and I gave it to him today. We went to lunch, just the two of us, and then we spent a profound afternoon together in Lithia Park. Our relationship is so precious to me that it is hard to imagine I would be more grateful to have him in my life if I had borne him from my own womb.

July ~ Full of Wonder

July 9

I want to spend time writing today. I do hope *Slippers* can help others, but surely there is healing for me in this process. In all the three and a half years since Mother died, I've never reread any of my journals. It's interesting to read some of the insights I had that helped me through that challenging time. And it's interesting to read about the pain and confusion, and not experience it in the same way anymore. I am removed from the intensity now, and even though I remember the pain as I read it, I am not wracked with it. Now I am experiencing the healing, and it is a gift.

July 26

Back from Ben and Julia's wedding. I am so thrilled to have shared it with them and with Julia's clan. The ceremony was profound and full of wonder, full of love and kindness and goodwill. The party was fun and not overwhelming at all. Lance and I both had a great time.

I helped in the hostess role and introduced myself to a lot of people who poured love on me, strangers who are no longer strangers. And I was made to feel, and *chose* to feel, absolutely welcome as a parent in every way—by Ben and Julia, by Lance and Nancy, and by Jeff and Deb, too. Any anxiety and feelings of not knowing how I fit in have dissipated. I feel rich and full and *honored*.

———

Before we left for our trip home, we were all sitting around Jeff and Deb's cabin talking, and I gave Ben a little massage on his shoulders. Julia came by and said, "Oh Ben, do you have a headache?" And Ben responded, acknowledging the affection between us, "No, I have a Fagel." It was a joy to hear him speak of me with such warmth in his voice.

What a fine thing to have a son. I never expected, so late in life, to feel the joy of it, and now I have a daughter, too. They are full of love for each other, and for all that touches them. It's moving and sacred to see, and I'm grateful to witness it, and to receive their love.

Lance and I were aware all during the trip, and especially at the wedding celebrations, of our abiding love for each other. The deep love is there, but also it bubbles to the surface like a spring, and I feel the joy of it and the giddiness of it and the dance of it in our lives. It's a wonder-filled thing. I wish that for Ben and Julia, that they can know that richness.

I didn't write anything the whole time we were away. Sometimes I am so full of living life, it's hard to take time to record it. So, many of the nuances of the past days will be left unwritten—but I'm sure other things will find their way to paper in time. The best thing is that we have loved and shared this all together—an incredible blessing.

Each of the parents spoke at the wedding. I adapted "A Family Prayer," by J. Harry Berger, from my favorite prayer book, *Renew Our Days: A Book of Jewish Prayer and Meditation*.

Wedding Blessing for Ben and Julia

Eternal One, we come to you in gratitude
    for what we have and for what we are.
Help these two young people, Ben and Julia,
Create of their home a sanctuary,
Warmed by reverence, adorned by tradition,
With family bonds that are strong and enduring,
Based on love, truth, trust, and affection.

Grant them gratitude enough to look backward
    and be thankful,
Courage enough to look forward
    and be hopeful,
Faith enough to look inward
    and be humble,
Kindness enough to look outward
    and be helpful.

And in the years ahead,
Help them to live their lives
As a blessing to each other,
And to all beings.

August ~ She Did Share

August 2

Here's an insight: The less self-absorbed we are, the more we can be fully who we are. Sounds like a paradox, but I think it means that the less we can be engaged by matters of the ego, the closer we can be to our essence.

Saturday, August 5, 7:00 a.m.

Thursday was Mother's birthday. Dad and Ger and I went to the cemetery in Jacksonville. Afterward we went to eat on the patio of the Jacksonville Inn. It was a surprisingly cheery dinner. Pop was horsing around, teasing a little, and Ger was *kibitzing* with the waiter. The food was good, the atmosphere was nice, and I'm glad we went.

⟶

This weekend we are celebrating Ben and Julia's wedding, part two, with the Oregon friends and relatives in Takilma, the little homestead community where Ben grew up.

Monday, August 7 – Takilma

Fabulous, fabulous weekend. We've stayed long enough for me to really get what Lance and Nancy and Ben love about this place. Kind, welcoming, generous people and a beautiful, woodsy setting.

The party came off well. Nancy is a talented organizer, a master, and the caterers were so efficient that the party flowed seamlessly. I was truly able to be a guest. Lots of work before and after, and lots of fun during the party itself.

The food was delicious and beautifully served, and the setting, lovely. Twilight at the farm. I was moved by the ceremony—all those circles within circles of people gathered around loving Ben and Nancy and Lance, and their love extended to the rest of the family, as well. Julia's parents came out from Colorado to be with us, and Dad and Ger were there. We enjoyed the people and the music, which was jazzy during dinner and light rock afterwards. Ben's friend Matt played his guitar on the breaks, and he's *good*. Lance and I danced more dances than we ever have before, and we danced well together. What a joy. We didn't even leave the party until half past eleven.

August 19

I was looking at a picture of Mom and me that's on my altar. It's from our wedding day. She looks wise and beautiful, and the way we are sitting made me remember what good friends we were—are. I have spent the last three and a half years wishing she had shared more of herself with me, but now, when I think back, I see she did share a tremendous amount, even in words.

I wanted to know everything, the answers to all my questions.

She shared much more than I could remember in those times of wanting it all. Maybe I can finally let go that craving. Maybe I can be thrilled at all the little details I do remember, now I've stopped feeling sorry for what I cannot have.

⤙⤚

Dad's giving us money to redo our yard. We're going to have a flagstone patio and a pond. We need to develop a master plan with the landscaper. Lance and I drove around last evening and found some gardens here in town that we'd like to show him. I want to show him plants I like in the Japanese Garden, too.

⤙⤚

Kevin is giving me herbs for my feminine parts—trying to get good circulation going in preparation for my appointment with Holly Granger. I gave my word I'd permit another biopsy if there was no improvement to my cervix this time. Whatever the outcome, I've had a lot of insights as a result of this, and I've done a lot of letting go, which always helps me.

⤙⤚

I'm in a cleaning-out mood, and I'm giving away some of Mom's clothes. Someone else might as well enjoy them. Is this my preparation for the High Holy Days? Maybe so. I want to feel empty inside, instead of cluttered. Outside, too.

Monday, August 28

Had the biopsy this morning. As Holly was finishing up, I started shaking violently. Tears came, and painful memories of a stupid thing I'd done, a sexual experience I'd had as a young woman.

Holly held my hands and got quiet and said, "I'm getting the word 'forgiveness.' I don't know whether it has to do with the perpetrator or yourself. This release has something to do with your legs."

I see now that it had to do with my failure to walk away from a dangerous situation. Now I am more intuitive, less likely to put myself in danger. At the time I didn't know how to protect myself, and I didn't know how to change my mind without losing face.

It's good to see that I'm no longer the shy, unassertive person I was then. It felt good to me to feel "in charge" of this medical procedure—that is, to really hear Holly's advice, but to wait until I was ready. I appreciate that she respected my need to make those decisions for myself.

September ~ Wise-Old-Woman Time

September 4

Just came home from Dad's. He asked me to clean out his linen closet. I realized that all the blue towels on the rack by the bathroom scale were the same ones from when Mom was there—maybe never even washed—same wash cloths and hand towels. It was an odd thing. Like an altar. Strange he never took them down.

No wonder Pop wants to get rid of stuff all the time. The house still feels full to the brim, in spite of everything we've already given away. And I want to clear out my own stuff right now, not spend time doing it at his house. He'd love it if I'd go through stuff every time I'm there.

This is tough. I know he'd like my help, and I don't want to give it, and I know it's not just the time it would take. Part of me still can't accept that this will never be a normal, functioning household again. Oh, I miss Mom!

September 7

I've noticed I can't wear black anymore. Every time I put on something black and look in the mirror, I take it right off again. I can't do it. I don't know whether it's my newest way of pulling back from the grieving process, or what. I never wore black before Mother died. Then, after she died, it felt just right. Now, it doesn't.

—◆—

Yesterday, Carolyn and I had breakfast and a walk. We were talking about how you get to a point in your life when living—staying alive—ceases to be as important as how you live. Lately I read about a survey in the end-of-life issue of *Modern Maturity*. It indicated that the more people aged, the more they felt that way. It's an important kind of letting go.

September 8

I've been feeling an undercurrent of sadness for some days. Not sure what it's about. Guess I'll just let it ripen and see what it is—or not. I'm in put-one-foot-in-front-of-the-other mode. I guess that's as good a mode as any.

Ben and Julia have been staying in town since their Takilma reception earlier this summer. I've loved having them around. Had another nice evening with them yesterday. I'd been yearning for a quiet evening at home, but when the kids proposed dinner at Wiley's Pasta Company, we went, and we had a lot of good laughing. I'll miss them. They're good playmates.

September 9

More and more lately, I am aware of things I know about Mother, about the way she felt about things. Little one-liners keep popping into my mind, small conversations we shared, passing moments filled with information and insight. All I need to do is to listen, to be attentive. One small sentence at a time she taught me the philosophy of her life, her way of being in the world. The more I open myself to those memories, the deeper is my knowing.

Before this, grief was in my way. I only could focus on what was lost. But truly there is a richness beyond description that is slowly revealing itself. I feel like I have opened a treasure chest. I am thrilled to think of going deeper into it, pausing over each beautiful thing I discover, pondering, wondering, taking into myself each pearl of wisdom, each diamond drop of woman knowledge.

I have my mother's diamond pendant. It is a symbol of her light and her wisdom. I hope I shall someday be ready to wear it. From time to time I look at it, sparkling from its depth as it meets the sunlight. As she did.

I am grateful for this latest insight. These are some things I have learned: I know it is important to make love into old age. I know it is important, when one is in pain, to remember that the pain will not go on forever. I know that one must fight with courage and accept fate with grace. There is much I know from her.

September 10

Yesterday I had a headache and Lance gave me a massage. While he was working on me, I started sobbing. He lay on the bed next to me, and held me while I cried. I haven't cried that way since Mother died. A wisp of thought, more impression than thought, flitted around in my mind: *I'll never bear a child.*

I'm grieving on a cellular level. My emotions are flip-flopping all over the place, and a tempest rages in my body—boiling hot, flushed, and sweating one moment, chilled and clammy the next. The confusion I feel, and the dismay at not knowing what to expect, are reminiscent of grieving. Lance has been suggesting that I read about menopause to see if I can learn anything useful. Maybe now I'm ready to. I've never been ready before.

This connection between menopause and grief interests me. I wonder if it is built into women—at least in our culture. If a woman is meant, at some level, to bear children, and she hasn't, or she can't anymore, there is a loss. A loss sustained must be dealt with, even as one moves with joy toward new beginnings.

I wasn't living at home when Mother began her grieving over Grandma, and I wasn't home when she experienced menopause. That is a loss for both of us—two things we didn't share. But she survived them both, and so shall I. Somehow, seeing these changes in my body as occasions for celebration *and* grief makes sense to me.

Many things to celebrate: more spontaneity, no more diaphragm, no more concern about having a child too late, no more menstrual cramps, a recognition that I am reaching the wise-old-woman time of life. Interesting that, as Mother once told me about herself, I don't remember I'm a gray-hair until I look in the mirror.

And the grief. Why might I grieve? I shall never bear a child and watch it grow, my body is no longer young, I am moving into another part of the Unknown, I am experiencing a life cycle event which carries me one step closer to old age, and I must come to terms with my own mortality. So far I do not grieve these things on a conscious level, but perhaps my *body* begins to grieve nevertheless.

September 11

Oh dear. I was supposed to see Holly Granger today about the biopsy results, and I missed my appointment. I got involved with Annie at the nursing home and totally spaced it. I was forty-five minutes late. Now I have to wait until tomorrow. I'm disappointed in myself. It's hard for me to accept it when I make mistakes.

Interesting to me that I'm having all these peri-menopausal symptoms—feeling disoriented, forgetting things, bumping into things, and that they are some of the same symptoms of grief I had when Mother died. So. I am in grief/menopause. I must let myself experience it without condemning myself. Life goes on with or without one's doctor's appointments. Probably.

September 12

Really nice talk last eve with Dad about knowing who we are, and accepting our own shortcomings, and doing what we want to do. Then we sat on the porch, and reminisced, and watched the stars come out.

Sometimes I have a hard time figuring out what Pop wants to do. He's pretty noncommittal. He tries to be accommodating. Sometimes I'm like that, too. What makes us yearn so to please? What if we didn't?

When I think about saying meaningful things to people through my writing, my throat spasms, almost slams shut. I need to find the cause of this fear and resistance to creative expression, to sharing my insights.

This is an old theme for me—withholding my creativity. I see it in my dancing, weaving, writing, public speaking. I don't do what I have the capacity to do. This reminds me of my childhood parent-teacher conferences. Mother would come home every time and regretfully report that my teacher felt I wasn't working up to my potential. Hopefully writing will provide, finally, the creative outlet I need. Voice constrained. Cervix coated over with plaque like dust on stored furniture. I must find a way to open myself up and celebrate who I am and what I have to offer the world.

Later

Lance and I spent some time talking about my *Slippers* project. I am compelled to write this book. I need to find my own voice, speak my piece, be visible with my own power and wisdom. In the past I've invested my energy in backing up people who are already in touch with their own power—Mary Margaret, Rabbi Marc, others. I haven't wanted to be a public person, didn't like being so visible. Maybe it's time to speak for myself.

September 22

It occurred to me this morning in the shower—my best thinking place—that part of my difficulty in moving into this creative process with *Slippers* is my fear that it will not be well received, that no one will want it.

Publishing a book carries with it the intention to sell it, the desire for people to read it, to buy it. The question is, would it feel like failure to me to do all the work and expend all the time and effort and money to get it published and then find that the book didn't sell? I wonder if I would feel discouraged, or if I could simply say to myself, which is true, that I wrote it because I needed to, and let it go.

Clearly something is moving me to do this work, and I trust the time is well spent. If the book is meant to be published, it will be—when everything is ripe. Until then, I'll work on my project and learn a lot in the process.

September 24

Today no plans. I'm thrilled to have time for myself. I want a puttering day, with time to read and write and work on my *Torah* portion, and maybe start turning that silk and linen fabric I wove into a *tallit*. I like the idea of wearing a prayer shawl I wove myself.

I've been listening to the tape Paul Perper made for me. Lance recorded one whole side of a cassette with just my *Torah* portion over and over again. I can sing pretty well with the tape, but I haven't tried chanting from the printed text yet, because I always listen in the car.

⌒⟶⌒

The kids are leaving tomorrow for their honeymoon on Maui. I've loved spending all this time with them this summer. It's been a great opportunity to get to know Julia better. They've been staying at Nancy's house, but Julia's been with us a lot while Ben's been guiding on Mount Shasta.

⌒⟶⌒

Terrible, terrible tragedy yesterday. A mountain climber, a friend of Marc and Catherine's from the Oregon Shakespeare Festival, who was married only last January, fell several hundred feet and badly injured his head. Not clear whether he'll survive, or in what condition.

This accident really brings home what dangerous work it is that Ben does. It's true what Julia says, though, and a comfort to us all, that Ben and his work partners are well trained and well prepared to do what they do. It reduces the risk significantly.

⌒⟶⌒

Almost *Rosh Hashanah*. It's on *Erev Shabbat* this year. I'll cook with Carolyn. We're not having company. Neither of us feels like it. This is a low-key time of the year for us.

⌒⟶⌒

Yesterday I finished transcribing the journals for *Slippers*, and now I've started editing. I'm making notes about parts I might need to expand. It's fun, and I'm excited to have begun.

Writing this book begins to feel like a research project—research about the self I used to be. I need to figure out what about my life would be interesting to someone else.

I saw while I was talking with a friend yesterday that it can be okay if I don't sell the book. I have several friends who've asked to read it, and if nothing else happens, it will give us an opportunity to share this experience. There's value in that, whether or not the book becomes known in broader circles. The main job for me is to write it and then be unattached to what follows.

October ~ It's Not Old That's Hard

October 1

October already. Next month, four years since Mother is gone. Dad has been in heavy grief mode for a while—maybe since Mom's birthday August third. I don't know how to help him.

We talked yesterday, just the two of us, and I asked him how he feels about going to *shul* these days.

"I don't like to go anymore," he said.

"It's too hard to be there without Mom?"

He nodded.

I told him I could barely walk in there after Mom died, and the feelings only started to leave after I was working there every day. Now it's comforting instead, but in the beginning, all I felt was loss when I was there.

"It hasn't changed for me," he said.

I still get stuck in anticipating Dad's death. How long will he go on? I love having him in my life. It's crazy to taint this time I have with him with fear of his passing. I shall truly miss him. But who knows? Maybe he'll live past a hundred, and then I'll have spent all these years worrying, instead of fully enjoying our time together.

I wonder if this fear is connected with a thing that has come up before. Dad always told me, "I will take care of you until you have a husband to do it." Well, this dear husband of mine is absolutely on my side, adores me, communicates with me, supports me in what I do. Financially, we'll be fine.

So what is my concern? Do I fear that the Universe will think I don't need Dad anymore? *What will happen to me*, says this small child inside of me, *when Daddy's gone?* He is still my refuge. I still go to him for some unexplainable comfort. How shall I stay safe inside my own deep spirit? I must remember that I *am* safe.

I see Dad looking old. That's rare unless he's actively grieving. It's not old that's hard, but frail. And the last few weeks, he's not hearing well. I must remember to ask him about his ears. Maybe he gets lost in his grief, and he forgets to listen. Maybe he has wax.

October 7

The young man who was injured on Mount Shasta has died. It's a terrible tragedy. Yet, it comes with a gift. Catherine told me he was an organ donor, and that many people will receive life-saving or health-renewing organs and tissue at his bequest.

One must remember every day that we are alive by Grace. Nothing reminds us so much or so poignantly of our mortality as the death of a young, vital person. And nothing reminds us so much of the delicate balance of our lives. Better count blessings every day. Never know what tomorrow will bring.

October 9, 6:30 a.m. – *Yom Kippur*

I've enjoyed attending services this High Holy Day season. I've been moved and inspired, filled with emotion. I'm finding a joy in community I haven't experienced in a long time, a renewed joy at sharing Jewish community on a spiritual, as well as cultural and ritual, level. I like exploring with my rabbi how Judaism lights the way.

This morning I wish to go inward, as Rabbi Marc says, "to the inside of the inside." Perhaps this *Yom Kippur* will be the one which will bring me to that sacred, secret place. Perhaps.

I shall, as always, spend much of the day with Ger, in the park or in the woods. Since Mother died, we've been coming home in time to go to the *Yizkor* service with Pop. I like being in *shul* then. Both parts of the day are special.

October 13 – *Erev Shabbat*

Had a great visit on the phone with Auntie Mim last night. I told her I've been having hot flashes (a friend calls them "power surges"), and she told me some women have them a long time, even, occasionally, in their eighties. It helps that she talks to me about these things, things I can't talk about with Mom.

I took Auntie Mim on a phone tour of our garden, described the fruit trees, the calendula, the roses, the progress on the new landscaping. Then she gave me some tips for taking care of my cold—like gargling with salt water, which I'd forgotten about, and using Vick's VapoRub, which didn't help.

Auntie Mim's like comfort food for me. I always feel better when I talk with her. She cheers me up, even if we're talking about sad things. Same with Mother and Dad. I wonder where I'll find my comfort when they're all gone.

—•—

I'm reading *The Wheel of Life: A Memoir of Living and Dying*. It was written by Elisabeth Kübler-Ross. Again, I am entranced by her writing and her spirit. She is truly one of the great influences in my life. I wonder what place there is for me in this realm. I am not a scientist, not a therapist, but I do have things to say about living and dying.

Lance and I took a class on self-publishing a few years ago. The instructor said once you write a book about something, people begin to think of you as an expert on the subject. Perhaps that's as good a way as any other to become an expert, so long as you only talk about the things you know about.

October 15

Bill and Judith Moyers produced an intense and powerful documentary, *On Our Own Terms*, about end-of-life care and choices. We saw the second of four segments on PBS last night. Was intense, because this segment was about a woman, much younger than Mom, who was dying of ovarian cancer. It reminded me of our own situation, and her family expressed much of the gratitude we felt that we were able to share Mom's ending time at home together. This woman suffered horrible pain though, and again I was grateful that Mother didn't seem to. I can't help but feel that the Essiac, and her visualizations, and her decision against chemotherapy are what saved her from that agony.

I called our hospice nurse Eileen today to ask if she'd ever invited Mother to talk about her concerns during her hospice visits. "There was no fear," she said. "But your mother cried a little and said that her great sadness was to leave all the people she loved, and also that she knew you would all be terribly sad after she was gone. She could accept that she was near the end. She was at peace with that. But there was the great sadness."

October 18

I had an interesting insight about my fear of losing Dad, in spite of his general good health. When I was a baby, maybe three, I saw Dad having a terrible appendicitis attack. I was standing in front of him, and he got an agonized expression on his face and doubled over toward me in pain. I still can see a vision of this beloved gigantic person toppling toward me.

And when I went away to college for the first time, he was in the hospital with diverticulitis. Since he and Mom couldn't drive me up to Berkeley, I had to go with another family.

Then, while I was living in Israel and Mom was scheduled for joint replacement, Dad was hospitalized with a bleeding ulcer, and Mom's surgery had to be postponed.

These health crises of Dad's were so dramatic, it's no wonder they affected me at some deep level. It's no wonder there have been psychological repercussions.

October 18

Beth and Ed were here from Los Angeles, and Beth and I had an especially good visit. I read her the revised sections of *Slippers*. She said she found them helpful.

Thursday, October 19

I've been home from work with a terrible respiratory infection. Last night I had horrible coughing spasms that went on for over three hours. At one point, I fell asleep and dreamed that loving spirits were gathering up my things to help me get ready to die.

When I saw Kevin for acupuncture today, I mentioned that I have had more respiratory problems lately than I've had in many years. He said a lot of old grief is coming out. I'm surprised I hadn't thought of that myself. It all fits in—seeing Beth, *Yizkor, yahrzeits, Yom Kippur,* the stuff in the book about dancing. I cried a lot when I was reading *Slippers* to Beth. It all comes together.

And when I told Kevin about my death dream, he said, "That's a transformation dream." Again, I was surprised not to have caught that myself. Now we need to see what changes the transformation will bring.

October 21 – *Shabbat*

Lance and I had a good talk. I told him it was a relief to be able to stop, take time to heal, not have to *do* anything. "It takes a lot of effort sometimes to be a good wife, good daughter, good sister, good friend, good employee, housekeeper, gardener, writer," I said.

"The thing I notice," he said, "is that you said 'good' before every one of those things—*good* wife, *good* daughter. . . ."

I saw that I expend a lot of energy trying to be good at what I do—that is, dutifully doing the best job I can, because the right thing to do is to do the job well. (I wonder what would happen if I didn't.) I think the key word here is "trying." It's the trying that drains me. The doing itself comes naturally. The things I do in life give me pleasure. I doubt much would change on the outside if I stopped trying. Everything that's meant to be done will be done, and in its own time, too.

I'm encouraged by the way I feel this morning. I had only one not-very-bad coughing spell early this morning. What a relief. Maybe I can go back to work next week. I feel for the first time that it's a realistic goal.

October 23

I was listening to a tape from a psychic reading I had years ago. The woman talked about my relationship with Mom, and how Mom had trained me to be like her. She said it was time for me to decide who I wanted to be, keep the stuff I wanted and let go what was unhealthy. I couldn't listen to the rest of the tape. Guess I'm not ready to hear that.

During a massage with Nirvesha today, I remembered a vision I had years ago in Taos. It reminded me that from the age of four, maybe earlier, I have believed I could help people by taking on their pain, whether physical or emotional. I would take it into my body and carry their sadness and sometimes manifest symptoms—always bronchitis.

This is the vision: my little-girl self dances at the edge of the Vastness, is weighed down by the fear and the pain, comes back, catches bronchitis. My spirit couldn't soar while my job was to hold pain. Tough to get off the ground when you're holding pain. No time for soaring.

I cried for a long time as Nirvesha worked, partly because I can't help people by taking on their pain, partly because I feel sad for their challenges, and partly because it is tragic that I have carried other people's pain with me all these years. So much sadness!

This feels connected to my pattern of trying, to the "good girl" stuff. Some part of me believed I was supposed to take away the pain, to make the owies go away. If I learned this from Mother, maybe this is part of what caused all *her* illness, especially the rheumatoid. What was she carrying around, and for whom? And why did I pick that part of her to emulate? Did she get it from *her* mother? There were many other healthier, more joyous parts of Mom and Gram. I am glad I have taken on some of those, as well.

I wonder what else I still carry around that was Mother's. I can cherish Mother's memory without carrying her baggage. Perhaps I fear if I don't keep it all, I'll feel disloyal to her.

Now it is time to release the pain of others. I no longer choose to live that way. I can be loving without rescuing. I can be kind without *trying* to be kind. I can be peaceful and centered without feeling guilty that other people are not. I don't need to take on anyone else's pain. It doesn't help them, and it certainly doesn't help me!

October 26, 2 a.m.

I'm so furious. I'm just starting to get over my flu, and now I'm having these stupid night sweats and sleeplessness. How will I ever get well when I feel like this all night? I can't stay home from work indefinitely. I am so angry.

Maybe I just have to accept that I'm angry instead of trying to get over it. I don't allow much space for anger in my life. I can't stand being angry. I don't have a good way of dealing with it. I usually just talk myself out of it, or I keep it inside—like Mom. Here's one part of her I am definitely willing to send on its way. I don't want to take my anger and stuff it into my joints.

Fourth Yahrzeit

November ~ A Time of Negotiation

November 1

November again. I hope no one else dies.

Wednesday, November 8

Dreadful few days.

Pop and I were planning a shopping trip to Medford for Sunday, but Ger called that morning to say Dad was still sleeping, that he'd been up all night with abdominal pain and nausea. Then Ger called again to say he was taking Pop to the emergency room. Lance and I met them there. The doctor examined Dad and took X-rays and tests and admitted him to the hospital for observation.

Pop was not happy to be admitted. He wanted to go home. "How about if I go home now and come back later for tests?" he said to the doctor. He never did lose his sense of humor, kept joking around with the staff. They took him all the way off food and ran a saline drip so he wouldn't dehydrate, and Sunday night he slept well. No pain. But his belly was tender to the doctor's probings, and they didn't know why.

On Monday Pop rested in the hospital and took a purgative to get ready for a colonoscopy and endoscopy on Tuesday.

"I'm sorry, Mr. Mandell," said Dr. Wong. "There is a large tumor in your colon, and it's malignant. I couldn't get past it with the scope to see how big it is. It's almost entirely blocking the bowel. I can't tell with the scope whether it has metastasized.

"You basically have three choices. One is to do nothing. Eventually, maybe in a few weeks, the tiny passage that's left in the bowel would close and require emergency surgery and cause you a lot more pain. The second choice is palliative surgery. You'd wind up wearing a bag."

"Not an option," said Dad.

"The third choice is curative surgery. They go in, take out the tumor, resection the bowel, and you have normal digestion after that."

"That's what we'll do," said Dad. "Might as well take care of this as quickly as possible."

They are doing the surgery today. Dad is not thrilled that he'll have to stay in the hospital for a minimum of ten days. He *really* likes to be at home.

It's hard to tell how Pop's feeling. He doesn't talk much. He doesn't complain. He just throws out an occasional one-liner that says a lot. I need to listen carefully to those. When we were alone he said, "I guess this is what happens when you outlive your life expectancy."

It was sort of a joke, but not really. He's resigned to doing what he has to do, and he's graceful about it. He seems at peace with it, really. Maybe "resigned" is the wrong word. I wonder if you can go into something like this without being fearful.

I certainly feel, have felt, afraid these last days. Fear lurks, waiting for me to fall out of mindfulness. It waits for me and sucks me up like quicksand and makes me cry.

—◆—

What I keep hearing in my mind, somehow a comfort, is *Ani baMakom*, a phrase inspired by the *Torah* portion I will chant. "I am in this place." I must turn my attention here. I must be in this moment, in this place. *Makom* means "place," but it is also a name of God.

—◆—

"Don't go there," people are saying to me. I have been going to a lot of places I don't want to visit. Into the future an hour, a day, a week, a month. Maybe there's a lot of pain there. When I stay here, I feel love for my family, gratitude for our blessings—peace, even. When I go there I feel fear, ugly possibilities, pain, trouble coping, immobilization, loss.

So, I ask myself, *Why go there?* The decision to stay here is, as Gerry says, a no-brainer. Remembering to make that decision in every moment is not always easy. *Ani baMakom.* It helps me.

I'm sitting at my altar, and Mom's candle is flaring—almost ready to go out. Today I want to catch it, to light the new one from that flame. Feels important. I especially need Mom's help today. Well, always.

I felt Mom with me yesterday, reminding me to walk tall through the hospital corridors. I felt my shoulders curling in toward my heart, as though they could somehow shelter it, could keep it from breaking.

It's not time for a broken heart. Dad is in excellent health except for the tumor, and hopefully it hasn't spread. Dr. Hudson (the same surgeon we had for Mom) will see what else is or isn't there when he goes in.

Dr. Wong cautioned us not to bring Mom's experiences into this situation. The two cancers are different, and the treatments for this one are far less toxic. This is a less aggressive cancer. It may have been in there ten years already. Strange nobody ever knew.

I want to sit quietly with Pop. Just be with him. We need to build that in. Ger is going over to the Rogue Valley Medical Center in Medford with him this morning, and I'm going to do some stuff at work so I don't fall behind, and go over later. It's too bad we can't have the surgery in Ashland, but Dr. Hudson doesn't work at the Ashland hospital. Anyway, they don't have pulmonary and cardiology experts here. They say the extra support is a good precaution for someone who's eighty-eight years old. How many temptations there are in each moment to think of scary things. *Ani baMakom.*

Ani baMakom. My new mantra. I hope I can remember to say it. And think, *Silence.* And feel Mom. All those things help me. And Lance is here, as he always is when I need him.

The kids are coming home from their honeymoon today. I'm thrilled they'll be here with us for the next days. They're so comforting. I felt sorry to tell Ben about Dad on the phone last night, but the words just came out. I didn't think about not telling him.

Nancy has been wonderfully supportive. She told Dad yesterday, "English doesn't have any description for our relationship, but you feel sort of like a stepfather-in-law."

Ger said, "Dad, I think what Nancy is trying to tell you is that she gives a damn!"

Then Nancy said in her droll way, "Well yes, that is in there."

Even now, when things are dreadful, we find humor. I'm so grateful we can laugh. And to think I didn't used to appreciate Dad's and Ger's sense of humor. Dad's still kidding around with the nursing staff. It takes some of them a while to catch on.

⟶

Drew Angel Cards: Power, Patience, Freedom, Integrity. I was asking for guidance for this day, but that's a great description of Pop.

Friday, November 10, 3:30 a.m.–
Rogue Valley Medical Center, Medford

Wednesday was a tough day. Dr. Hudson was going to do Dad's surgery in the evening. Then it was scheduled for the afternoon, at a quarter to four. Just before noon, Carolyn called me at work.

"They're taking Dad right now. Ger's not here. He's down in the cafeteria taking a break. They're trying to page him." I could hear the anxiety in her voice.

Earlier, Dad had asked me, "Are you going to come over and wait with me at the hospital today?"

"Would you like that, Pop?" I asked.

"I always like to have you with me," he said.

"Then I will," I told him.

I felt terrible I hadn't come back yet when they took Dad down to surgery. After Carolyn called, I picked up Lance and we came right over. The pink ladies at the surgery information desk got the nurses to let me into the pre-op area to see Dad. He was already heavily sedated, but I woke him up to tell him I was here, and I kissed him on the cheek.

I have some kind of magical notion that if only I can stay with him, I can protect him and help him heal.

All of us kids sat in the surgery waiting room—again. That's a tough place to spend time. The surgery took longer than expected—two hours and forty-five minutes. Pop has a lot of scar tissue that the doctor had to get through.

So here's the report: the tumor appears to have been self-contained and large, about the size of a man's fist. Dr. Hudson took out everything he could see, but, it's possible that some cells may have gone outside the bounds of the colon. He said some of the lymph nodes may be involved though the fact that they are hard could also mean they're having a normal immune response to the invasive cells. He also saw some spots on the liver. They might be a result of stuff that happened a long time ago, but they could be an indication of liver involvement.

God willing, the pathology report will show that the tumor was self-contained and that the other tissue is healthy. God willing. Dr. Hudson said chemo for someone Dad's age is probably not indicated. It would imperil the quality of his life and wouldn't be curative, so no point, especially if the cancer hasn't spread. He said colon cancer cells are slow to reproduce.

So today we're waiting for the pathology report. Should be here this afternoon.

———✦———

Lance told me Dr. Hudson's mother died yesterday, unexpectedly. I am so sorry for his loss. And still he came in to check on Dad instead of sending another surgeon. What dedication that is. I wonder how he's managing. Maybe the reality hasn't hit him yet. Or maybe working is what will get him through.

———✦———

I saw a lot of people at work yesterday. It was trying. There were many well-meaning, sincere, nonintrusive good wishes, and a few upsets. It was, for one thing, hard to get any work done. But the thing that surprised me most—that is, the thing that triggered the most surprising reaction in me—was someone kindly reaching out to say, "We went through this with my Dad, and please know that if you ever feel like talking, I am here for you."

I thanked her, but I felt annoyed and confused. How does she know what "this" is? We haven't been telling people. From the way she said it, I inferred her father had had colon cancer. But until we get the pathology report back, we ourselves don't know for sure what we're dealing with. I felt invaded, that our privacy was at risk.

Judy reminded me that what is private to one person may not seem private to someone else, and she helped relieve my exasperation. It helps to see things from a different point of view.

One of the board members came downstairs from a meeting and gave me a hug.

"Someone must have told the *Torah* study group information we hadn't intended to share," I said.

"I did," she said. "I'm sorry. I didn't realize you weren't ready to talk about it."

"We're a pretty private family," I told her. "If you're ever wondering whether to share something about us or not, you can probably just figure you shouldn't."

I wasn't as annoyed with her by then because of my conversation with Judy, but I could still hear the sarcasm in my voice. She's lucky she didn't come down earlier. I'm lucky, too.

November 15

Four years tomorrow since Mother died. Amazing to me that so much time has passed, and that we have healed as much as we have. And still, last night when Dad and I were talking about going home from the hospital, I felt it acutely that Mom wouldn't be there to welcome him—physically, at least.

That keeps coming up. It seems like Mother, or whatever Mother is at the moment, has really been helping me get through these days. When I feel dejected and exhausted walking back through the hospital corridor after sitting with Dad, something (Mom) always helps me manage to straighten my creaky, aching back and hold my head up and walk tall. There's always a "You can do this" message attached, and I am grateful.

I'm thrilled that Dad is coming home today. He hates being in the hospital. He hasn't complained much to me, but he's been pretty outspoken with Ger. I have concerns for his safety at home, but I dearly hope we can manage to provide him with as much independence as will satisfy him.

Ger and I agree with the doctors that Pop needs company around the clock. Someone needs to track on his meals, meds, and safety in order to avoid an interim nursing home stay. I hope Dad's willing to have help. I pray we can find a gentle, reasonable way to tell him we need to bring somebody into the house. Rabbi Marc says this is a time of negotiation for us. Everyone will just have to give a little to accommodate each other's needs.

I need to deal with my fear and overprotectiveness. The first time Dad got up to go to the bathroom after his surgery, I felt like a mother who had just watched her kid climb a tree for the first time. Part of me wants to protect him, but in my heart and mind I don't want to take away an ounce of his independence. He's still the head of the family. He's still Dad. I hope we can find a respectful balance.

I'm coming to see myself in the role of listener. If I can help everyone feel heard, I think it will help a lot. We all have our private concerns. I hope I can help us all to be present with them. First challenge is to stay present myself. I had a helpful talk with Marc yesterday. What a dear and wise friend he is.

Had a run-in with Ger in the morning—a big brother / little sister encounter about personal responsibility. It sent me right into feeling offended, then into self-doubt, and I came out questioning whether I was being responsible about my job at the *shul*.

Rabbi Marc assured me that I *am* being conscientious about my work. He said that when I notice I am going into that self-doubt place, I can recognize it as an old pattern and choose not to go there. It was a good reminder. He also said the synagogue wants to honor employees' personal needs. He made a big space for me to create a balance which will keep things going at work *and* honor my own needs and family responsibilities. What a blessing to have his support.

So. Pop is coming home today. Rabbi Marc recommended Mary Sanders as a caregiver. Apparently she's great, and she's able to be present and attentive without chatting all the time. That's important. She's coming this afternoon to meet us. She's actually trained in hospice work, but will do whatever home care is needed. It's not clear how long we'll need her help. We'll have to see how quickly Dad heals, and how quickly he becomes reoriented. He's been pretty vague since the epidural. God willing, he'll be more lucid when he's at home.

The SOLIR class on the brain that I took with Annie and Dad reassures me. The instructor said older people have a lot of data stored in their brains. It takes them longer to process stuff, but they are eventually able to retrieve things, especially if they don't stress over it. I need to remind Dad of that, and the rest of the family, too. Oh, I think that was the topic of the lecture the day Dad decided not to stay for class.

Wow! I just remembered. Dad told me the afternoon of that class that his stomach had been bothering him, so he rested in the car and then went home. I wonder how long he'd been suffering with this tumor without telling us. How lonely it must have been to fear it (*Did* he fear it?) and not talk about it. I wonder why he didn't go to the doctor sooner. Same old thing, maybe—not wanting to hear the diagnosis. We've all been there.

◆

I'm afraid we're at the beginning of another challenging journey. I hope I can stay steady with it. God willing, I've gained some strength coping with Mother's ending time.

Interesting to me how much more conscious I am of Dad's mortality now he's been diagnosed with another cancer. I mean, he *is* 88. His relatively good health and active lifestyle had shoved my fear of losing him back a little. I just hope he—we—can manage a peaceful, pain-free ending time when we get there.

November 18

Last night we went to *shul* to say *Kaddish* for Mom. Funny, I cried during the *Misheberach*, the healing prayer for Dad, but not during

Kaddish. But, of course, the *Misheberach* has always been the one to get me. The Debbie Friedman melody we sing was Mother's favorite, and it took me years after Mother died to be able to hear it without weeping.

———

Dad and Mary Sanders are hitting it off well enough. He beat her at Gin Rummy yesterday. Today I'll teach her how to play Five Hundred.

Mary says Dad's worried that his memory is failing him. I don't think it's time to worry yet. That is, I don't think it's dementia. I think it's still the effects of the epidural, and that he's grieving and having an emotional response to what he's been through. I remember how absentminded he got when he was worried about Mother before she died. But as he began to heal, he was more present again.

I wonder if I could talk with him about this stuff. I want to talk about the grief, not only related to Mother's fourth *yahrzeit*, but to finding out he has another cancer, to finding himself needing someone around all the time, to being old and having lost so much over the years.

I wonder if, when one is old, loss and grief are nearly always present, at least in the background.

I wonder if I'll ever have the guts to broach such subjects with him.

November 23 – Thanksgiving

Carolyn planned the whole Thanksgiving dinner and did the shopping. It was kind of her to take that on. It's a stretch for me to even want a holiday meal this year.

Thanksgiving is my least favorite holiday now. So many hard hits associated with this time of year. Still, we have much to be thankful for.

More challenges brewing. Now that Dad is feeling better, we need to reevaluate what is a reasonable amount of help to provide, and who will provide it, and how we will balance that with the needs and demands of the rest of our lives—spouses, work, social life, respite. These have been intense weeks. All of us kids have spent a lot of time at Dad's house. We've put a lot on hold. Totally acceptable so far. But we each have different expectations as we move into this next phase, and we don't see our options in the same way. We need to come to terms with our differences and find the common ground. It's not clear yet whether Dad is fine on his own, or not.

The important thing is for Dad to have the independence and privacy he wants, and also the right amount of companionship and diversion.

November 29

Dad has a urinary tract infection. I'm afraid we're in some sort of downward spiral. I only hope his last years aren't filled with doctors and discomfort. The uncertainty of these days is a challenge for me. Everything is new, and I am always on the edge of concern that doing my best won't be good enough. Here's a pertinent question: good enough for what? I certainly can't keep my father alive if it's his time to go on. Perhaps I can't even keep him comfortable by my own volition.

Here we are again: one must surrender one's illusion of control, drop into Silence, find peace there, and resume activity without anxiety. What an assignment! And yet, when I do think to drop into Silence, it is there to receive me and comfort me. I only have to turn my thoughts to it, and I am there.

How relevant this is to the *Torah* portion I'm chanting for Mother's *yahrzeit* next week. "God is in this place and I, i did not know it." Here we are, God and I, and I didn't even realize we are in this together.

I haven't heard it quite that way until this moment. If only I can remember. So here's the message: God and I will get through this as we have done every other thing, and I need to remember that.

Last night I saw that I need to let go of Dad, of my claim on him.

I asked him why he doesn't tell me when he doesn't feel well. "Is it that you want to protect me?" I asked, still seeing it as his way of not trusting me to be a grown-up.

He nodded, and I saw the satisfaction in his face. He's doing his job. He's taking care of his daughter, even now, at a time in his life when he himself needs so much support. What a noble man he is, and how true to what he values. I have to shift my perception, my way of being with his reticence, now I've seen this. I would never do anything intentionally to undermine his dignity. Here I am, at age almost fifty-four, and still learning how to be a daughter.

November 30

I am fine-tuning the trope for my *Torah* portion with Paul Perper this morning, and studying the text with Rabbi Marc at noon. I'm excited—and nervous. What an adventure. I'm having trouble remembering the trope today, even the parts I knew well a few days ago.

⤙

I went to put away the Angel Cards today and "Humour" fell out. Interesting to think of humor in connection with studying *Torah*—but why not? Who has a better sense of humor than God, judging by what I see around me. Watch a pigeon walk, listen to a hyena cackle, look at human nature in all its machinations. Can get pretty funny.

Well, better study some more. And I want to mark the insights I've had in my journaling about the *Torah* portion, so I can share them with Rabbi Marc during our meeting.

Later

Study with Paul and Rabbi Marc went well. It was exciting to do the *chevruta,* the one-on-one *Torah* study, with Rabbi Marc. Paul helped me write musical notation for the words and phrases that were hard for me.

After my lesson, Paul told me about his uncle who was a violinist, and about his mother who learned *Talmud* by listening while her brothers, and later her husband, studied aloud. Women weren't permitted to study openly in those days. It sounds like the fact that women did study was accepted, but not acknowledged, because Paul remembers her singing quietly in the kitchen and calling out comments from there to augment the men's discussion. I'm glad I live in *these* times.

December ~ Remarkable Day

December 2 – *Shabbat*

A hard thing happened after the service last evening. I was standing with some family friends and talking with a young woman, a new pediatrician in town. One of our friends told her, "Fayegail's father is eighty-eight and just had surgery for colon cancer." My anger flared.

I was shocked that our friend would share our private information with a stranger. It felt like mindless chatter. I decided earlier this morning that I'd call and tell her Dad values his privacy and would prefer that people not share the details of his health. He can tell people himself if he wants them to know.

But later, in the shower, I had a terrible realization. After Mom was diagnosed with ovarian cancer, and I was in shock, I told close friends and relatives without even considering whether she would want it known. And Mom probably would not have shared it herself. I can rationalize that she received an abundant outpouring of love and prayer and other kinds of support during her last year as a result of that disclosure, but the bottom line is, I did not consider her privacy. I only did what I needed to do for myself at the time. I wanted comfort and reassurance, and that's what I did to get it.

As I write, another part of me is watching myself resist self-criticism. I could be entirely immersed in self-deprecation right now, go into Drama Queen mode. How could I be so inconsiderate? How could I break confidence for my own mother? How could I not discuss it with her first?

I don't want to go there. I did what I did. Mother might not have told people herself. She was probably more private than that. But as usual, she accepted it with grace. It happened, and she moved on.

I asked my humbled self another thing in the shower this morning: *Is this privacy issue my own, or am I getting it from someone else?* I think Dad wants privacy, but it occurs to me that I'm not sure. I've been thinking it's not my issue, but I found myself writing about privacy in an e-mail I sent to Catherine. I was telling her I don't like it when people call the office on business and enquire about the health crises of my family. I had no idea how much of a charge that carries for me. Interesting that I don't simply interpret it as concern.

Later

I think I'll let this whole privacy thing go. This desperation to control information seems futile to me anyway. The word is out and is apparently being shared freely. Trying to convince a few people to be more discreet wouldn't have much impact on the big picture. Besides, it would add more stress.

What *about* this need to control? I remember that as Mom lost control over her health, she tried harder to control the little day-to-day things. Why do we need to feel in control, anyway? Maybe life would be easier if we'd just surrender to the vaster plan without a fight.

Monday, December 4

Dream

I walk into an upscale art gallery where two of my weavings are hanging. When I walk in, I see that the gallery attendant has taken one of them from the wall. It's on the table in front of her, and she's holding a pair of scissors. She has clipped off several strands of yarn, and she thinks she has improved the look of the piece. Grace and fluidity gone.

I am furious. I can't believe someone would have the chutzpah *to alter another person's (my!) piece of art. I am all caught up in whether she had the right or not. Even though the gallery had bought it outright, did she have the right to change it? Would she have done that to a painting? Doesn't she perceive tapestry weaving as art?*

Later in the dream, I see the creator of the piece. She is a handsome, radiant, Semitic-looking woman—dark hair and clear dark eyes. Doesn't look like me. I don't know how I know she's the artist. We gaze deeply into each other's eyes.

Maybe the point is that I am only the hands of the Artist. I have no claim on what is created. It is the process that concerns me, and I need to let the product go.

It's interesting to me that I'm making such an unconventional *tallit*. It's more like a small poncho or a *tallit katan* than like the usual piece of rectangular cloth. I suppose it's the artist in me. She's been seriously repressed since I've been back in America. But, of course, one can be artistic in the way one lives a life, no matter the product of one's endeavors. I guess I needed that reminder.

December 7

My *tallit* turned out well. I took it in to work yesterday to show Marc and Judy and they like it a lot, too.

I met Paul Perper for final touches on my *Torah* portion this morning. Carolyn came by as I was finishing my lesson. She gave me a delicate silver *yad*, the pointer one uses to hold the place while chanting. She gave it to me especially to welcome me into the community of those who chant *Torah*. She brought it back from Jerusalem, and she's used it herself to chant, so whenever I chant, she will be with me. When she gave it to me, I cried.

Interesting insight: In all the times I've heard Carolyn chant so movingly, it never occurred to me that I could, or would, chant myself. It wasn't until I heard Catherine chant, who had never chanted before, that I realized it was something I could do.

Friday, December 8

Rabbi Marc and I talked today after lunch about tomorrow's service and about my decision to chant *Torah* but not to have a formal *bat mitzvah* celebration the way some women do. He took out a piece of paper and drew a picture of a river, and he told me, "When you're kayaking, you look at the river, and you decide which way to take it. Some routes are slower, some faster. Each one creates a different experience, not better or worse, just different."

Yesterday I questioned my decision to hold my process close, but today Rabbi Marc reassured me with his analogy about the river. I am taking a slow, deep, quiet way, and it has been rich and meaningful.

We spoke of how this journey is bringing together the many parts of myself: employment, spiritual journey, community, inner work, family, mindfulness, study, even fiber art with the *tallit*. He said, "You are a weaver, and that is what you do. You are weaving together the strands of your life."

He asked me whether I would like him to share anything of our journey with the community, or whether I wanted to talk about what I had learned. And he wanted me to understand that if he didn't talk about it publicly, his silence would be honoring my process, just the same. He wanted me to know he does understand the depth of its importance to me. What a kind and loving man he is. I am blessed that he's my rabbi—my teacher—and my friend.

Lance's generous and unending support of my journey inside is a huge help. He's coming tomorrow to hear me chant *Torah*. Dad and Ger are coming, too, just for the *Torah* service at eleven. Dad and Carolyn will share the *aliyah,* the *Torah* blessings, for the portion I'm chanting. Carolyn will chant the first portion, I, the second, and Gail Frires, the third.

December 9 – *Shabbat*

Well, this day has finally arrived. I meant to write this morning, but no time. Now it is the middle of the afternoon, and I am sitting all cozy in front of the little upstairs heater where I sometimes read before bed.

What a remarkable day this has been—a *Shabbat* to remember for my whole life. I told Lance when I was getting ready this morning, very carefully, that I felt as though I were dressing for my wedding.

I wore Mother's black knit suit with the colorful cross-stitched jacket. I wore her locket on my white cambric blouse and Grandma Mandelblat's pearl earrings.

A little synchronicity: I noticed this morning that the first word in my *Torah* reading is *va-yi-katz*. Katz was Grandma Mandelblat's maiden name. When Mother and Dad were married, Mother promised Great-grandma Katz that she would always light *Shabbos* candles, and Mother did, each *Shabbos* ever after.

I sat with Carolyn during the service. She taught me how to say the special blessing and put on my *tallit*.

The service was full of singing. It is the music of our prayers that most touches my heart—more than the words themselves. It transports me.

We sang *Modah Ani,* and I was back in my retreat at Mount Angel, just after I realized I wanted to chant in Mother's honor, and just before I knew it was time to write *Slippers. Modah Ani,* I am grateful. That was a meaningful part of my healing. I chanted that prayer all the time when I was there. It was my mantra, and it was the heart of my walking meditation.

I saw Carolyn turn around, and I realized that Dad and Ger had come in. I went to greet them. That's when the tears hit—of gratitude that we five could share this; and of sadness that Mother isn't physically here; and of gratitude, as I watched Lance come in a few moments later, for all that we share as a family and for our closeness; of gratitude that Dad is well enough that he could come today. He hardly even seemed frail—just himself, as he always is.

And then it was time for the *Torah* service.

I liked the way Rabbi Marc invited people up for the *aliyot.* For the first one, he called up Eliza and her Dad, Erv, who is visiting from out of town, and he included anyone else who wished to honor their parents, so I went, and Judy went, too. Carolyn's chanting was exquisite, full of depth.

Then my portion. Carolyn and Dad were honored with the *aliyah.* I was moved to be standing on the *bimah* with them, and of course Mother was right there with us, and Ger and Lance too, from across the room.

I could never have imagined, when I began this journey, what the actual experience of chanting *Torah* would be like. I found my place in the scroll and touched it with my silver *yad.* I began to chant, and I felt as though I entered into an altered state. That is, I was exquisitely present, and I could see the words and hear my voice, but my body felt strange—distant, maybe, and I was somehow not my usual self. I have no idea how to describe it. My voice was enchanting—I *felt* enchanted. Then it was over, and people were saying "*Yasher koach,* go forward in strength." People began to sing a song of celebration, and I stood there with tears streaming down my face.

Lance told me afterwards he will remember for as long as he lives how my face looked while I was chanting. Leona whispered to me as Gail was getting ready to chant that I sounded like an angel.

Then our close family friends, the Dratches, were honored with the third *aliyah*, and Rabbi Marc announced to the congregation that they are moving to Fort Collins, Colorado, in January. People were shocked and saddened to think of their leaving our community. We'll miss them a lot.

I'm afraid I wasn't able to listen very well as Gail chanted. I was still under the spell of my own experience.

After the *Torah* reading, we all stayed on the *bimah*, and Rabbi Marc said a blessing for the people who had been called up to the *Torah*. He made the blessings very personal. He said a special blessing of healing for Pop. Then, he started telling the Dratches how much they mean to our community, but he was overwhelmed, and had to stop. When he'd regained his composure, he said, "I guess that says it all." So there it was, the whole *bimah* filled with people I care about deeply, and I felt—am still feeling—awed by the whole thing.

The service was perfect, beautiful and meaningful, and the *Torah* study was interesting. I was still in awe, and quietly happy to be there, and grateful that Dad was well enough to come, and I wasn't very focused on the discussion. But one part of the *Torah* study stood out for me: that the ladder in Jacob's dream was not separate from himself. That we are the connection between the world above and the world below, between the numinous and the mundane, and it is our job to continually bridge the two.

—◆—

People came up to me after the service and thanked me for my chanting. I think this is the same thing that happened in Ventura during my *aliyah* for Mom and Dad, except that then my body didn't feel so strange. My voice was transformed into something other than *my* voice. Something responded to my *kavanah* today, to the intention in the depth of my being, and brought that voice through me. I was chanting about awe and experiencing awe—*HaMakom*—in the same moment.

Kathy and Lisa Dratch commented on the angelic quality of my voice, and I said, "Maybe it was not *my* voice."

"I wondered about that," Kathy said. I'm glad they were there today.

It is the experience, what happened in my body and my consciousness, that is so remarkable, ineffable. No wonder our ancestors taught us not to pronounce *Yod-Hey-Vav-Hey*, the most sacred name of God. How ever could one manage to find words that could even come close to that experience of the One?

Paul Perper has offered me private lessons to learn trope so I can chant without relying on tapes. He said he'd meet with me mornings before work, since I can't come to class during the day. It's such an honor to learn with him.

My first thought when he offered to teach me was that I want to return to *HaMakom* where I was this morning again and again and again. But I know one mustn't expect that, or try to get back, even. I sense those experiences happen only by the grace of God to encourage us along our way.

—✦—

I'm feeling like I used to feel after I completed a major tapestry—especially the one called "Exaltation" that hangs in my office—that feeling of gratitude and completion and awe, and also the feeling of emptiness that comes after I have put my whole self into something for a long time, and I am doing so no longer. There's a time, then, when I must simply sit quietly, be present, be empty, a time when I must wait for the vessel, which is myself, to fill up again.

Epilogue

I Love You, Sweetheart

Friday, August 3, The Following Year –
Mom's Birthday – Ashland

I wrote this letter to Pop and took it over to him this morning:

Dear Daddy,

I've loved spending all this time with you lately. You mean so much to me. I'm glad you found the part of *Slippers* I read to you to be beautiful. I wanted so much for you to like it.

Dad, I've been thinking about you a lot lately—so what else is new? It seems like a pretty challenging thing to have all these changes going on in your body and not understand why. I can imagine it might be frustrating, discouraging, even scary.

I know Mom was your confidante, and that you still talk with her all the time. I can imagine that right now you miss her more than ever.

Poppy, after Mother died, you gave me Mama's slippers and you said, "Now you will walk in Mother's shoes." I have tried to be worthy of that gift, and to celebrate the ways I am like her.

Like Mom, I think, I am a strong person. Even though I let my feelings show more than she did, I feel strong and solid inside. And, Dad, I think I'm a pretty good listener, too.

I'm writing this because it was a little hard for me to say this out loud, but I want you to know that I want to be here for you in every way that I possibly can—as a helper, and a listener, and in whatever other ways are needed.

You have always been a wonderful father, loving and supporting me and protecting me through all the challenges of my fifty-four years of life. I am deeply grateful. For now, I'm going to let you off the hook just a little bit. You don't need to protect me from your feelings, Pop. I want to share them with you—even if it's hard. I want—if *you* want—to listen if you're scared, or just hug you, or hold your hand, if that's what you'd prefer.

I love you, Dad.

Fagel

⤙⤙

Dad read my letter. He took my hand. "I love you, Sweetheart," he said. "I want to keep this in my vault at the bank. I wish Mom could have read this."

"Maybe she has, Poppy."

⤙⤙

Ger came over, and we went with Dad to see Jeff Elder. What a dear, caring doctor he is. He gave us the results of Dad's tests. He was very gentle. Dad's colon cancer has metastasized, as Dr. Hudson suspected it might. It's in his liver. That means it's incurable, and Jeff referred us to hospice.

When we left Jeff's office, we stopped to buy a bouquet of summer flowers and headed for Jacksonville for a birthday visit to Mother's grave. For the first time, Dad stayed in the car. When Ger and I got back to him, Dad quoted the inscription on the gravestone, "Together forever—sailing into the sunset." He's been waiting a long time.

Thank God Daddy's not in pain. Thank God hospice will help us manage the nausea. Thank God Pop lives near us. Thank God we have each other.

August 6

Dad asked me last night when I think I'll be finished with the first draft of *Slippers*. Poignant moment.

"I don't know, Daddy. I really want you to read it. Maybe I can read you the sections as I finish them. I'll hurry."

He nodded.

Lance says I must be careful not to set myself up, not to make myself crazy trying to finish in time. He's right, and yet, I do so want to do that—for Dad, and for myself.

August 11

I've been working on *Slippers* every moment I've had. I've been sitting with Dad, keeping him company, helping when he needed something, and working like one possessed.

"I've had the feeling," I told him, "that you have been waiting to join Mom until you felt like we were ready to go on without you, and until I'd come to terms with my grief, and you knew I would be okay."

He nodded.

Working on *Slippers* has given me strength. I have grown enough and deepened enough that I shall manage this time with more grace than I did after Mother died.

Dad's on morphine now, and floats in and out. Gerry came in to give Dad another dose this evening when I was nearly finished with the book. I asked him to wait just a few minutes so I could tell Daddy I was finished before he went under again. He didn't want to wait at first. He thought maybe I was withholding comfort from Dad to do something for myself. But I knew it was important to Dad.

"Five minutes isn't going to matter out of four hours," I told him, and he agreed to wait.

I finished the manuscript at six-forty-three and turned to Pop. "Daddy, I've finished it. I've finished the book."

Pop looked at me tenderly, with pride, and his eyes teared up. "I love you, Poppy. I love you."

August 14, 7 a.m.

Today is the day of my father's funeral. I wonder when it will really sink in that he is gone. I stroked his hair as he died, and yet it is not real.

Ben and Julia brought us photos from their Takilma wedding reception. I'm looking at a photo of Dad and me. Pop's wearing his navy blue dress-up shirt with the tiny white dots. He's listening to me, totally absorbed. I'm speaking to him earnestly, with my hands. He is cherishing me.

During the memorial service, I shall read from *Slippers* in Dad's memory.

I am numb, I think.

Peace

January 20 – Lowden's Beachfront B&B, Brookings

Five months since Daddy died. Mother and Dad are together again.

I've been coming here a weekend a month since October—here to the beach, to the mouth of the Winchuck River, to sanity and healing—and I go home renewed, ready to manage everyday life again. I've given myself this gift. Barb Lowden says she keeps the place open for people like me, for people who need a place to turn inward.

Surf and wind roar at the edge of my consciousness as I write. The rain has stopped for now, but the tide is high, and the surf surges up the mouth of the river in front of the house. Bare twigs that are the shrubs beyond the lawn thrash and shimmy with each gust. Tumult all around me, yet in my heart, at this moment, is peace.

Dancing Lesson

Stillness.
Only Mother.
I am dancing.
She moves me as a breeze moves flame.
Quietly.
Her angel's fingers caress me.
She is gone six years and
she is present, vast, unbridled.
Vast.
She has no edges, only space.
Vast.
There is no Mother, only space.

I know her for her tenderness.
She brings no thoughts or guidance, no opinions.
And yet, she moves me.
I am sensing,
following her, with my body, with my being.
Sensing. And watching.

This I know:
Mother feels no pain.
She does not suffer.
She does not yearn for me.
She does not yearn,
she who is not she, but all.
Her vastness comforts me.

I am dancing,
deep in this place she has carried me.
I am purely present,
in no space,
in no time,
only in the music that is Mother's vastness.
No thinking,
no wanting,
only Mother.

Grief unfolds into movement
and escapes.

Hebrew/Yiddish Glossary and Pronunciation Guide

Note: ch *is pronounced like a guttural h (kh), not like the ch in cheer.*

aron (ah-ROHN). The Holy Ark where the *Torah* scroll is kept; burial casket, traditionally made of pine or another simple wood and without nails.

aliyah (ah-lee-YAH); pl. aliyot (ah-lee-OT). Literally, to go up; to be called up to the *bimah* to bless the *Torah*. To make *aliyah*: to become an Israeli citizen.

Amidah (ah-mee-DAH). Standing prayer which is central in Jewish liturgy.

Ani baMakom (ah-NEE bah-mah-KOHM). I am in this place, I am within God.

bar/bat mitzvah (bar/baht MITZ-vah). Son/daughter of the commandments; celebration of the transition from childhood to adulthood within the Jewish tradition.

bikkur holim (bee-KOOR hoh-LEEM). The *mitzvah* of visiting the sick.

bimah (BEE-mah). The raised area in a synagogue where the Holy Ark is located and where the *Torah* is read.

bracha (brah-KHAH); pl: brachot (brah-KHOHT). Blessing.

chai (KHY, rhymes with eye); pl. chayim (khy-IM). Life, equal to the number eighteen in the Hebrew numbering system. Gifts of money are commonly given in multiples of eighteen to signify a gift of Life. *L'chayim:* a toast, "To Life."

challah (KHAL-lah). The ritual braided egg-bread eaten by Jews on *Shabbat.*

Chanukah (KHAH-nu-kah). A Jewish festival of eight days commemorating the rededication of the Holy Temple in Jerusalem and the rekindling of the Holy Light.

chanukiah (khah-nu-kee-AH). Candelabrum *(menorah)* with nine lights used during *Chanukah.* Each of eight lights corresponds to one of the eight days of *Chanukah.* The ninth light is used to kindle the other eight.

charoses (Yiddish: khah-ROH-sis). A mixture of chopped apple, nuts, cinnamon, and wine, used at the Passover *seder* to represent the mortar used by the slaves in Egypt.

chevra kadisha (KHEV-rah kah-DEE-shah). Jewish burial society.

chevruta (khev-RU-tah). A traditional form of *Torah* study in partnership.

chutzpah (Yiddish: KHUTZ-pah [u, as in push]). Audacity.

erev (EH-rehv). Evening; the eve of a Jewish holiday. The Jewish Sabbath and holidays begin at sunset.

gimilut chasadim (gim-ee-LOOT khah-sah-DEEM). Acts of lovingkindness.

haftarah (hahf-tah-RAH). Literally means conclusion. Refers to the concluding part of the *Torah* Service, which consists of a reading from the Book of Prophets. The tradition began when Jews were not allowed to read *Torah*, so they read a portion from Prophets which reminded them of the weekly *Torah* portion.

haolam haba (hah-oh-LAM hah-BAH). The world to come.

HaMakom (hah-mah-KOHM). The Place; a name of God.

Imah, Imahleh (EE-mah, EE-mah-leh). Mama, little mama; an affectionate name.

Kabbalat Shabbat (kah-bah-LAHT shah-BAT). A late afternoon/ early evening service of songs and psalms which welcomes in *Shabbat*.

Kaddish (KAH-dish). A Jewish prayer recited in community which glorifies God's name; one version is the mourner's prayer.

kavanah (kah-vah-NAH). Intent; one prepares to pray by gathering oneself and focusing intent.

kibitzing (Yiddish: KIB-its-ing). Joking, fooling around.

Kislev (KISS-lev). Ninth month of the Hebrew Calendar.

koach (KOH-akh). Strength.

Kol Nidre (Hebrew: kol nee-DRAY; Yiddish: kol NIH-dra). Solemn prayer chanted just before sunset on the eve of *Yom Kippur* which declares a release from religious vows made unintentionally or under duress.

kugel (Yiddish: KUH-g'l [u, as in push]). Pudding, usually made of noodles or potatoes, also bread or rice; can be sweet or savory.

Magen David (mah-GEHN dah-VEED). Star of David, national symbol of the state of Israel.

matzoh (MAH-tsah). Crisp, thin, unleavened bread used during Passover.

maven (MAY-vin). Expert, a knowledgeable person.

mazal tov (Hebrew: mah-ZAL tohv; Yiddish: MAH-zel tuhv). Congratulations. Good luck. Literally, good stars, or, may your planetary influences be favorable.

menorah (meh-NOH-rah). The oldest Jewish symbol. A seven-branched candelabrum used in the Holy Temple in Jerusalem.

met. The body of a deceased person.

mikvah (MIK-vah). Ritual and spiritual immersion in water from a natural source.

minyan (Hebrew: min-YAHN; Yiddish: MIN-yuhn); pl. minyanim (min-yahn-EEM). Group of ten Jews who gather for formal communal prayer.

Misheberach (mee-sheh-BEHR-akh).
"May the one who blessed. . ." The beginning words of special blessings done after reading *Torah* on occasions such as birthdays and anniversaries, or when there is a need for healing.

mitzraim (mitz-RAH-eem). Egypt; narrow place.

mitzvah (MITZ-vah); pl. mitzvot (mitz-VOHT). Commandment(s) required of Jews; a responsibility; a good deed or charitable act.

Modah Ani (MOH-dah ah-NEE). I am grateful.

Pesach (PAY-sakh). Jewish festival of freedom. Literally, to pass over. In English known as Passover. The holiday lasts for eight days and commemorates Israel's deliverance from enslavement in Egypt.

Rosh Hashanah (ROSH ha-shah-NAH). The Jewish New Year, one of the High Holy Days. Literally, head of the year.

seder (SAY-dehr). Literally, order. Passover service and ritual meal that tells the story of the Exodus from Egypt.

Sefer Torah (SAY-fehr TOH-rah). *Torah* scroll.

Shabbat (shah-BAHT); Ashkenazi pronunciation—by Jews of central and eastern Europe: Shabbos (SHAH-bus). The Jewish Sabbath. A day of rest and renewal which begins Friday at sunset and lasts until three stars appear in the sky on Saturday night.

Shavuot (Shah-voo-OHT). Feast of Weeks. Jewish holiday commemorating the revelation of the Law at Mount Sinai.

Shehekianu (sheh-heh-kee-AH-nu). Jewish prayer of gratitude: You abound in blessings, Eternal One our God, Sovereign of all time and space, who has kept us in life, sustained us, and allowed us to reach this moment.

shiva (SHIH-vah). The first week of the year-long formal Jewish mourning period observed in the home of the deceased, during which friends visit, pray with, and comfort the bereaved.

shloshim (shloh-SHEEM). The formal thirty-day mourning period during which the bereaved begin to re-enter normal life, but with restricted activity.

shomer (SHO-mer). Guard.

shomrim (shohm-REEM). Members of the *chevra kadisha* who sit with the body, helping the transition from this world to the world to come. They also protect the body from any unnecessary disturbance.

shuk (u, as in push). Middle-Eastern market or street of shops.

shul (Yiddish: shool; oo, as in food). Synagogue.

simcha (SIM-kha). Joyful occasion.

sukkah (SU-kah; u, as in push). A temporary structure made with leaves and boughs built by Jews during the fall harvest festival *Sukkot* to commemorate the dwellings used during the time in the desert after the Exodus from Egypt.

tallit, tallis (Hebrew: tah-LEET; Yiddish, TAHLL-iss). Prayer shawl made with ritually tied fringes at the four corners to remind one of God's commandments.

tallit katan (tah-LEET kah-TAHN). A small fringed, four-cornered garment (see *tallit*) worn daily, often under the shirt.

Talmud (TAHL-mud; u, as in push). A collection of discussions and stories by the rabbis who lived between 200 and 500 C.E. which constitute and elucidate Jewish religious and civil law.

Tashlich (tash-LEEKH). Ceremony done at a body of flowing water on the first day of *Rosh Hashanah* to cast away the mistakes and heaviness we are ready to surrender to prepare for the new year.

tikkun olam (tee-KOON oh-LAHM; oo, as in food). The commandment to repair the world.

Torah (Hebrew: to-RAH; Yiddish: TOH-rah). Depending on the context, it may refer to the Five Books of Moses, to the sacred canon of Jewish religious writings, or to all Jewish holy writings. One could say one studies *Torah* to do *Torah* to be *Torah*.

Vayetze (va-yeh-TZAY). The seventh weekly portion in the annual cycle of *Torah* reading. Genesis 28:10 – 32:3.

vayikatz (vah-yee-KAHTZ). Awoke. From the *Torah* portion Genesis 28:16, "Jacob awoke from his sleep."

yad (yahd). The pointer used to hold the place while chanting *Torah*.

yahrzeit (German: YAHR-tzite; Yiddish: YOHR-tzite). Anniversary of a death, commemorated by the recitation of *Kaddish*.

yasher koach (YASH-er KO-akh). Go forth in strength, a way of saying "Good job."

Yetziat Mitzraim (yeh-tzee-AHT mitz-RAH-eem). The Exodus from Egypt. Literally, going out from narrow places.

Yizkor (Hebrew: yiz-KOHR; Yiddish: YISS-ker). Memorial service conducted on *Yom Kippur, Shavuot, Pesach,* and *Sukkot.*

Yom Kippur (Hebrew: yohm kee-POOR; Yiddish: yum-KIP-per). Day of Atonement or "at-one-ment." A Jewish High Holy Day.

yontif (Yiddish: YUHN-tiff, u, as in sun; Hebrew: yom tov (o, as in home). Literally, good day, holy day.

Questions to Ponder: A Guide for Readers

1. What is *Dancing in My Mother's Slippers* saying to you?

2. Which characters in this book remind you of people in your life? Who, and in what way? How are the relationships in the book similar to or different from relationships in your life?

3. Do certain parts of the book resonate with you more than others? In what way?

4. Are there parts of the book that are especially painful for you to read? Comforting? Joyful? Why do you think that is so?

5. How do you feel about the explicit physical details in the book? Have you had similar experiences as a caregiver or patient? What has it been like for you?

6. Fayegail writes about the influence of Judaism, faith, and spirituality upon her healing process. What roles do religion, faith, and spirituality play in your own loss, bereavement, and healing process? In other areas of your life? Has *Dancing in My Mother's Slippers* influenced you in those realms?

7. What is your relationship with your community? How is it similar to or different from Fayegail's community involvement?

8. Fayegail contemplates her dreams as one way of looking more deeply into herself. Do you have your own version of dream work? How is it similar to and different from Fayegail's approach?

9. What questions arise in you as you read the book?

10. How has this book affected you? Has it changed you? How?

11. How might *Dancing In My Mother's Slippers* help you with your own grief?

12. How does this book compare with similar books you've read?

13. Is this a book you would recommend to others? Why or why not?

If you would like to share your comments about *Dancing In My Mother's Slippers* with Fayegail, please visit her website at www.griefandhealing.net and click on the guest book link.

A Conversation with Fayegail

1. "Dancing in My Mother's Slippers" is a provocative and powerful title. Where did it come from?

Originally, the title was *In My Mother's Slippers,* because after Mother died, I had the feeling I was expected, somehow, to take her place in the world. But as I healed, I realized that title wasn't dynamic enough, didn't show enough movement and change. I love dancing. Life is one long improvisational dance. We turn and flow and stop and double back and *express* ourselves. Mom and Dad were great dancers. One of my favorite childhood memories is of watching them waltz around our family room.

2. What was it like for you to write this book? Was it hard to go back into the journal? Did you see healing?

Writing this book has expanded my capacity for gratitude. I'm grateful that I kept the journal. Sometimes it was painful to read it. More often, reading my journal brought me into the experience again, but with a new point of view. I remember reading about a particularly challenging time and being aware, in that moment, that I wasn't crying. Healing was present. Sometimes, as I was working, I'd go back into active grief, and even then, I knew it would never be as hard as it had been in the beginning. My feelings were, as my husband, Lance, says, part of The Procession, and I knew they would pass.

There is another aspect of creating the book from the journal that I want to mention. When I wrote the journal, I was trying to digest and understand my raw experience. The act of creating the book for a larger audience was my memorial to Mother, and a delicious awakening in me of a new art form. Dad was with me all the way. I shared sections with him, and we discussed how to handle various parts. He also loved to write, and he was a great storyteller. It was a precious sharing that we had around the transformation of the journal into the book. It was important to him that I share Mom with the world.

3. When did you actually start working on the manuscript?
I started transcribing the journal four and a half years after Mother died. I hadn't re-read any of the entries before that. Once they were transcribed, I started my editing process.

4. Why have you left the year off the dates in your journal entries?
I want there to be a sense of timelessness about the book. I want people reading it in 2050—or 2150—to feel its relevance to them. Loss is a universal experience. I don't want people to look at the book and say, "Oh, that happened a long time ago. It doesn't have anything to do with me."

You'll also notice that I've included few descriptions of people in *Slippers*, few descriptions of our homes, gardens, vehicles. I want readers to imagine themselves on this healing journey, to plug their own details into the story.

5. How did you translate the immediacy and the emotion of your journal into what eventually became *Dancing in My Mother's Slippers*? What was your process?
I had to make the language and the narrative work for readers—to explain who people were and add dialogue to show the flavor of our conversations. I started with about 750,000 words from my journal, and pared it down to about 75,000 words. I needed to simplify.

It is interesting to me how many people pass through our lives. Until I had to cut dozens of people out of the story, I don't think I fully appreciated this. I also cut incidents and meanderings from the journal that weren't relevant to the story I was telling.

6. Does time itself bring a measure of peace to the healing process, or do you think it was your spiritual journey that brought you peace?

I think both are true. With the passage of time, I was able to think of Mother without crying, to feel more level when I'd get a "zinger." That's what I call it when I come across a poem in my mother's handwriting, or one of her recipes in my box, or a photo in an unexpected place.

But mindfulness was also an important part of my healing. I watched myself. I tried hard from the beginning to be attentive to my feelings and not suppress them. I cried when I needed to, and I excused myself from activities that gave me no space to be present with what was going on inside me. Being willing to grieve was crucial.

7. Many people seem to expect that they will grieve for a year and then move on. What is magic about that length of time? Is it normal to grieve longer than that?

Once a year has passed, a mourner has experienced an entire cycle of holidays and other annual events. Sometimes a person thinks, *At least I've made it through it all one time. It will never be as hard again.* But it is certainly normal to grieve longer than a year.

In the Jewish tradition, the *public* period of mourning is a year-long prescribed grieving practice, which often ends with the dedication of the gravestone. But *private* grief goes on as long as it has to. Each year Jews mark the date of death of our loved ones by reciting the *Kaddish*, the prayer which praises God and asks for the blessing of peace. We recite this prayer in community, not alone. We expect grief to be a part of life. We're not told to hurry up and get over it.

8. What surprised you about your grieving process?

Memory loss, disorientation. A failure of competence. I thought at one point that I was losing my sanity. I felt irrational and self-critical. I'd forget to do things. I'd lose things. Then I read in Therese Rando's book, *How to Go On Living When Someone You Love Dies,* that the behaviors I found upsetting in myself were well within the range of normal grieving behavior. That was deeply comforting.

9. Would *Dancing in My Mother's Slippers* be meaningful for someone who wasn't close to his or her mother? For someone whose mother is still alive? For someone whose mother died a long time ago?

Slippers has been meaningful to women and men who weren't close to their parents. And yes, reading it can help in addressing anticipatory grief. People have mentioned to me that they, like me, feared the death of their parents even before their parents were ill. Reading *Slippers* can help people look at and come to terms with those fears. One friend who read the manuscript told me that even though her mother had died thirty years earlier, *Slippers* brought up unresolved grief she hadn't known she carried with her.

I also believe that reading *Slippers* can influence a reader's relationship with his or her own children. It provides a good opportunity to take stock and to make needed changes now, instead of waiting until the end of life.

10. Can a person who is not of the Jewish faith benefit from this book?

Yes. The spirituality in the book transcends any particular religion. I have always been interested in learning about other faiths. To complement my Jewish upbringing, I have encountered Buddhism, Taoism, and Native American shamanic practices, Sufism, Hinduism, and many forms of Christianity. There is a unity in all life. There is a dance between my personal spirituality and Jewish practice and ritual. *Slippers* could resonate with readers of any faith, and, hopefully, with those who are searching for meaning.

11. What surprised you most about readers' reactions?

My friend Georgia read the manuscript and asked if she could share it with her mother, Grace, who is approaching the end of her life. I sent the electronic file so the text could be printed in a larger font, and Grace devoured it. I was astonished. I thought I was writing *Slippers* for the daughters and sons. Then I realized that of course, Grace was a daughter, too, and still had feelings about her own mother's death. But the most wonderful thing was that *Slippers* prompted a dialogue between Georgia and Grace about death and what they were experiencing and what they were feeling, and they decided to share parts of that dialogue with me. What could be better than that?

I was also interested and pleased to learn that men as well as women are drawn to the book, and that what I have written is relevant to losses other than death.

12. As you were finishing *Dancing in My Mother's Slippers* your father died. Did writing the book help you as you grieved for him?

Yes. Living in the constant presence of the manuscript helped me remember that I was capable of healing. That time would help. That mindfulness would help. The work held for me a promise. Even in the depth of my pain, I knew that I could heal, because healing always surrounded me—in the profound grief, and in the gradual and wondrous transformation.

13. What other observations would you share about grief in our American culture?

In mainstream culture, people often feel they are expected to get back to business, to return to work or school, to act as if they have put grief behind them, even within a few days of a life-shattering loss. But that really is an act. Failing to acknowledge grief is like stepping into the river at the base of Niagara Falls and thinking you won't be swept away.

I remember the day I announced at a meeting with colleagues that I was leaving my job because I realized, after a year, that I needed to take more time to grieve my mother. People came to me after the meeting with tears in their eyes and said they wished that they had made that choice. One woman told me it had taken seven years for her to begin grieving her mother. I remember feeling that day that, in taking time to grieve, I was also grieving for all the people who couldn't or wouldn't do their own grief work.

I think about how we deny the power of grief, and how often we ignore the opportunity it offers for personal growth. I look around me at the anger, despair, fear, illness, the imbalance of our society, and I suspect that many of the people I see acting out in pain and frustration are walking around with unresolved grief. Our lack of awareness is injuring us. This would be a healthier nation if we would face death, acknowledge our grief, do our grief work, and move in our lives with the compassion that comes from that work.

Resources

The following are books, articles, videos and other items of interest which have helped me along my way. Some are mentioned in this book. Others are books about grief, healing and spirituality I've enjoyed reading at other times in my life. Many are books I refer to frequently. I've also included some memoirs and autobiographical works I like. – FMB

Aigen, Rabbi Ronald. *Renew Our Days: A Book of Jewish Prayer and Meditation*. Montreal: Congregation Dorshei Emet, 1996. This is my favorite prayer book, and it contains my favorite translation of Psalm 30 (on page 99). It also contains "A Family Prayer," by J. Harry Berger, (on page 601) which I adapted for Ben and Julia's wedding.

Albom, Mitch. *Tuesdays with Morrie: An Old Man, A Young Man and Life's Greatest Lesson*. New York: Doubleday, 1997.

Bartholomew. *"I Come as a Brother": A Remembrance of Illusions*. Taos, New Mexico: High Mesa, 1984.

———. *From the Heart of a Gentle Brother*. Taos, New Mexico: High Mesa, 1987.

———. *Reflections Of An Elder Brother: Awakening from the Dream*. Taos, New Mexico: High Mesa, 1989.

————. *Planetary Brother.* Taos, New Mexico: High Mesa, 1991.

————. *Journeys with a Brother, Japan to India: Bartholomew and the Dalai Lama in the Himalaya.* Taos, New Mexico: High Mesa, 1995.

Brener, Anne. *Mourning & Mitzvah: A Guided Journal for Walking the Mourner's Path through Grief to Healing.* Woodstock, Vermont: Jewish Lights, 1993.

Byock, Ira. *Dying Well: Peace and Possibilities at the End of Life.* New York: Riverhead, 1998.

Callanan, Maggie, and P. Kelley. *Final Gifts: Understanding the Special Awareness, Needs and Communications of the Dying.* New York: Bantam, 1997.

Chopra, Deepok. *The Seven Spiritual Laws of Success.* San Rafael, California: Amber-Allen and New World Library, 1994.

Eliot, George. *Daniel Daronda.* Vol. 16–18 of *The Writings of George Eliot.* Boston and New York, Houghton Mifflin, 1908.

Gilman, Dorothy. *A New Kind of Country.* New York: Fawcett Crest, 1978.

Jampolsky, Gerald G. *Love Is Letting Go of Fear,* rev. ed. Berkeley, California: Celestial Arts, 1988.

Kaufman, Barry Neil. *Happiness is a Choice.* New York: Fawcett Columbine, 1991.

————. *To Love Is To Be Happy With.* New York: Fawcett Columbine, 1977.

Kaufman, Barry Neil, and Samharia Lyte Kaufman. *A Sacred Dying.* New York: Fawcett Columbine, 1996.

Kübler-Ross, Elisabeth. *On Death and Dying.* New York: Touchstone, 1969.

————. *Death: The Final Stage of Growth.* Englewood Cliffs, New Jersey: Prentice-Hall, 1975.

————. *Living with Death and Dying*. New York: Macmillan, 1982.

————. *The Wheel of Life: A Memoir of Living and Dying*. New York: Touchstone, 1998.

L'Engle, Madeleine. *A Circle of Quiet*. The Crosswicks Journal Book 1. San Francisco: HarperSanFrancisco, 1972.

————. *The Summer of the Great-Grandmother.* The Crosswicks Journal Book 2. San Francisco: HarperSanFrancisco, 1974.

————. *The Irrational Season*. The Crosswicks Journal Book 3. San Francisco: HarperSanFrancisco, 1977.

————. *Two-Part Invention*. The Crosswicks Journal Book 4. San Francisco: HarperSanFrancisco, 1988.

Lamm, Maurice. *Consolation*. Philadelphia: The Jewish Publication Society, 2004.

Lamott, Anne. *Bird by Bird: Some Instructions on Writing and Life*. New York: Anchor Books, 1995.

Lerner, Harriet Goldhor. *The Dance of Anger: A Woman's Guide to Changing the Patterns of Intimate Relationships*. New York: Harper & Row, 1985.

Levine, Stephen. *A Year to Live*. New York: Bell Tower, 1997.

Moyers, Bill, and Judith Moyers. "On Our Own Terms: Moyers on Dying." A four-part PBS series by television journalist Bill Moyers that focuses on end-of-life care in the U.S. The videotape and related resources about end-of-life issues are available on this exceptional website: http://www.pbs.org/wnet/onourownterms, and other valuable resources are available on this PBS website: http://www.pbs.org/witheyesopen/.

Perlman, Debbie. *Flames to Heaven*. Wilmette, Illinois: RadPublisers, 1998.

Pipher, Mary, Ph.D. *Another Country*. New York: Riverhead, 1999.

Rando, Therese A. *How to Go on Living When Someone You Love Dies*. New York: Bantam, 1991.

Remen, Rachel Naomi. *Kitchen Table Wisdom*. New York: Riverhead, 1997.

———. *My Grandfather's Blessings*. New York: Riverhead, 2000.

Richards, Paul, and Patty Richards. *Energetic Empowerment Level One: Path, Practice, and State of Being*. Ashland, Oregon: The Senté Center for Energetic Studies, 1999. For more information about this body of work, visit this website: www.sentecenter.com.

Schmall, V.L., S. Bowman, and D.G. Vorhies. *Driving Decisions in Later Life*. Pacific Northwest Extension publication # PNW 0510. October, 1998. To purchase online: http://cru84.cahe.wsu.edu/cgi-bin/pubs/PNW0510.html.

Stern, Chaim. ed. *Gates of Prayer for Weekdays and at a House of Mourning*. New York: Central Conference of American Rabbis, 1992.

Thomas, Richard. *The Essiac Report: Canada's Remarkable Unknown Cancer Remedy*. Immunocorp, 1994.

Veary, Nana. *Change We Must: My Spiritual Journey*. Blue Hill, Maine: Medicine Bear, 1990.

Acknowledgments

Trying to express my gratitude, in a page or two, to all of the people who have supported me in the creation of my current self and in the creation of *Dancing in My Mother's Slippers* is like trying to stuff a king-size down comforter into the front pocket of my jeans.

Each of you has contributed much, and my gratitude is boundless. You have loved me, inspired me, taught me, supported me, provided technical advice, read, re-read, and listened to various versions of the manuscript for seemingly endless hours, and met with me to discuss the manuscript for hours more. You have coached me and cried with me and listened to my tales of joy and tales of woe. You are my community, my family, my beloved friends.

I offer my thanks to all of you who have contributed to the creation of this joyful project, whether or not you are specifically mentioned here.

My deepest gratitude to my beloved husband, Lance, for all the conversations at two and three and four in the morning, for reading the entire manuscript aloud to me so we could feel the sharing of it, for the editing, the brainstorming, the computer support, for the kindness when I was grumpy, and for hanging in when it got too hard. For the Love, always the Love.

Immense gratitude to my mother, of blessed memory, who brought me into this world and guided me through it and loved me and cared for me and inspires me to this day, and to my father, of blessed memory, who loved me and believed in me and stretched for me, who took care of me and supported me in countless ways, who wanted this book to be written. To my big brother, Gerry, who has always been my advocate and has always encouraged me to be myself, and to do what was important to me to do, even when it wasn't comfortable for him, and to my sister-in-law, Carolyn, who is the sister I always wished I'd had, and who loves me, even when it's not easy. To Cousin Beth who listened and listened and listened to revisions. To Cousin Lee, who is always ready to talk with me about creativity. To the aunts and cousins, and to Nancy and Ben and Julia, who cheered me along on this project, and to all the rest of you who are part of our loving family.

My abiding gratitude to you who have been my spiritual teachers: To Mary Margaret, who understands me better than anyone on earth, who brought the vastness of the Teachings of Bartholomew into my life, and who has shared with me countless moments of love and friendship, support and wisdom—and laughter. To Joseph, who taught me that we of each generation must be willing to grow beyond our parents. To Jean Marc, who kindled in me a love of contemplative movement and of a Taoist view of the world. To Helen, who taught me non-profit management as a spiritual practice. To Rabbi Marc, my teacher, my work partner, my friend, who encouraged me to write this book, who read the manuscript twice, and has given me invaluable writing advice, who has listened with all possible patience, who has supported all the parts of me—except the Drama Queen. To Paul, my mentor and my writing coach, who has opened my eyes in new ways and expects excellence. To EC, who has shown me the beauty of a disentangled life.

Thank you to friends who have supported me in myriad ways as I learned my way into writing a book: To Catherine, who read twice through the manuscript, acting as my sensitivity agent and coaching me in the creation of dialogue. To Ann, who also read it twice and read with a perspective that is different from mine. To Olive, who sat for hours in Lithia Park, in restaurants, at her kitchen table while I read to her aloud from the manuscript and listened as she brought her wisdom and years of grief counseling experience to our conversations. To Sister Dorothy, who first talked with me about the book project and about bereavement literature, and assured me that there is a place in the world for such a book. To Georgia and Grace, who showed me a new dimension of the book. And to all the other early readers who shared with me your experiences and told me how *Slippers* pulled you in and pushed you away, touched and comforted you, left you unsettled and left you joyous—your insights were invaluable.

My thanks to members of our Jewish community and our Senté community and our Mediation Works community who have helped me feel I belong, and to all my other friends who haven't directly supported the book process, but who have loved me and listened to me and shared dinners and lunches and dancing and music and plays and lectures and walks and hikes and picnics and all the things that make life rich, I thank you. You know who you are.

Thank you to the folks at hospice and WinterSpring, and to the dedicated health professionals who support our family and our community.

And thank you to my writing teachers and to all the members of my writers' groups who have encouraged me and have witnessed my transformation as a writer. You read and critiqued and held me in your gentle honesty and gave me skills I never dreamed existed. I am grateful for your patience and your vision.

My thanks, also, to Carolyn Bond, who edited the first draft of *Slippers*—and the last—and whose astute observations and suggestions helped me create a better book. To Barb and Gary Lowden, who made space for me to write. To Christy Collins of Confluence Book Services, who designed the cover and the interior, and to Gary Kliewer, Kait Fairchild, and Kelli Crispin, also of Confluence, for all the ways they helped. To David Wick and Irene Kai of Silver Light Publications, who shared excellent advice and recommended just the right professional helpers, and to Mary Margaret Moore, Yossi Abramowitz and Marilyn Edwards for their insights and suggestions about publishing. To Sara Glaser for sharing her experience with layout and book production. And to Amy Blossom of the Jackson County Library for scheduling the first public reading of *Dancing in My Mother's Slippers*.

To all of you, my heartfelt thanks.

About the Author

Fayegail Mandell Bisaccia lives in Ashland, Oregon, with her husband, Lance, and their cat, Maya. *Dancing in My Mother's Slippers* is her first book.

Please visit her website at www.griefandhealing.net.

Share this book with a friend...

♦ **To place on-line / credit card orders,** please visit our website at www.weaverbirdpress.com.
♦ **To place postal orders,** mail the form below with your check or money order to:

> Weaverbird Press
> PO Box 688
> Ashland, OR 97520

Please send _____copies of *Dancing in My Mother's Slippers* to:
(Please print clearly.)

Name _____

Address _____

City _____State _____ Zip ____

Telephone _____

E-mail Address _____

For more information, call us toll-free at 888.804.7787 or e-mail us at: orders@weaverbirdpress.com.

Shipping:
U.S. (by air): $4.00 for the first book, $2.00 for each additional book
International: Call or e-mail for current rates.

> _____copies @ $16 = $_____
>   Shipping $_____
>   Total Enclosed $_____

Privacy policy:
We will not share your contact information with anyone.

I would like to be notified via e-mail by Weaverbird Press about:
_____ Book events in my area.
_____ Discussion groups about *Dancing in My Mother's Slippers* forming in my local area.